中外翻译理论教程

第二版

CHINESE AND FOREIGN TRANSLATION THEORIES: A COURSEBOOK

主编◎黎昌抱　邵　斌

参编◎陈向红　余晓燕　缪　佳　吴　侃

ZHEJIANG UNIVERSITY PRESS
浙江大学出版社
·杭州·

图书在版编目（CIP）数据

中外翻译理论教程：英文 / 黎昌抱, 邵斌主编. —
2版. — 杭州：浙江大学出版社, 2023.12
ISBN 978-7-308-22782-7

Ⅰ.①中… Ⅱ.①黎… ②邵… Ⅲ.①翻译理论—高
等学校—教材—英文 Ⅳ.①H059

中国版本图书馆CIP数据核字(2022)第111615号

中外翻译理论教程（第二版）
ZHONGWAI FANYI LILUN JIAOCHENG (DI ER BAN)
黎昌抱　邵　斌　主编

策划编辑	李　晨	
责任编辑	李　晨	
责任校对	郑成业	
责任印制	范洪法	
封面设计	闰江文化	
出版发行	浙江大学出版社	
	（杭州市天目山路148号　　邮政编码　310007）	
	（网址：http://www.zjupress.com）	
排　版	杭州林智广告有限公司	
印　刷	杭州宏雅印刷有限公司	
开　本	787mm×1092mm　1/16	
印　张	20	
字　数	580千	
版 印 次	2023年12月第2版　2023年12月第1次印刷	
书　号	ISBN 978-7-308-22782-7	
定　价	60.00元	

前　言
Preface

　　翻译是一项历史悠久的人类行为，人类自从有了交流史，就开始有翻译活动。翻译研究是一门综合性、交叉性学科，它包括描写现实世界翻译现象的"描写分支"、确立可以解释这些现象的"理论分支"，以及将从描写分支和理论分支中产生的知识应用于翻译实践和教学的"应用分支"①。翻译研究作为一门独立的学科在 21 世纪得到了迅速发展。

　　党的二十大报告指出："构建人类命运共同体是世界各国人民前途所在。万物并育而不相害，道并行而不相悖。只有各国行天下之大道，和睦相处、合作共赢，繁荣才能持久，安全才有保障。"② 为推动构建人类命运共同体做出积极贡献，要下大气力加强国际传播能力建设，形成同我国综合国力和国际地位相匹配的国际话语权。因此，培养高素质翻译人才是新时代加强国际传播能力建设，促进文化交流、文明互鉴，进而实现和睦相处、合作共赢、繁荣安全的迫切要求。令人欣喜的是，翻译专业、翻译硕士、翻译学都已分别作为单独的本科专业、专业硕士学位和独立学科正式列入国家本科专业、专业硕士教育和学科目录。然而，虽然目前我国已有各类翻译教材多达数百种，但涉及翻译理论的教材并不多见。

　　首先，在中国翻译理论方面，这些书籍多以中文著述，概括起来，大致有三类：

　　一是以论集的形式呈现，如罗新璋的《翻译论集》、中国译协的《翻译研究论文集》等。

　　二是以史论的形式呈现，如马祖毅的《中国翻译史》、陈福康的《中国译学理论史稿》和王秉钦的《20 世纪中国翻译思想史》等。

　　三是对某译论家理论进行个案研究，如沈苏儒的《论"信达雅"——严复翻译理论研究》、顾钧的《鲁迅翻译研究》等。

　　然而，对于外语专业学生而言，翻译理论课教学一般应以外语授课为主，所以与之对应的教材最好是外文教材。以英文教材为例，虽然也偶有关于中国翻译理论的英文译本，如中国香港的张佩瑶等编译的《中国翻译话语英译选集》和陈德鸿的《20 世纪中国翻译理论》，但前者仅限于古代佛经的传译，后者只涉及 20 世纪。如果作为教材，似乎仍有不妥。

　　其次，相比之下，西方翻译理论书籍则相对较多，且不乏英文教材，但其读者往往是以

---

① 方梦之. 中国译学大辞典[M]. 上海：上海外语教育出版社，2011：43-44.
② 习近平. 高举中国特色社会主义伟大旗帜 为全面建设社会主义现代化国家而团结奋斗——在中国共产党第二十次全国代表大会上的报告[R]. 北京：人民出版社，2022：62.

英语为母语的翻译研究工作者，内容往往较为宏大，语言通常较为艰深，如莫娜·贝克（Mona Baker）主编的《翻译研究百科全书》、道格拉斯·罗宾逊（Douglas Robinson）主编的《西方翻译理论》。苏珊·巴斯奈特（Susan Bassnett）编著的《翻译研究》所面向的读者是对西方翻译有一定了解的学者，因此提纲挈领有余，详尽阐述似有不足。杰里米·蒙代（Jeremy Munday）的《翻译学导论》侧重现当代的翻译理论，对历史上的西方翻译理论梳理似乎不很充分。此外，虽然也有关于西方翻译家流派和个案研究的英文著作，但它们更适用于翻译研究。还有一些中国著名学者用中文编纂的西方翻译理论著作，似也不宜作为教材使用。于是，这本《中外翻译理论教程》应运而生。

《中外翻译理论教程》是浙江省高校重点教材建设项目成果，是一部面向高校外语院系（英汉）翻译理论学习者，涵盖中西方重要翻译理论，既简明易懂又基于原典的中外翻译理论英文教材。

全书分 Part Ⅰ 和 Part Ⅱ 两大部分，各 17 章，共 34 章。在理论体系上，本书强调"三抓"：一抓主线，即抓住中西翻译史上的主要事件；二抓主角，即抓住中西翻译史上的主要代表性人物；三抓主题，即中西翻译史最具代表性的翻译理论和思想。为此，在内容编排上，本书具有三大特点。

（1）编写思路与众不同。本书把中国翻译理论和西方翻译理论合二为一，融入一书。在具体篇章中，以译家个案为主线，以流派作为暗线加以处理，并以历时分期逐一编写，有利于将某个译论家的重要译论全面系统地反映出来，也有利于读者了解某个时期某个译论家或流派的重要译论。

（2）编排形式别具一格。本书每一章一般由"正文"和"附录"两大部分组成。"正文"部分包括"译论家的生平和翻译活动介绍""译论家的重要翻译理论"（包括学界后人对其译论的评价）、"译论家的翻译实践"（Part Ⅰ 尤为突出）。其中"译论家的翻译理论"是最重要的主体部分，注重对于译论家原典的阅读，所以尽量从译论家的著作、序言等原典文献中选取，让学生接触原汁原味的译论家理论和思想。正因为此，所以本书在用英文编写 Part Ⅰ 的同时，还着重在一些地方分别附注标明相关中国译论家的汉语原文。"附录"部分由"课后练习"和"参考文献及进一步阅读文献"构成，以满足学生复习和课后进一步学习的需要。

（3）理论实践密切结合。本书在突出译论家翻译理论的同时，还注重对其翻译实践的讨论，通过征引译论家自己的翻译实践来佐证或反证其翻译理论的可行性和一致性。如果译论家的翻译实践涉及学生不熟悉的语种，或者译论家是一位纯理论家，缺少相应的翻译实践，本书则征引其他相关的翻译实例，进一步阐明其翻译理论的内涵和指导意义。这样，可以让学生感同身受地体会到翻译理论的重要性，以及翻译理论对翻译实践的指导作用。

本书初版由浙江财经大学外国语学院翻译教学团队于 2013 年编写，为更好地适应翻译学发展趋势以及满足翻译理论教学需要，编者对初版内容加以修订，新增了 4 章内容，修订及新增内容达全书的三分之一，其中 Part Ⅰ 新增 "Wang Zuoliang's Translation Theory and Practice" 和 "Hu Gengshen's Translation Theory and Practice" 两章，Part Ⅱ 新增 "Pierre Bourdieu and *The Field of Cultural Production*" 和 "Mona Baker and *Corpus Linguistics and Translation Studies*: *Implications and Applications*" 两章。本书再版编写人员及具体分工是：陈向红修订完成 Part Ⅰ 的第 1、2、3、4、5、6、7、8、9、10 和 17 章；余晓燕修订完成 Part Ⅱ 的第 1、2、3、4、5、6、7、8、10、13 和 14 章；缪佳修订完成 Part Ⅰ 的第 11、12、13、15、16 章以及 Part Ⅱ 的第 9、11、12 和 15 章；吴侃完成 Part Ⅱ 的第 16、17 章；黎昌抱完成 Part Ⅰ 的第 14 章；邵斌完成本书初版 20 章内容的编写；黎昌抱负责本书再版的组织策划及全书的审稿、统稿工作。

最后，要感谢国内多所高校的外语院系以及相关教师多年来一直使用本教材，并为本书再版提出了宝贵的修订意见和建议！感谢浙江大学出版社李晨女士为本书的顺利再版提供帮助！

囿于编者水平，书中谬误和疏漏之处，自知不免，敬请读者不吝指正。

编　者

2023 年 11 月 15 日

目 录
Contents

Part I   Chinese Translation Theory

Part II Western Translation Theory

Part I

Chinese Translation Theory

Chapter One

Translation of Buddhist Scriptures

① Introduction

There have been waves of translation throughout Chinese history, sometimes predominantly into Chinese, and occasionally predominantly out of Chinese into other languages. The introduction and dissemination of Buddhism into China from the 2nd century was dependent on translation, and the movement brought a new development to the Chinese language. The period of Jesuit mission in China in the 17th century in the Ming Dynasty, brought another substantial impetus to the activity of translation. A third major wave was that of the late 19th and early 20th centuries, when China became acutely aware of the need for modern Western science and technology. The adoption of foreign writing in vernacular Chinese during the first half of the 20th century might be regarded as the fourth. Now, in the 21st century, on the one hand China is integrating into global economy and culture; on the other hand the western world has woken up to China, and has realized that the biggest nation on earth does not necessarily write in English. So now we are embracing the fifth translation wave.

At the very beginning, Chinese translation theory was born out of contact with vassal states during the Western Zhou Dynasty (1046 BC–771 BC). Early texts contain various words for "interpreter" or "translator." *The Classic of Rites* claims that there is one word for each direction. The people living in different regions of the country could not understand one another's languages. Their likings, needs and desires were all different. There were officers whose duties were to comprehend these people's minds and ideas, and communicate their likings and needs. These officers held the post of "ji" in the east, "xiang" in the south, "didi" in the west, and "yi" in the north (中国戎夷，五方之民。东方曰夷。南方曰蛮。西方曰戎。北方曰狄。五方之民。言语不通。嗜欲不同。达其志。通其欲。东方曰寄。南方曰象。西方曰狄鞮。北方曰译。) It has been claimed that "yi" (译) finally survived and became the sole character for "interpreter" or "translator" because in the Han Dynasty and the period of disunion, most translation activities were involved with the north.

Other words referring to "interpreters" are "tongue person" (舌人) and "return tongue" (反舌).

The large-scale translation activities in ancient China, however, are accompanied by the introduction of Buddhism. It is agreed that translation of Buddhist scriptures into Chinese in great numbers did not begin until the end of the Eastern Han Dynasty, that is, the middle of the 2nd century, when An Shigao and Lokaksema (支娄迦谶) came to Luoyang. With the middle of the 2nd century as the starting point, translation of Buddhist scriptures in China from the end of the Eastern Han Dynasty to the end of the Northern Song Dynasty (12th century AD) can be divided into four stages: initial period, and the periods of development, prosperity, and decline.

2 Initial Period

In the early part of this period, leading translators of Buddhist scriptures were mainly Buddhist missionaries who had journeyed over the Silk Road and made their way into China from Central Asia, as represented by An Shigao and Lokaksema.

An Shigao (?–168 AD) was a prince of Parthia, nicknamed the "Parthian Marquis" (安侯), who renounced his prospect as a contender for the royal throne of Parthia in order to serve as a Buddhist missionary monk. *An* in An Shigao's name is an abbreviation of *Anxi* (安息), meaning *Parthia* in ancient Chinese. In 148, An Shigao arrived in China at the Han Dynasty capital of Luoyang, where he set up a centre for the translation of Buddhist scriptures. He translated thirty-five texts from the Theravada and Mahayana schools of Buddhism, including works on meditation, psychology, and techniques of breath control, introducing the basic Abhidharmic doctrine and the meditative method of the Hinayana school of Buddhism and, for some Chinese scholars, originating what later developed into the study of Zen.

Zhi Qian (支谦) was a Kushan Buddhist monk of Yuezhi ethnicity who translated around thirty-six Buddhist sutras into Chinese between 222 AD and 253 AD. His origin is described in his adopted Chinese name by the prefix *Zhi* (支), abbreviation of *Yuezhi* (月支). Zhi Qian studied with Zhi Liang, who was one of the disciples of Lokaksema. The name "Lokaksema" means "welfare of the world" in Sanskrit. He translated a large quantity of scriptures. The earliest record of a *Heart Sutra* (《心经》) text is a translation attributed to him.

Zhi Qian wrote a preface in the translation of *Dhammapada* (《法句经》). The preface is the first work whose purpose is to express an opinion about translation practice. It recounts an historical anecdote of 224 AD, at the beginning of the Three Kingdoms period. A party of Buddhist monks came to Wuchang. One of them, Zhu Jiangyan by name, was asked to translate some passage from scripture. He did so, in rough Chinese. When Zhi Qian questioned the lack of elegance, a monk from India, named Vighna (维只难), responded that the meaning of the Buddha should be translated simply, without loss, in an easy-to-understand manner: literary adornment is unnecessary. All present concurred and quoted two traditional maxims: Laozi's "beautiful words are untrue; true words are not beautiful" and Confucius' "speech cannot be fully recorded by writing, and speech cannot fully capture meaning."

Zhi Qian's own translations of Buddhist texts are elegant and literary, so the "direct translation" advocated in the anecdote is Vighna's position, not Zhi Qian's.

③ The Period of Development

The second period lasts from the early 4th century to the 7th century, with Dao'an as a representative. Dao'an (道安, 312–385) was a Buddhist monk of the Eastern Jin Dynasty, originating from what is now Hebei Province. Mainly important today as a translator of Buddhist scripture, he was active in Xiangyang until Emperor Xiaowu took the city in 380 and asked Dao'an to live in Chang'an. He spent the last years of life translating and interpreting scripture as well as compiling a catalogue of scriptures. He also advocated monks and nuns taking *Shi* (释) as a surname, from the Chinese for Sakyamuni.

Dao'an played an important role in the development of Buddhism in China. Dating back to the Eastern Jin Dynasty, the translation of Buddhist scripture was in disorder. Numerous translations of Buddhist scriptures were the sheer departure from the originals. His greatest contributions are: observing the existing problems and trying to address them from the aspect of theories, summing up the doctrines of the two schools of dhyana and prajnaparamita which had been popular in China since the Han Dynasty, collecting and systematizing various Chinese versions of Buddhist scriptures, and compiling the first collection of Chinese versions of Buddhist scriptures: *A Comprehensive Catalogue of Various Sutras* (《综理众经目录》). He also directed the translation of Buddhist scriptures in the translation center.

He was a prolific author and commentator. In his commentarial work, Dao'an was one of the first to acknowledge the need to break dependence on the translation method of matching the meanings of Buddhist philosophical concepts with pre-existent Daoist terms, desiring instead the establishment of an independent Buddhist system of terminology. His great contribution in translation theory is that he pointed out Five Losses and Three Difficulties in translation. The five points indicated the losses of original meaning through translation, and the three difficulties refer to the three things, revealing that the translation is a backbreaking job. The five points are as follows.

(1) Sanskrit and Chinese are in reversing word order in sentence structure, as far as the grammar is concerned. (2) Sanskrit prefers to be simple and straight forward, while Chinese prefers to be complex, polished in writing. (3) Sanskrit tends to be repetitive for important points while Chinese does not. (4) Sanskrit always contains sentences within sentences, while Chinese does not. (5) Sanskrit writing is repetitive in subsequent passage, while the repetitions are deleted in Chinese translations. (五失本，即胡语尽倒而使从秦，一失本也；胡经尚质，秦人好文，传可众心，非文不合，二失本也；胡经委悉，至于叹咏，丁宁反复，或三或四，不嫌其烦，而今裁斥，三失本也；胡有义记，正似乱辞，寻说向语，文无以异，或千五百，刈而不存，四失本也；事已全成，将更傍及，反腾前辞已乃后说而悉除，五失本也。)

Another important translator in this period is Kumarajiva (鸠摩罗什). He was born in Kucha (龟兹) in Central Asia. Kumarajiva was a Kuchean Buddhist monk, scholar and translator whose father was from an Indian noble family, and whose mother was a Kuchean princess who significantly influenced his early studies. He had been proficient in buddhist scriptures since he was young. He settled in Chang'an. He is mostly remembered for his prolific translation of Buddhist texts written in Sanskrit to Chinese that he carried out during his later life. Among the most important texts translated by Kumarajiva are the *Diamond Sutra* (《金刚经》), *Amitabha Sutra* (《阿弥陀经》) and *Lotus Sutra* (《妙法莲华经》). His translation was distinctive, possessing a flowing smoothness that reflects his prioritization on conveying the meaning as opposed to precise literal rendering. Because of this, his renderings of seminal Mahayana texts have often remained more popular than later, more exact translations.

Kumarajiva preferred to adhere to the original meaning. The story goes that one day Kumarajiva criticized his disciple Sengrui for translating "heaven sees man, and man sees heaven" (天见人，人见天). Kumarajiva felt that "man and heaven connect, the two able to see each other" (人天交接，两得相见) would be more idiomatic.

In another tale, Kumarajiva discussed the problem of translating incantations and panegyrics at the end of sutras. In the original, there is attention to aesthetics, but the sense of beauty and the literary form (dependent on the particularities of Sanskrit) are lost in translation. It is like chewing up rice to feed people (嚼饭与人), losing the flavor and inducing disgust.

④ **The Period of Prosperity**

The period of the Tang Dynasty (618–907) witnessed not only the most splendid flourishing of Chinese literature, but also the most splendid flourishing of the translation of Buddhist scriptures in China, when the enterprise entered its stage of great prosperity. Although foreign missionaries continued to travel to China and to play an important part in the translation of Buddhist scriptures into Chinese, when Xuanzang returned to Chang'an from India in 645, the days when they could dominate this enterprise were gone forever. The leadership in translating Buddhist scriptures into Chinese was taken over by eminent Chinese monks with a profound knowledge of Buddhism and a good command of both Chinese and Sanskrit.

Xuanzang (600–664), better known as "Sanzang Fashi" (Master Tripitaka), came from a noble family in China. He became a Buddhist monk at Luoyang at the age of fifteen, Having learnt many canons or treatises from various distinguished scholars, he felt that no conclusion could be reached as the doctrines varied, and determined to go to India for further studies. He spent seventeen years in India, touring more than one hundred states. Early in 645 AD, he returned to China, bringing back with him 657 Buddhist scriptures, unprecedented in both number and variety. Since then, Xuanzang dedicated himself to the career of translating Buddhist scriptures. He worked as Chief Translator at the translation center in Chang'an. In 19 years, he and his associates rendered into Chinese of 75 Buddhist scriptures, 1,335 fascicles in all. He produced over half of the total number of the new translations made in the Tang Dynasty. He also wrote *Journey to the West in the Great Tang Dynasty* (《大唐西域记》) in 646–648,which recorded all his experience during his travel, and later his biography.

His great contribution to translation theory is the advocacy of *Five Untranslatables*, the five instances we cannot translate the meaning of the original, but refer to transliteration as a resort. They are described as follows. (1) Secrets, for example, Dharani, a Sanskrit curse; (2) Polysemy, Bhagavan for instance for this Sanskrit word has six meanings; (3) None in China: Jambul for example, a kind of tree that does not grow in China; (4) Deference to the past: Anubodhi for a special kind of knowledge. This transliteration is an established usage; (5) To inspire respect and righteousness: Prajna instead of "wisdom." (玄奘法师论五种不翻：一秘密故，如陀罗尼。二含义多故，如薄

伽梵具六义。三此无故，如阎浮树，中夏实无此木。四顺古故，如阿耨菩提，非不可翻，而摩腾以来长存梵音。五生善故，如般若尊重，智慧轻浅。)

In addition, the excellence of his translations of the Buddhist scriptures is due above all to Xuanzang's mastery of both Sanskrit and Chinese, and to his profound knowledge and understanding of Buddhist doctrines. Earlier great translators were either ignorant of Sanskrit, like Dao'an, or lacked a proficiency in Chinese, like Kumarajiva. The quality of their translations was inevitably affected because they had to depend on something other than the source text or something. That is why they had to first produce a word-for-word translation structurally identical to the original. This first version then was put into grammatically correct Chinese before it was polished. In the case of Xuanzang, the division of duties was even more detailed, yet the translation was basically made by himself. In other words, he abandoned the old process of having the scripture put into interlinear Chinese first. Instead, he put the Sanskrit text directly into good Chinese. As to the style, Xuanzang's translations can be considered literal in contrast with Kumarajiva's which retained the gist of the original only, but free in contrast with Yijing's translations which were full of difficult or unpronounceable words.

The organization of the translation center led by Xuanzang was further perfected, and more than ten duties were established:

> (1) The Yizhu or Chief Translator (译主) who, as the head of the translation center, had a good knowledge of both Chinese, Sanskrit, and Buddhist doctrine.
>
> (2) The Zhengyi (证义), the assistant to Chief Translator who discussed with Chief Translator all the differences in meaning between the translation and the Sanskrit text.
>
> (3) The Chengwen (澄文), who was in charge of finding out possible errors in the original Sanskrit text.
>
> (4) The Duyu (度语), who interpreted Sanskrit into Chinese.
>
> (5) The Bishou (笔受), who recorded the Chinese interpretation and turned it into the first draft of a translation.
>
> (6) The Zhuiwen (缀文), who put the translated version into grammatically correct Chinese.
>
> (7) The Canyi (参译), who not only proofread the original for possible errors but also used the translation to find out if the original contained variant readings.
>
> (8) The Kanding (刊定), who was in charge of deleting redundancy and repetition due to differences in style between Chinese and Sanskrit.
>
> (9) The Runwen (润文), who polished the Chinese translation rhetorically.
>
> (10) The Fanbai (梵呗), who read or recited the translation in the way of reading or

reciting the Sanskrit text to see if the translation sounded harmonious and appropriate for monks to read.

The decline of the translation of Buddhist scriptures in the Northern Song Dynasty was not so much one of quantity as of quality. With the patronage of the emperors the translation center getting even better organized, and the scriptures translated were as many as 284 books of 758 rolls. Yet in terms of quality, translations of Buddhist scriptures produced during this stage prove definitely inferior to those rendered during the Tang Dynasty, especially to the translations by Xuanzang, which have always been acclaimed as the acme of perfection.

5 Exercises

(1) Summarize the different translation styles of the great Buddhist scriptures translators mentioned in this introduction.

(2) Select some translated classic scriptures paragraphs to analyze if the comments of the translators are pertinent or not.

6 References and Further Readings

(1) CHEUNG, M P Y. Volume 1: From Earliest Times to the Buddhist Project [M] //An Anthology of Chinese Discourse on Translation. Manchester & Kinderhook: St. Jerome Publishing, 2006.

(2) 王宏印. 中国传统译论经典诠释: 从道安到傅雷[M]. 武汉: 湖北教育出版社, 2003.

Chapter Two

Translation of Western Science by Jesuit Missionaries in the Ming Dynasty

① Introduction

The period from the 16th century to the 18th century witnessed a high tide of translation ranging over a very wide field. Christianity was reintroduced when Michael Ruggieri, a Jesuit missionary from Italy, set foot on Chinese soil in 1580 and established a chapel in Zhaoqing, Guangdong, In 1601 Matteo Ricci (1552–1610), who arrived in China in 1582, went to Beijing, gained a foothold in the capital, and established a church there, so that Catholicism established legal status in China. Chinese versions of the Bible and the Imitatio Christi were produced and many treatises on the Catholic religion were written by Jesuit missionaries in China during this period.

The historical role the Jesuits played in China went much beyond that of missionaries who introduced a religion to China. Their translations were therefore not confined to religion only. To better pave the way for the acceptance of Christianity by the Chinese, Jesuit missionaries doubled their efforts to introduce Western Science into China. With the arrival of western Christian missionaries, Jesuits in particular, China came into contact with Europe which had begun to overtake China in various scientific and technological fields. To facilitate their relations with Chinese officials and intellectuals, the missionaries translated works of western science and technology as well as Christian texts. Between 1582 and 1773 (Early Qing Dynasty), more than seventy missionaries undertook this kind of work. They were of various nationalities: Italian (Matteo Ricci, Longobardi, De Urbsis, Aleni and Rho), Portuguese (Francis Furtado), Swiss (Jean Terrenz), Polish (Jean Nicolas Smogolenshi), and French (Ferdinand Verbiest, Nicolas Trigaut).

Numerous books on science were translated into Chinese, covering astronomy, mathematics, physics, chemistry, mechanics, mining and metallurgy, military technique, anatomical physiology, biology, and cartography. Translated into Chinese at the same time were works of Western scholastic philosophy and theology. The philosophy of Aristotle and Thomism, the theological and philosophical doctrines of Thomas Aquinas which formed the basis of 13th century scholasticism, were introduced into China with translations of *On the Soul*, *On Heaven*, *Logic*, and *Ethics*. Working with Jesuit missionaries at the translation were some of the Chinese elites who converted to Christianity, and the most distinguished of these Chinese translators was Xu Guangqi (1562–1633) who, in cooperation with Ricci, produced one of the most influential translations in the history of China — *Euclidis Elementorum* (《几何原本》), written by Clavius, a German mathematician.

In the meanwhile, many Chinese works were translated into the West by the Jesuit Missionaries. The most important translation of this period is the translation of Chinese classical works, especially the doctrines of Confucianism. The missionaries realized that Confucius was respected by all the Chinese at that time and tried to find similarities between Confucianism and Christianity to help them propagate their religion. However, the translation of Chinese classics into the West also had great influence on the cultural communication between China and the West.

2 Matteo Ricci and Xu Guangqi

Matteo Ricci (利玛窦) was an Italian Jesuit priest, and one of the founding figures of the Jesuit China Mission, as it existed in the 17th–18th centuries.

In August 1582, Ricci arrived at Macau, a then Portuguese trading post on the South China Sea. At the time, Christian missionary activity in China was almost completely limited to Macau, where some of the local Chinese people had converted to Christianity and lived in the Portuguese

manner. Once in Macau, Ricci started learning Chinese language and customs. This was the beginning of a long project that made him one of the first Western scholars to master Chinese script and classical Chinese. In 1601, Ricci was invited by the Emperor to become an adviser to the Imperial court of the Wanli Emperor; the first Westerner to be invited into the Forbidden City. This honor was in recognition of Ricci's scientific abilities, chiefly his predictions of solar eclipses, which were significant events in the Chinese world. He established the Cathedral of the Immaculate Conception in Beijing, the oldest Catholic Church in the city. Ricci was given free access to the Forbidden City, but he never met the reclusive Emperor Wanli (1563–1620). Wanli did grant him patronage, however, with a generous stipend. Discovering that Confucian thought was dominant in the Ming Dynasty, Ricci became the first to translate the Confucian classics, such as analects of Confucius and moral views of mencius, into a western language, Latin, with assistance from the scholar Xu Guangqi.

Matteo Ricci, together with Sabatino de Ursis (1575–1620) and Xu Guangqi, translated Euclid's *The Elements* (《几何原本》) into Chinese. However well acquainted with the Chinese cultural tradition and language, Matteo Ricci could not have made a Chinese translation of *The Elements* without a competent native partner. Fortunately, for the Jesuit Order as well as for the Chinese society, he met a most open-minded and able cultured person in late Ming China, whose name was Xu Guangqi. Only with the ardent support and cooperation with Xu, could he make the essence of classical Greek mathematics known to Eastern Asia. If Matteo Ricci can be called "the first man of the world," having studied Chinese classics earlier than any Westerners, Guangqi must be surely said to have been, to contemporary Western people, "the first Chinese to have a face," for he was the earliest man in China to turn his front directly to European culture.

Xu Guangqi (1562–1633) was born in Shanghai and after having passed at the age of forty the final imperial examination destined to higher officialdom, became a member of the Hanlin Academy (翰林院), an academic institution at which all elite group of scholars studied and worked for the emperor's politics and administration. In his subsequent career until death as an imperial officer and minister, Xu worked very hard in particular for the reforms of calendar, agriculture and military affairs. It was in 1600 that he met Ricci for the first time in Nanjing, and two years later, he became a Christian. Ricci and Xu seem to have been engaged in the translation of Euclid for one year and half from 1606. It is said that while serving at the Hanlin Academy in Beijing, Xu visited Ricci's residence every day to have a long discussion of the text of *The Elements* and continued to render everything he had learned into a "lucid, imposing and defiant style," until they finished translating the first six books that are the most necessary.

The text on which they based their translation was a Latin version edited by Matteo Ricci's teacher at the Jesuit Collegio Romano in Rome. As Xu Guangqi could not understand Western languages, he must have listened attentively to Ricci's exposition in rough Chinese and asked him about every obscure point each time before putting some amount of Latin passages into a smooth, traditional style of Chinese. To perform such a highly intellectual and technical job as the translation of *The Elements*, he had to coin so many new terms and to select carefully the accurate expressions of mathematical concepts and contexts from the wide vocabulary of Chinese. Although his translation of *The Elements* simply says at the beginning that it was "transcribed" by Xu Guangqi, one will easily imagine that this kind of work could not be accomplished by an ordinary court scholar specialized alone in making literary compositions, but only by an exceptional figure having also all outstanding ability of logical thinking as well as a genuine interest in different culture and science.

When they worked for one year and a half and revised three times their manuscript of the first half, Xu Guangqi suggested Matteo Ricci that they should continue their job to the end of *The Elements*. But Ricci wanted to stop there, in order to make Xu rest for a while and to see what effects their partial translation would exercise on Chinese intellectuals. Thus in 1607 the first six books of his translation of *The Elements* were published with Ricci's "Preface" (《几何原本》引) and Xu's "Prelude" (《几何原本》杂议). Unfortunately, Ricci passed away after three years, so that the complete version of Euclid did not appear until as late as two and a half centuries afterwards. It was in 1859 that a British missionary Alexander Wylie and a Chinese mathematician Li Shanlan (李善兰) published their translation of the remaining nine books of *The Elements*.

To sum up, Xu was a great translator in the Ming Dynasty, for stretching the field of translation to science and technology. Before him, the field of Chinese translation was limited in religion and literature. Moreover, he was a preeminent patriotic personage. He dedicated himself to introducing foreign technology to China, making remarkable contribution to the development of Chinese science and technology. However, he failed to synergize all his translation theories. Thus, his insights into translation didn't merge into a system.

③ Li Zhizao and Yang Tingyun

Li Zhizao (1565–1630) was a Chinese mathematician, astronomer and geographer whose

translations of European scientific books greatly contributed to the spread of Western science in China. Born in Hangzhou, originally from a military family, Li was made a *metropolitan graduate* (进士) , the highest scholar-official title in imperial China in 1598. In 1601, he met an Italian Jesuit Matteo Ricci. To gain acceptance, Ricci had first learned the Chinese language and culture, which in turn enabled him to spread knowledge of Western science and religion. Li was greatly attracted by Ricci's teachings, although he only consented to be baptized by him in 1610, shortly before Ricci's death. Li was regarded as one of the most important Christian converts in the late Ming Dynasty Roman Catholic mission. In 1613, Li assumed a position as an official in Nanking and worked with Xu Guangqi. Both men edited and translated numerous Christian literatures into Chinese. Li Zhizao saw the importance of opening up to the Western world. Li was eager to translate Western literature into Chinese. He helped to translate Matteo Ricci's books into Chinese. At a certain moment Li proposed that an institution should be set up to translate books from European languages into Chinese.

Li began his collaboration with the Jesuits by engraving and printing numerous copies of Ricci's world map, which altered many Chinese views of world geography. The German Jesuit Christopher Clavius (best known for the Gregorian calendar) had been Ricci's teacher and, together with Li, Ricci translated his arithmetic primer *Epitome arithmeticae practicae* (1585; "Selected Arithmetic Methods") as *Rules of Arithmetic Common to Cultures* (《同文算指》, 1614). This book systematically introduced European-style mathematical notation, while Li included complementary elements from traditional Chinese mathematics. Li also wrote a short treatise on geometry dictated by Ricci. Together with the Portuguese Jesuit Francisco Furtado (1589–1653), Li also translated *Commentarii Collegii Conimbricensis e Societate Iesv: In Vniversam Dialecticam Aristotelis Stagiritæ* ("The Exploration of the Patterns of Names"). Based on Aristotle's *On the Heavens* (4th century BC), this book was originally used as a textbook at the College of Coimbra in Portugal. In 1629 he was recommended by Xu Guangqi to work at the Imperial Astronomical Bureau (钦天监) on *Astronomical Treatises of the Chongzhen Reign* (《崇祯历书》) (1628–1644), a compilation of European mathematical and astronomical books. Li wrote the *Plea to Translate Books on Western Calendar Methods* (《请译西洋历法等书疏》), which was submitted to the Ming Dynasty Wanli Emperor, beseeching him to hire missionaries and have them make corrections to the Chinese calendar.

His works included numerous engraved and printed copies of Ricci's world map, which altered many Chinese views' of world geography. Li and Ricci translated Christopher Clavius's arithmetic primer *Epitome arithmeticae practicae* ("Selected Arithmetic Methods") as *Rules of Arithmetic Common to Cultures*, printed in 1614. This book systematically introduced European-style mathematical notation, while Li included complementary elements from traditional Chinese mathematics. He also brought together and published in 1629 a series of books composed by the Jesuits with Chinese help, *First Collection of Writing on the Heavenly Learning* (《天学初函》). These writings concerning Heavenly Studies are divided into those pertaining to principles (理) and to concrete things or objects (器). Li also wrote many prefaces for the Jesuit writings he edited.

To conclude, First, Li Zhizao occupied a certain position in the history of scientific translation in China. He made an outstanding contribution to the cultural and technological exchanges between China and the west. And the influence of Li Zhizao's scientific translation is listed as follow: First, Li Zhizao was the first to introduce the knowledge of astronomy, written calculation and formal logic to the Chinese, and corrected people's limited understanding of the geographical scope of the world, so that broadening the vision of the people in the late Ming Dynasty. Secondly, he triggered a new trend of learning science, pouring major energy into the development of science and technology in China. Moreover, Li translated many scientific terms into Chinese, facilitating the spread of western scientific knowledge in China. In addition to translation practice, Li Zhizao's serious attitude towards the translation of Western works has set a good example for later translators

Yang Tingyun was born in Hangzhou in 1557, and died in Hangzhou in 1628, at the age of 71. Yang Tingyun was a scholar-official. He studied the Confucian classics for many years, but was also interested in Buddhism. He held several very important posts, including that of vice-governor of Peking. He met Matteo Ricci in Peking during the years 1602–1608 and was deeply influenced by him, but entered the Catholic Church only in 1613, in Hangzhou, after much persuasion by Li Zhizao. He was then 55.

Yang Tingyun was Giulio Aleni's (艾儒略, 1582–1649) good friend and important collaborator. In 1623, Aleni, at the request of some of his friends, who were interested in European knowledge and scholarship, wrote *Summary of Western Learning* (《西学凡》). In it, Aleni offered an outline of studies then given at European universities, namely, rhetorica, philosophia, medicina, leges (law), canones (canon law) and theologia. *Summary of Western Learning* provided also information on medical training in Europe and on different charitable institutions of the church, such as hospitals and orphanages. At the beginning of the book there is a preface by Yang Tingyun. At the end of the book, Aleni revealed an ambitious project that he had in mind, namely, to gather a number of scholars who would devote their time to the translation of books into Chinese. It might take ten-odd years for these books to be published, but he was confident that they would come out successfully. Yang Tingyun in his preface gave full support to Aleni's project. He stressed emphatically that one should not let slip the knowledge which Aleni had introduced in his book. "Give me a decade and with the help of scores of hands we shall bring our work to its completion." He spoke of the 7,000-odd volumes that were being sent from Europe to China through the efforts of Nicolas Trigault. Unfortunately, both Yang Tingyun and Aleni died before their great project could be realized; it remained only an aspiration.

Yang Tingyun was not a scientist nor a mathematician or a cartographer like Xu Guangqi or Li Zhizao. He was a deep thinker and a very good writer. He was a humble man and had a good sense of humour. These qualities can be seen in a very amusing incident he refers to in one of his prefaces to Ricci's books. Yang Tingyun writes that, when he was in Peking, he often went to Ricci's residence. He enjoyed the evenings he spent listening to Ricci's talks on science, mathematics. He admits though that quite often he couldn't follow Ricci's reasoning. One night, he says, "Ricci looked at me, made a deep sigh and said, 'In Peking I have found only two intelligent persons: Xu Guangqi and Li Zhizao!' "

In fact, Yang Tingyun's contribution to the spread of western scientific technology was not great for his lack of scientific knowledge. The only scientific work, which he helped editing and prefacing, was Aleni's *On Geography* (《识方外纪》).

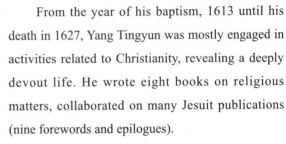

From the year of his baptism, 1613 until his death in 1627, Yang Tingyun was mostly engaged in activities related to Christianity, revealing a deeply devout life. He wrote eight books on religious matters, collaborated on many Jesuit publications (nine forewords and epilogues).

Technical translations during the Ming Dynasty facilitated the scientific and technological development of ancient China, and thus foreign missionaries whose main purpose was to promote Christianity became the first group of disseminators of Western knowledge.

Translations during the Ming Dynasty had two distinguishing characteristics: (1) The subject of translation shifted from Buddhist scriptures to scientific and technological knowledge; (2) Translators in this period were mainly scientists and government officials who were erudite scholars, and the Western missionaries who brought Western knowledge to China. The effect of the translations was that China was opened to Western knowledge, and translation facilitated the scientific and technical development.

So successful were the Ming translators as pioneers on technical translation, that some of the translated technical terms are still in use today. However, translation practice was overstressed and no translation theories were developed during the Ming Dynasty. By comparison with the large scale of translation of the Buddhist scriptures during the Tang Dynasty, translation during the Ming Dynasty was not so influential in terms of the history of translation in China. During the Tang Dynasty, there was translation practice accompanied by a quest for systematic translation theories, while during the Ming Dynasty, the main purpose of translation was to introduce Western technical knowledge.

4 Exercises

(1) Try to do a field work regarding the influence of Li Zhizao and Yang Tingyun in the development of Christianity in Hangzhou.

(2) Study the terms in Ricci and Xu Guangqi's translation of *The Elements*, to see if they are well translated and if they are preserved in modern mathematics.

5 References and Further Readings

(1) STANDAERT N. Yang Tingyun. Confucian and Christian in Late Ming China: His Life and Thought [M]. Leiden: ej Brill, 1988.

(2) 孙尚扬. 利玛窦与徐光启[M]. 北京: 新华出版社, 1993.

(3) 赵晖. 耶儒柱石: 李之藻、杨廷筠传[M]. 杭州: 浙江人民出版社, 2007.

Chapter Three

Translation of Science in the Late Qing Dynasty

By the latter half of the 19th century China was beset with difficulties both at home and abroad. With repeated defeats suffered since the Opium War (1840–1842) and more and more treaties of national betrayal and humiliation signed under coercion, particularly after the loss of the Sino-Japarese War of 1894–1895. The whole empire was on the verge of disintegration. Drawing a lesson from this bitter experience, Chinese bureaucrats and intellectuals of deep in sight finally came to realize the cost of their parochial arrogance and the great urgency of constitutional reform and modernization by means of learning from the West. Although the aim of the Westernization Movement (洋务运动) initiated in the later half the 19th century by comprador bureaucrats was to introduce the techniques of capitalist production, what was actually imported from the West later was not confined to advanced technology only. "西学", which means Western learning, a late Qing Dynasty term for Western natural and social sciences, was introduced together with Western literature. A new wave of translation swept China.

① The Introduction of Modern Science by Protestant Missionaries

Even after the British victory in the First Opium War, which led to highly favorable trade agreements for Britain and a resumption of the flow of opium to China, Western missionaries had only limited influence in China. Yet Protestant missions were significant for the introduction of modern science: they principally funded the new translations, newspapers, and schools that introduced it in the 1850s.

Once the East India Company decided to permit missionaries into its territories, Protestant denominations quickly organized. Similar groups organized in mainland Europe, and even the Jesuit order regrouped to enter China again. The London Missionary Society (LMS), founded in 1795, played an important role in China throughout the 19th century. Similarly, the American Board of

Commissioners for Foreign Missions organized in 1810. The Protestant mission in China laid the foundation for future work by arranging a corpus of Christian literature for printing. It also provided groundwork for gathering books in Chinese by the missionaries. Robert Morrison (1782–1834), for example, who worked for the LMS, put together an impressive library collection that included works on traditional Chinese medicine and mathematical astronomy. Morrison's collection contributed to the development of LMS Press. Established at Malacca in 1818 at the Anglo-Chinese College, the LMS Press later moved to Hong Kong and then to Shanghai in 1842, where it was renamed Inkstone Press. After 1847, when Alexander Wylie (1815–1887) began to supervise its operation, Inkstone Press became the publishing mecca of missionary activities.

Daniel Jerome Macgowan (1814–1893) and Benjamin Hobson (1816–1873), both physicians, were the key pioneers in the late 1840s and early 1850s. The American Macgowan initially served as a medical missionary in Ningbo. Later he became a freelance lecturer and writer, as well as a member of the Qing maritime customs service. After moving to Hong Kong, Hobson, an English medical missionary, pioneered a series of medical and science translations, coauthored with the Chinese, for his premedical classes in Guangzhou. Meanwhile, Alexander Wylie came to Shanghai from England to join the LMS Inkstone Press as its printer. He had been selected by James Legge (1815–1897), who pioneered the translation of the Chinese Classics at Oxford with the help of Wang Tao (1828–1897).

Hobson produced a series of works to educate his medical students, including the *Summary of Astronomy* (1849), *Treatise on Physiology* (1851), *First Lines of the Practice of Surgery in the West* (1857), *Treatise on Midwifery and Diseases of Children* (1858), and *Practice of Medicine and Materia Medica* (1858). Hobson's work *Treatise on Physiology* presented modern anatomy and reintroduced the centrality of the brain and the nervous system, which Jesuits had tried unsuccessfully to do in the late Ming and early Qing.

Hobson's work represented the first sustained introduction of the modern European sciences and medicine in the first half of the 19th century. His 1849 digest of modern astronomy, for instance, presented the Copernican solar system in terms of Newtonian gravitation and pointed to God as the author of the works of creation. Thereafter, Newtonian celestial mechanics, which was based on gravitational pull, was increasingly presented in Protestant accounts of modern science.

By including sections on physics, chemistry, astronomy, geography, and zoology for his Chinese medical students, Hobson unexpectedly attracted the interest of literati unsuccessful in the civil examinations. They used Hobson's *Treatise* to catch up with findings since the Jesuits. This group, which included Xu Shou and Hua Hengfang (1833–1902), also carried out experiments. After fleeing the Taiping rebels in the early 1860s, they were invited by Zeng Guofan, the leader of the victorious Qing armies, to work in the newly established Anqing Arsenal. Hua began translation projects with Alexander Wylie and Joseph Edkins, while Xu worked on constructing a steamboat based on Hobson's diagrams.

British and American Protestants in China recognized that Chinese literati were interested in the sciences that the missionaries accepted as part of their Christian heritage. Like their Jesuit predecessors, British and American missionaries viewed science as emblematic of their superior knowledge systems. Consequently, their introduction of modern science and medicine to China was not only a missionary tactic; it was a way of showcasing the wealth and power of Western nations.

Among treaty ports, Shanghai by 1860 was the main center of foreign trade, international business, and missionary activity. The LMS Press in Shanghai became the most influential publisher of Western learning after 1850. It published translations from a distinguished missionary community, which included Alexander Wylie and Joseph Edkins, and worked with outstanding Chinese scholars such as Li Shanlan and Wang Tao, who had moved to Shanghai after failing to gain a place in the imperial civil examinations. Wang went to Shanghai in 1849 and was invited to serve as the Chinese editor at the Inkstone Press.

A talented missionary printer and translator, Alexander Wylie produced the *Shanghae Serial* monthly for thirteen issues in 1857 and for two more issues in 1858. Wylie was also busy during this period making some remarkable inquiries about Chinese science and mathematics with the help of Li Shanlan. Through this interaction, Li successfully completed the transition from the traditional craft of algebra to understanding the modern calculus. Around 1860, Wylie and Li also started but left unfinished a complete translation of Newton's *Principia.* It presented for the first time in Chinese his laws of motion. About 1868, Li Shanlan completed the translation in the Jiangnan Arsenal's Translation Department with the help of John Fryer, but the work was never published because it was too hard to understand. After 1899, the manuscript was lost. The title for the Li-Fryer version of the *Principia* in Chinese meant "Investigating and Extending Knowledge of Mathematical Principles."

Wylie's and Li's 1859 translation of *The Outline of Astronomy* (1851) by John Herschel grew out of their early collaboration. In 1855, Wylie and Li Shanlan also translated books seven through fifteen of Euclid's *Elements of Geometry,* which had been left out of the Jesuit versions. In 1853, Wylie prepared his *Compendium of Arithmetic* with the help of his Chinese student. This primer contained the rudimentary rules of arithmetic, the theory of proportion, and logarithms, but Wylie also solved traditional Chinese mathematical problems to make the translation accessible. Wylie and Li Shanlan also published through Inkstone Press an 1859 translation of the 1836 work *Elements of Algebra,* which in turn had been taken from the original by Augustus De Morgan. Wylie and Li stressed modern algebra as a mathematical language for the natural sciences. In particular, they related modern algebra to traditional Chinese mathematics by substituting it for procedures solving equations with a single unknown or four unknowns.

While collaborating on the *Shanghae Serial,* Li Shanlan and Alexander Wylie also translated a work that they entitled *Step by Step in Algebra and the Differential and Integral Calculus* (1859), which reintroduced the Cartesian algebraic symbols rejected in 1712 by the Kangxi Emperor. Wylie noted in his English preface the effect the calculus would have: "There is little doubt that this branch of the science will commend itself to native mathematicians, in consideration of its obvious utility. A spirit of inquiry is abroad among the Chinese, and there is a class of students in the empire, by no means small in number, who receive with avidity instruction on scientific matters from the West. Mere superficial essays and popular digests are far from adequate to satisfy such applicants. "

After Qing armies defeated the Taiping, the calculus spread through the new arsenals first established in the 1860s. The practical applications of the differential and integral calculus for arms manufacture and shipbuilding made it essential for Chinese working in the arsenals' new technical schools under British or French advisers. A new understanding of European mathematics among Chinese literati emerged that emphasized the integration of Chinese and Western mathematics. This emerging mixture no longer favored Chinese origins. Until the 19th century, literati had understood mathematics as a tool. With the introduction of advanced algebra and calculus after 1850, the Chinese began to view mathematics as a field of learning with its own principles.

2 John Fryer and the Translation of Terms of Chemical Elements

John Fryer (傅兰雅, 1839–1928), an Englishman of humble origins, was the most prolific translator of books on "Western learning" in 19th-century China. Between his arrival in Hong Kong in 1861 as a largely self-educated Protestant missionary and his relocation to Berkeley, where he was appointed the Louis Agassiz Professor of Oriental Languages and Literatures in 1896, Fryer participated in the translation or compilation of close to 100 books. In addition, he engaged in a broad range of activities devoted to translating more practical aspects of Euro-American science and technology into late imperial China, for instance, as editor of the periodical *The Chiness Scientific Magazine* (《格致汇编》), the first scientific magazine in China, director of the Shanghai Polytechnic Institution and Reading Room (格致书院), and proprietor of the Chinese Scientific Book Depot (格致书室).

In 1867, Xu Shou and Hua Hengfang, initiated a Translation Department at the Jiangnan Arsenal, which Zeng Guofan enlarged in 1868 to include a school to train translators. John Fryer worked at the Jiangnan Arsenal after he left the Anglo-Chinese School in Shanghai in 1867. Before that, Fryer was professor of English in the School of Foreign Languages in Beijing from 1863 to 1865. When Fryer officially joined the arsenal as a translator of scientific books, he indicated that he welcomed the appointment over teaching, which he did not enjoy, and over missionizing, for which he was considered too secular. He stayed for twenty-eight years before accepting the Aggasiz Chair in Oriental Languages at Berkeley University and leaving for California in the summer of 1896. Fryer completed 129 translations at the arsenal, with seventy-seven published by the arsenal itself (fourteen of those were released between 1896 and 1909 when Fryer was in California). Fifty-seven of Fryer's seventy-seven arsenal translations dealt with the natural sciences. His translations of physics were concentrated in the years between 1885 and 1894. He also completed five works on mathematics in 1887–1888 compared to seven from 1871 to 1879. Forty-eight works dealt with applied science, with eighteen on manufacturing. Because the Chinese government prioritized machinery, Fryer early on stressed Chinese adaptations from *The Engineer and Machinist's Drawing Book,* published in Britain in 1855.

Writing in May 1886 at a symposium on "The Advisability, or the Reverse, of Endeavoring to Convey Western Knowledge to the Chinese Through the Medium of Their Own Language," Fryer noted, "Next if we examine Chinese secular literature we find astronomy and mathematics with kindred subjects have always been popular among the Chinese. The most highly prized books on these subjects are the translations or compilations made by the Jesuits two or three centuries ago. These are found in the library of every Chinaman who has any pretensions to general scholarship. Coming down to more times that are recent. There is strong demand for whatever useful knowledge foreigners have to impart. The cry on all sides is for more books." In 1880, Fryer rejected the missionary view that the Chinese language was inadequate for scientific discourse. Moreover, Fryer discarded the notion that English would become a universal language or that China would ever be ruled by foreign powers. He then described the method of translating that he and his co-workers employed and noted the translators' efforts to establish a systematic nomenclature in a report entitled *An Account of the Department for the Translation of Foreign Books at the Kiangnan Arsenal Shanghai* (《江南制造局翻译西书事略》).

(1) Using existing nomenclature. (a) To search in the principal native works on the arts and sciences, as well as those by the Jesuit missionaries and recent Protestant missionaries. (b) To enquire of such Chinese merchants, manufactures, mechanics, etc., as would be likely to have the term in current use; (2) coining new terms. Where it becomes necessary to invent a new term there is a choice of three methods: (a) Make a new character, the sound of which can be easily known from the phonetic portion, or use an existing but uncommon character, giving it a new meaning. (b) Invent a descriptive term, using as few characters as possible. (c) phoneticize the foreign term, using the sounds of putonghua, and always endeavoring to employ the same character for the same sound as far as possible, giving preference to characters most used by previous translators or compilers; (3) constructing a general vocabulary list of terms and proper names.

Based on his translation experience in Kiangnan Arsenal, Fryer put forward some essential features of China's system of scientific nomenclature in his report entitled *Scientific Terminology: Present Discrepancies and Means of Securing Uniformity* (《科学术语:现存的分歧和获取一致的方法》).

(1) New terms ought to be translations, where possible, and not mere transliterations.

(2) New terms, if positively untranslatable, must be transliterated by the most suitable Chinese characters obtained.

(3) New terms ought to accord as far as possible with the general construction of the language.

(4) In the next place, new terms should be short and terse.

(5) New terms must be accurately and clearly defined.

(6) New terms must bear an analogy with all others of the class they belong to.

(7) Lastly and briefly, new terms must be elastic.

At that time, China lacked scholars with sufficient knowledge of Western languages. Although the Westerners who came to China had a relatively good grasp of the Chinese language, it was difficult for them to translate Western books into Chinese on their own. For this reason, the prevalent way of rendering Western works on sciences and technology was collaboration between a Westerner with some knowledge of the Chinese language and a Chinese scholar. This practice was commonly referred to as "oral translation (by a Westerner), recorded with the brush (by a Chinese scribe)" (口译笔述). John Fryer described the translation practice at the Jiangnan Arsenal as follows:

"The foreign translator, having first mastered his subject, sits down with the Chinese writer and dictates to him sentence by sentence, consulting with him whenever a difficulty arises as to the way the ideas ought to be expressed in Chinese, or explaining to him any point that happens to be beyond his comprehension. The manuscript is then revised by the Chinese writer, and any errors in style, and the like, are corrected by him. In a few cases, the translations have been done over again by the foreign translator, but in most instances such an amount of trouble has been avoided by the native writers, who, as a rule, are able to detect errors of any importance themselves, and who, it must be acknowledged, take great pains to make the style as clear and the information as accurate as possible."

Xu Shou was one of the founders of the most important official organization for translation — the Translation Department at the Jiangnan Arsenal; John Fryer was Xu's main collaborator and the most productive "oral translator" of the Translation Department. Together, the two rendered five specialized works on chemistry into Chinese.

(1) *Mirroring the Origins of Chemistry* as《化学鉴原》, 1871;

(2) *A Sequel to Mirroring the Origins of Chemistry* as《化学鉴原续编》, 1875;

(3) *A Supplement to Mirroring the Origins of Chemistry* as《化学鉴原补编》, 1882;

(4) *Chemical Analysis* as《化学考质》, 1883;

(5) *Seeking Numerical Patterns in Chemistry* as《化学求数》, 1883.

Mirroring the Origins of Chemistry, as the first work on chemistry in the Chinese language, exerted considerable influence during the later half of the 19th century.

The technical terminology employed in the *Mirroring the Origins of Chemistry* can be divided into one part concerned with chemical substances (mainly elements and chemical compounds) and dealing with chemical concepts. The efforts by Xu Shou and John Fryer to coin translated terms for the chemical elements were particularly successful. Xu and Fryer were the first to propose a consistent program for the translation of chemical elements into Chinese:

In the West, the names of substances often have many "characters" and are difficult to pronounce. If one translates them into Chinese, it is impossible that they fully correspond [to the original]. Here we use one character for each term designating a chemical element…With respect to the names of compounds we combine the terms of the elements. Many of the elements were known in ancient China. Their names we retained, for instance, "金" (gold), "银" (silver), "铜" (copper) , "铁" (iron) , "铅" (lead), "锡" (tin) , "汞" (mercury), "硫" (sulphur) , "磷" (phosphorus) and "炭" (carbon) . We also retained names that had already been translated appropriately, such as "氧气" (oxygen), "氮气" (nitrogen) and "氢气" (hydrogen). In addition, there are several dozen (elements) — which were either unknown to the ancients or which they knew of but designated with a name that was deficient in some respect—and which are covered more completely in Western books. Were one to translate their meanings, it would be extraordinarily difficult to be concise. Transliterating the whole name would be excessively complicated. We therefore used the first sound of the Western term and transliterated it with one Chinese character. If the first sound was unsuitable, we used the second sound. We then added a radical to distinguish the classes but retained the original pronunciation.

Moreover, Xu Shou and Fryer proposed the principle to use "官话" or putonghua as the basis for transliterations. Overall, these principles were comprehensive, simple and easy to understand. Not only did they make it possible to coin appropriate names for known elements, but they set a standard for naming elements that were to be discovered in the future.

In contrast, John G. Kerr (1824–1901) and He Liaoran applied no fixed principles in the translation of the elements in their *An Introduction to Chemistry* (《化学初阶》), sometimes using semantic renderings and sometimes transliterations. Some of the characters they devised for the chemical elements had a very large number of strokes. If one compares the two systems, the advantages of Xu Shou and John Fryer's approach are obvious (see Table 3.1).

Table 3.1 Comparison of the names for chemical elements in
Mirroring the Origins of Chemistry and *An Introduction to Chemistry*

NO.	English	Mirroring the Origins of Chemistry	An Introduction to Chemistry	Modern Chinese
1	calcium	鈣	鉓	钙
2	potassium	鉀	鏩	钾
3	silicon	矽	玻	硅
4	sodium	鈉	鑥	钠
5	arsenic	鉮	窒	砷
6	cadmium	鎘	鐭	镉
7	cobalt	鈷	鎬	钴
8	uranium	鈾	鏾	铀
9	zinc	鋅	鋰	锌

The main reason why Xu Shou and John Fryer's translated names for the elements are still in use is that their method of translation was quite rational, and not simply, as has been suggested, that the books translated at the Jiangnan Arsenal enjoyed considerable circulation. In striking contrast, the overwhelming majority of the terms for organic and inorganic compounds and chemical concepts which Xu and Fryer proposed in the same works were not adopted by later generations and soon fell into oblivion.

At its peak, the Jiangnan Arsenal contained four institutions: the Translation Department, the Foreign Language School, the school for training skilled workmen, and the machine shop. In addition, the Jiangnan Arsenal had thirteen branch factories. By 1892, it occupied seventy-three acres of land, with 1,974 workshops and a total number of 2,982 workers. The arsenal acquired 1,037 sets of machines and produced forty-seven kinds of machinery under the supervision of foreign technicians.

③ Exercises

(1) What is the justification of collaborating translation in the translation of science in the Qing Dynasty?

(2) Is the translation method taken by Xu Shou and John Fryer still applicable in translation of modern chemical element?

(3) Make an investigation of the history of translating chemical elements in Chinese.

④ References and Further Readings

(1) WANG Y. A New Inquiry into the Translation of Chemical Terms by John Fryer and Xu Shou [M] //Michael Lackner, Iwo Amelung and Joachim Kurtz, eds. New Terms for New Ideas. Western Knowledge and Lexical Change in Late Imperial China. Leiden: Brill, 2001.

(2) WRIGHT D. Translating Science: The Transmission of Western Chemistry into Late Imperial China, 1840–1900 [M]. Leiden: Brill, 2000.

Chapter Four

Yan Fu's Translation Principles

① An Introduction to Yan Fu

Yan Fu (1854–1921), courtesy name Jidao, was a Chinese scholar and translator, most famous for introducing Western thoughts, including Darwin's idea of "natural selection," into China during the late 19th century.

He studied in the Fuzhou Shipyard School in Fuzhou, Fujian Province. Yan Fu first encountered Western science in the English-language section of the Fuzhou Shipyard School, where he studied arithmetic, geometry, algebra, analytical geometry, trigonometry, physics, mechanics, chemistry, geology and navigation. In 1877, he travelled to Britain, where he studied seamanship, first at Portsmouth, and then at the Royal Naval College in Greenwich. After returning to China in 1879 he taught at Fuzhou Shipyard School for a short time, before moving to the Beiyang Naval Academy in Tianjin, where he eventually became Principal. In 1902, the National University in Beijing set up the Bureau for the Compilation and Translation of Books, where Yan Fu became Director, working there for two years. In 1908 or 1909 he was invited by the Board of Education to work as the Head of the Bureau for the Revision of Terminology to make dictionaries and glossaries of terms. He worked there for three years, but, although an "astonishing number of draft glossaries" were prepared, most were never completed. It is said by one biographer that he used the Bureau merely as a means of earning a living and that he did not throw himself heart and soul into the work.

His heart was indeed not in technical translation, but in the transmission of the political ideas which he had discovered in the West, and which he felt to be of urgent relevance to the future of China. In the late 1890s, spurred by the national disasters he saw unfolding around him, he began translating a number of key works of modern Western thought, namely, in order of their year of publication.

(1) *Evolution and Ethics and Other Essays* by Thomas H. Huxley as 《天演论》, 1898;

(2) *The Study of Sociology* by Herbert Spencer as 《群学肄言》, 1902;

(3) *The Wealth of Nations* by Adam Smith as 《原富》, 1902;

(4) *On Liberty* by John Stuart Mill as 《群己权界论》, 1903;

(5) *A History of Politics* by Edward Jenks as 《社会通诠》, 1904.

(6) *System of Logic* by John Stuart Mill as 《穆勒名学》, 1905;

(7) *The Spirit of the Laws* by Montesquieu as 《法意》, 1909;

(8) *Primer of Logic* by William Stanley Jevons as 《名学浅说》, 1909.

② Yan Fu's Translation Theory

The manner in which Yan Fu approached this aspect of the task of translation is of interest for several reasons. He was by far the most influential translator of his generation, admired as much for his Chinese prose style as for his skill as the greatest contemporary interpreter of Western thought. He stands at the watershed between the translations of the missionaries and the early modern government schools and arsenals — carried out between 1840 and 1895 — and the wave of scientific translations from Japanese sources which dominated the period from 1900 to the May Fourth Movement of 1919. Finally, he himself played a direct though ambiguous role in the process of standardization of science terminology in China as Head of the State Terminology Bureau and other similar organizations in the dying years of the Qing regime.

Yan Fu's "Preface to *Evolution and Ethics and Other Essays*" was exceedingly well-timed to inaugurate 20th-century translation theory in China: it was published in 1901. Often regarded as the most important statement on translation and repeatedly debated by scholars throughout the past century, this short piece has assumed a prominence unequaled by any other theoretical work so far produced in the country. Opinions on Yan Fu's contribution to Chinese translation theory have been divided. His ideas about "信" (faithfulness, fidelity), "达" (fluency, comprehensibility) and "雅" (elegance, polish) have been said to exert influences both laudatory and detrimental. Also on the negative side, critics have pointed out that his actual practice, as demonstrated in his translation of Huxley's *Evolution and Ethics and Other Essays*, to which his Preface was presumably an introduction, was at great variance with his theory. The liberty he took with Huxley's text shows Yan to have been least concerned with xin, the first of his three principles.

Yan stated in his preface that "there are three difficulties in translation: faithfulness, expressiveness, and elegance." He did not set these three difficulties as general standards for translation and did not say that these were independent of each other. However, since the publication of that work, the phrase "faithfulness, expressiveness, and elegance" has been attributed to Yan Fu as a standard for any good translation and has become a cliche in Chinese academic circles, giving rise to numerous debates and theses.

(1) Translation involves three requirements difficult to fulfill: faithfulness, comprehensibility and elegance. Faithfulness is difficult enough to attain but a translation that is faithful but not comprehensible is no translation at all. Comprehensibility is therefore of prime importance. Since China's opening to foreign trade by sea, there has been no lack of interpreters and translators. But if you assign them any book to translate and tell them to meet these two requirements, few can do so. The reasons for their inability are: superficiality, partiality and lack of discrimination. This book is based on the new knowledge of the West acquired during the last fifty years and was one of the author's later works. My translation attempts to present its profound thought. It does not follow the exact order of words and sentences of the original text but reorganizes and elaborates. However, it does not deviate from the original ideas. It is more an exposition than a translation as it seeks to elaborate -- an unorthodox way of transmission. Kumarajiva said, "Whoever imitates me would fall." There will be many others coming after me in translation work; I sincerely hope that they will not use this book as an excuse for their failings. (译事三难：信、达、雅。求其信已大难矣，顾信矣不达，虽译犹不译也，则达尚焉。海通已来，象寄之才，随地多有，而任取一书，责其能与于斯二者则已寡矣。其故在浅尝，一也；偏至，二也；辨之者少，三也。今是书所言，本五十年来西人新得之学，又为作者晚出之书。译文取明深义，故词句之间，时有所颠倒附益，不斤斤于字比句次，而意义则不悖本文。题曰达旨，不云笔译，取便发挥，实非正法。什法师有云：学我者病。来者方多，幸勿以是书为口实也。)

(2) Terms in Western language texts are defined as they occur, somewhat similar to digressions in Chinese. What comes after elaborates what goes before and completes the sense and structure. A sentence in a Western language consists of from two or three words to tens or hundreds of words. If we should follow this construction in translation, it would not be comprehensible, and if we should delete and abridge, we might miss some of the ideas expressed in the original. When the translator has understood thoroughly and digested the whole text he will then be able to rewrite it in the best manner possible. Since the original is profound in thought and involved in style, which are difficult to convey together, he should correlate what precedes and what follows to bring out the theme. All this effort is to achieve comprehensibility; for only when a piece of translation is comprehensible can it be regarded as faithful. (西文句中名物字，多随举随释，如中文之旁支，后乃遥接前文，足意成句。故西文句法，少者二三字，多者数十百言，假令仿此为译，则恐必不可通，而删削取径，又恐意义有漏。此在译者将全文神理，融会于心，则下笔抒词，自然互备。至原文词

理本深，难于共喻，则当前后引衬，以显其意。凡此经营，皆以为达，为达即所以为信也。）

(3) *The Book of Change* says, "Fidelity is the basis of writing." Confucius said, "Writing should be comprehensible." He also said, "Where language has no refinement, its effects will not extend far." These three dicta set the right course for literature and are the guidelines for translation. In addition to faithfulness and comprehensibility, we should strive for elegance in translation. This is not just for extending the effects far. In using the syntax and style of the pre-Han period, one actually facilitates the comprehensibility of the profound principles and subtle thoughts whereas in using the modern vernacular one finds it difficult to make things comprehensible. Oftentimes, straining the meaning but slightly to fit the language can result in gross misinterpretations. Inevitably, I had to make a choice between these two media, not that I have a preference for the eccentric. My translation has been criticized for its abstruse language and involved style. But I must say this is the result of my determined effort at comprehensibility. The treatise in the book is largely based upon logic, mathematics and science as well as astronomy. If a reader is not familiar with these studies, even if he is of the same nationality and speaks the same language as the author, he won't be able to comprehend much, far less by reading a translation. (易曰：修辞立诚。子曰：辞达而已。又曰：言之无文，行之不远。三曰乃文章正轨，亦即为译事楷模。故信、达而外，求其尔雅，此不仅期以行远已耳。实则精理微言，用汉以前字法、句法，则为达易；用近世利俗文字，则求达难。往往抑义就词，毫厘千里。审择于斯二者之间，夫固有所不得已也，岂钓奇哉。不佞此译，颇贻艰深文陋之讥，实则刻意求显，不过如是。又原书论说，多本名数格致，及一切畴人之学，倘于之数者向未问津，虽作者同国之人，言语相通，仍多未喻，知夫出以重译也耶。）

3 Criticism of Yan Fu's Translation Theory

Many Chinese evaluations of Yan's translations acknowledged his contribution in introducing Western learning. For instance, Liang Qichao said that Yan, as one of the earliest overseas Chinese students to learn a foreign language and understand Western civilization, had begun the task of introducing new ideas to China directly from the West. Cai Yuanpei said that, among those introducing Western philosophy during the last fifty years, "Yan Fu ranks as number one." Hu Hanmin said, "Among the translations in the field of politics in recent years, Yan Fu's works are the most valuable." Kang Youwei regarded Yan as one of the two most talented translators in China.

Yan's translations, however, not only won applause but also provoked heated debates. The criticisms of his translations have developed to form a complicated discussion including not only criticisms of his work but also criticisms of these criticisms. The bulk of the arguments revolve around Yan's famous three principles of translation — "accuracy," "elegance" and "accessiblity." Almost all readers agree that Yan's translations were elegant, but many question their accuracy and accessibility.

I Issue of Accessibility and Elegance

Even though Yan was a pioneer in introducing Western learning and promoting new values, he resisted the burgeoning vernacular movement and used ancient writings to translate Western works as well as to write essays and personal letters throughout his life. For him, there was no contradiction between the importance of Western-inspired progress and ancient writings as the most precious and civilized way to express important ideas in Chinese. But in the 1890s, those favoring a more colloquial prose style (白话文) started to criticize ancient writings. So not surprisingly, therefore, many criticized Yan, holding that his prose style restricted his readership. In 1898, Wu Rulun wrote a preface for Yan's *The Theory of Natural Evolution*. He praised Yan's prose style as suitable for the task of translation but also pointed out, "When Master Yan presents us with a piece that has enduring prose value equal to the works of the pre-Qin scholars, I am worried that there exists a deep gap between him and his readers." Wu thus worried that Yan's elegant prose was not fully appreciated or even understood by some of the literati.

Although Liang Qichao surely had no problem reading Yan's classical Chinese, he worried about the difficulties faced by younger students. In 1902, he wrote a book review of *The Principles of Prosperity in New Citizen Journal* (《新民丛报》). Liang not only praised Yan's translation for helping Chinese readers understand the first important book in the history of Western economics but also approved of Yan's translations of economic terms — "Yan's translations of them are precise, suitable, and should not be replaced." Nevertheless, Liang worried that Yan's language was too elegant to understand by school students, and that the content of the book was too profound to fully grasp. He concluded: "Even though Master Yan is a worthy person, I cannot hide the fact that his elegant prose style will prevent his book from conveying civilized thought to the citizens. In response, Yan tried to rebut Liang's criticism, "Language is the tool for expressing thought and feeling. Coarse terms (i.e. the vernacular) cannot express sophisticated ideas and refined feelings." Moreover, "The expected readers of my

translations are not young school students but the literati, who are familiar with the classics. So if there is a problem of accessibility, responsibility for it lies with the reader, not the translator."

In 1905, when Hu Shi was fifteen years old, he read Yan's translations and works. Hu felt that Yan's prose was too elegant to understand by youngsters as he saw it, the older literati found Yan's translations elegant and readable, while the young people unfamiliar with ancient writings found them elegant but not readable. Hu, however, did not criticize Yan for lack of accuracy, His (Yan's) carefulness and seriousness in translating books is really admirable and can be taken as a model. It should be noted that even Hu Shi, who was the most famous liberal in the republican China and had a deep understanding of the English language and Western civilization, believe that Yan has accurately translated Western writings, including Mill's liberal ideas.

Another famous liberal and leader of the May Fourth Movement, Cai Yuanpei, had a similar opinion. In an article written in 1924, Cai said that, although it was not easy for the average reader to understand Yan's translations, the classical prose could still meet the needs of a significant number of intellectuals. Cai said that Yan's works seem to be old-fashioned and his literary style is difficult to comprehend, but the standard with which he selected books and the way he translated them are very admirable even today.

The appreciation of Hu and Cai of Yan's translations, however, was not typical of the May Fourth Movement as a whole. By the 1930s, the vernacular had become more popular, and so there were fewer readers interested in reading or even able to read Yan's translations. The comments of Qu Qiubai illustrated this point. In 1931, Qu wrote a letter to Lu Xun:

Yan Fu's translations put "elegance" above "accuracy" and "accessibility." Recently, the Commercial Press reprinted the eight famous books translated by Yan. I have no idea what their intention was! It is as though they were playing a joke on China's people and youths. How could the ideals of accuracy and accessibility be reached using classic Chinese?

In the 1980s, Wang Zuoliang compared Yan's using ancient Chinese in translation to a bitter pill coated with sugar. Wang pointed out that perhaps the real point about ancient-writing style is neither a linguistic nor a stylistic one. Yan Fu conducted translation with a purpose, i.e., to attract the attention of the people who he thought really mattered, namely, the intelligentsia... and he knew what a bitter pill these books contained for those still taking refuge in medieval dreams and so he sugar-coated it with something they treasured, a polished antique style. Elegance, in other words, was Yan's salesmanship.

II Issue of Accuracy

Another such problem was that of accuracy, and in time, criticism of the translations came to focus more on this one. At first, the complaints revolved around the lack of competence, such as an inadequate grasp of English and of the Western intellectual tradition and a tendency to paraphrase rather than to translate exactly. Wu Rulun was the first to bring up the question of inaccuracy. Wu argued that Yan failed sufficiently to respect the content of what he translated because he wanted to use his work to influence the thinking of the readers. Wu said translation was different from writing a book. If one wrote a book, one could write whatever one liked, but if one translated a book, one had to respect the original text. Thus, Wu criticized Yan for replacing Huxley's references to Western historical or literary loci classici with similar Chinese examples. He said, "Huxley had no ideas about these Chinese events and persons... It would be better (for Yan) to translate the original references faithfully."

The famous scholar Wang Guowei, who had a particularly brilliant grasp of Western thought, appreciated Yan's translations on the whole. Yet he also picked up inaccuracies. In an article in 1905, he gave several examples of inaccuracies, such as translating *Evolution and Ethics* as 《天演论》 (*The Theory of Natural Evolution*), ignoring "ethics" in the title, "evolution" appearing as "天演" (natural evolution or heaven's progress), "sympathy" as "善相感" (good at having feelings of mutual appreciation). And "space and time" as "宇" (infinite space) and "宙" (infinite time). He felt these translations were imprecise and loaded with meanings from Chinese culture.

④ Yan Fu's Translation Practice

(1) It may be safely assumed that, two thousand years ago, before Caesar set foot in southern Britain, the whole country-side visible from the windows of the room in which I write, was in what is called "the state of nature." Except, it may be, by raising a few sepulchral mounds, such as those which still, here and there, break the flowing contours of the downs, man's hands had made no mark upon it; and the thin veil of vegetation which overspread the broad-backed heights and the shelving sides of the coombs was unaffected by his industry. (Thomas H. Huxley: *Evolution and Ethics and Other Essays*)

> 赫胥黎独处一室之中，在英伦之南，背山而面野。槛外诸境，历历如在几下。乃悬想二千年前，当罗马大将恺彻未到时，此间有何景物。计惟有天造草昧，人功未施，其借征人境者，不过几处荒坟，散见坡陀起伏间。而灌木丛林，蒙茸山麓，未经删治如今日者，则无疑也。(Yan's version)

可以有把握地想象，二千年前，当凯撒到达不列颠南部之前，从我正在写作的这间屋子的窗口可以看到整个原野是一种所谓"自然状态"。也许除了若干突起的坟墓已在几处破坏了连绵的丘陵的轮廓以外，此地未经人工修葺整治。薄薄的植被笼罩着广阔的高地和峡谷的斜坡，还没有受到人的劳动的影响。（1971年科学出版社白话版本）

(2) To Strive, to seek, to find, and not to yield,

    It may be that the gulfs will wash us down,

    It may be we shall touch the Happy Isles,

    …but something ere the end,

    Some work of noble note may yet be done.

    (Thomas H. Huxley: *Evolution and Ethics and Other Essays*)

挂帆沧海，风波茫茫；

或沦无底，或达仙乡；

二者何择，将然未然；

时乎时乎，吾奋吾力；

不竦不戁，丈夫之必。

(Yan's version)

 5 Exercises

    Translate the following paragraph into Chinese and compare your translation with Yan's translation and summarize the differences.

    It may be safely assumed that, two thousand years ago, before Caesar set foot in southern Britain, the whole country-side visible from the windows of the room in which I write, was in what is called "the state of nature". Except, it may be, by raising a few sepulchral mounds, such as those which still, here and there, break the flowing contours of the downs, man's hands had made no mark upon it; and the thin veil of vegetation which overspread the broad-backed heights and the shelving sides of the coombs was unaffected by his industry. The native grasses and weeds, the scattered patches of gorse, contended with one another for the possession of the scanty surface soil; they fought against the droughts of summer, the frosts of winter, and the furious gales which swept, with unbroken force, now from the Atlantic, and now from the North Sea, at all times of the year; they filled up, as they best might, the gaps made in their ranks by all sorts of underground and overground animal ravagers. One year with another, an average population, the floating balance of the unceasing struggle for existence among the indigenous plants, maintained

---

itself. It is as little to be doubted, that an essentially similar state of nature prevailed, in this region, for many thousand years before the coming of Caesar; and there is no assignable reason for denying that it might continue to exist through an equally prolonged futurity, except for the intervention of man. (Thomas H. Huxley: *Evolution and Ethics and Other Essays*）

6 References and Further Readings

(1) SCHWARTZ B. In Search of Wealth and Power: Yen Fu and the West [M]. Cambridge, MA: The Belknap Press of Harvard University Press, 1964.

(2) 高惠群, 乌传衮. 翻译家严复传论[M]. 上海: 上海外语教育出版社, 1992.

(3) 沈苏儒. 论信达雅[M]. 北京: 商务印书馆, 1998.

(4) 俞政. 严复著译研究[M]. 苏州: 苏州大学出版社, 2003.

Chapter Five

Lin Shu's Translation Activities

1 An Introduction to Lin Shu

Lin Shu (1852–1924), was a traditional Chinese literatus and prominent translator, most famous for introducing the Western literary works into Chinese in the late 19th and early 20th centuries, despite his ignorance of any foreign languages. He collaborated with different interpreters to translate about 180 western literary works, mostly novels, from England, the United States, France, Russia, Switzerland, Belgium, Spain and Norway, etc. into classical Chinese.

Lin Shu was born in 1852 to a merchant family in Fujian province. When he was five years old, his father fell into a heavy debt due to a shipwreck so that he went to Taiwan to make a living. His mother and elder sister turned to needlework to support the whole family and they lived in poverty. The Lin family was too poor to support Lin Shu's education. Lin studied with different teachers but remained something of an autodidact. When Lin was eleven, he began to learn classical Chinese poetry. At the age of 16, he gave up his schooling and went to Taiwan to work in the family business, but he continued to learn by himself. In 1882, Lin Shu received the *provincial graduate* (举人) degree, a successful candidate in the imperial examinations at the provincial level, but failed to attain a higher degree after several attempts. Hence, he lost the chance to obtain a governmental position. Later he taught at a high school and Peking University.

Lin Shu was one of the influential literary figures in the late Qing Period and early Republic Period. Although he knew no foreign languages, he translated about 180 literary works written by various Western authors into Chinese in twenty years by collaborating with different oral interpreters. Of these works, the most influential ones are:

(1) *La Dame Aux Camelias* by Alexandre Dumas as 《巴黎茶花女遗事》, 1899;

(2) *David Copperfield* by Charles Dickens as 《块肉余生记》, 1908;

(3) *The Old Curiosity Shop* by Charles Dickens as《孝女耐儿传》, 1907;

(4) *Oliver Twist* by Charles Dickens as《贼史》, 1908;

(5) *John Haste* by H. Rider Haggard as《迦茵小传》, 1905;

(6) *Ivanhoe* by Sir Walter Scott as《撒克逊劫后英雄传略》, 1905;

(7) *Uncle Tom's Cabin* by Harriet Beecher Stowe as《黑奴吁天录》, 1901;

(8) *Don Quijote de las Manche* by Miguel de Cervantes as《魔侠传》, 1922;

(9) *The Sketchbook* by Washington Irving as《拊掌录》, 1907.

2 Lin Shu's Translation Motives

Although Lin was a Confucian conservative, he made valuable contributions towards the introduction of Western literature into China. He was the first translator who brought many of the important works of Western literature to the attention to the Chinese for the first time. And his translation influenced many Chinese intellectuals of his contemporary and of a later generation. Because of Lin's translation, the Chinese began to appreciate the value of the Western fiction. Prior to this time fiction was regarded as "minor way"(小道). When Liang Qichao and others began to advocate the use of fiction as educational and political tool, Lin Shu went even further. He proved that fiction was more than a tool through his translations.

I To Cultivate Patriotism

Lin Shu began his translation career by accident. As a traditional scholar in the late Qing period, he achieved greatly in arts and literary creations in the first half of his life. It was not until 1897 when Lin's wife died did he begin to translate Western literary works into Chinese. After the death of his wife, he was urged by his friends, who wanted to distract him from his bereavement, Lin undertook the translation of Alexandre Dumas's *La Dame aux Camélias*. Wang Shouchang (王寿昌, 1864–1926), who had studied in France, interpreted the story for his friend and Lin put what he heard into Chinese. The book (known as《巴黎茶花女遗事》in Chinese) was published in 1899

and was an immediate commercial success. Ten thousand copies of the book had been sold. As Yan

Fu commented, "What a sorrowful volume *The Lady of the Camellias* is, it broke the hearts of every affectionate young Chinese."("可怜一卷茶花女，断尽支那荡子肠。") Greatly encouraged by the sensational response from the readers, later he went on to translate more.

As a patriotic scholar, in many of Lin's prefaces and postscripts to his translations, Lin stated clearly that his translation intentions were to save the nation from subjugation and ensure its survival. Motivated by the national crisis and patriotic atmosphere in China, Lin Shu spoke of his political intention in a novel about slavery in America. In the epilogue of the translation of *Uncle Tom's Cabin*, Lin Shu stated that his intention of translation was "to cultivate patriotism and preserve the Chinese race." He also compared the miserable conditions of the Chinese workers in America with those of the black slaves in *Uncle Tom's Cabin*.

"The yellow race has been subject to worse treatment than even the black… I noted what the book relates about the Negroes and when I reflected that the yellow race too are facing subjugation, my indignation increased… Some Chinese think too well of the white race and, believing that Western powers treat their vassal states leniently, are actively campaigning for affiliating with them. To such people, this book I have translated ought to serve as a necessary warning." ("黄人受虐，或加甚于黑人……触黄种之将亡，因而愈生其悲怀耳……而倾心彼疾者，又误信西人宽待其藩属，跃然欲趋而附之。则吾之书足以傲醒之者，宁可少哉？") Lin Shu compared the Chinese laborers migrated to North and South America with African American slaves and appealed to the problem of race and nation, which made it one of the most famous translated works in the 20th century.

II To Educate the Public

Among Lin Shu's translated works, *Robinson Crusoe* (《鲁滨孙漂流记》) was one of the most popular adventure fictions. According to Lin Shu, the Chinese lack a pioneering and adventurous spirit, so he decided to translate the work to encourage the Chinese people. In his preface, he mentioned,

"The English man Robinson, because he is not willing to accept the golden mean as a doctrine of his conduct, travels overseas alone by boat. As a result, he is wrecked in a storm, and was caught in a hopeless situation on a desert island. There he walks and sits alone, lives like a primitive man. He does not go back to his native country until twenty years later. From ancient times to the present, no book has recorded this incident. His father originally wishes that he could be a man who behaves according to the doctrine of the golden mean, but Robinson goes against his will, and in consequence, pioneering extraordinary undertakings. Thereupon, the adventurous people in the world, who are nearly devoured by sharks and crocodiles, are all inspired by Robinson." ("英人鲁

滨孙者，惟不为中人之中，庸人之庸。故单舸猝出，侮狎风涛，濒绝地而处，独行独坐，兼
羲、轩、巢、燧诸氏之所为而为之，独居二十七年始返，其事盖亘古所不经见者也。然其父
之诏之也，则固愿其为中人之中，庸人之庸。而鲁滨孙乃大悖其旨，而成此奇诡之事业，因
之天下探险之夫，几以性命与鲨鳄狎，则皆鲁滨孙有以启之耳。") Obviously, Lin hoped that
the Chinese people could learn the pioneering spirit from reading the translation of the novel.

③ Lin Shu's Translation Methods

Lin Shu knew no foreign languages, so he had to cooperate with a collaborator who was
familiar with the foreign language and worked as an interpreter for him. The collaborator translated
the text into Chinese orally and Lin Shu wrote down what he heard in classical Chinese. Lin was an
efficient translator. It was said that as soon as the collaborator stopped speaking, Lin stopped writing
as well. But Lin Shu was not like a tape-recorded to copy what the collaborator said, instead, he
made some alternations taking into consideration the needs of the target culture, the acceptance of the
readers, the social, political or historical conditions, or even the untranslatability of the source text.

I Omission

In Lin Shu's translation process, he deleted the original for some reasons. Sometimes he
mentioned his reasons for omission in his preface or postscript to the translation. Actually, omission
is a very common practice in translation in Lin Shu's time. He deleted some contents for the sake of
Chinese literary norms and Chinese readers' taste.

At that time, the Western literature were quite novel to the Chinese readers. Taking the needs
of the Chinese culture and the Chinese readers' reception into consideration, Lin had to delete
something in translation. The Chinese readers are very familiar with the tradition of story-telling
in traditional Chinese fiction; therefore the psychological description in the novel may be deleted
because it has nothing to do with the development of the story.

Take the translation of *Uncle Tom's Cabin* as an example. The original work is about 446
pages, if it is translated into Chinese, the length of it should be about 600 pages in modern Chinese
and about 300 pages in classical Chinese. However, Lin Shu's version is about 206 pages and
124,000 words. While the late versions by Huang Jizhong, Zhang Peijun, and Wang Jiaxiang have
the length of 432,000 words, 438,000 words and 324,000 words respectively. Obviously, Lin made
some deletions in his translation practice. In addition, in the preface of the translation of *Uncle
Tom's Cabin*, Lin noted, "Too much religious material in the book constitutes nothing more than
redundancy. In light of the convenience of the readers, Wei Yi has omitted those that are somewhat

trivial, for which no censure is hoped from the readership (是书言教门事恐多，悉经魏君节去其原文稍烦琐者，本以取便观者，幸勿以割裂为责)."

II Addition

In his translation process, he made some additions to polish and improve the original and also to help the readers to understand the original. Lin Shu himself was a writer and very good at the writing techniques, so he had the impulse to embellish the original. In his translation, he always added something to make the translation more interesting and attractive and appealing. Qian Zhongshu mentioned Lin's addition in his translations. "When Lin Shu found a perceived void in the source text, he would add here and polish there so that the wording in the version was more concrete, the scene more vivid, and the description more substantial." For example:

The married couple were enjoying their honeymoon… (Harriet Beecher Stowe: *Uncle Tom's Cabin*)

彼夫妇在蜜月期内，两情忻合无间(蜜月者，西人娶妇时，即挟其妇游历，经月而归)。(Lin's version)

Here, Lin translated "honeymoon" literally into Chinese, but to help the Chinese readers better understand the Western tradition, Lin made a specific explanation here. Addition is quite a common phenomenon in Lin's translations. Lin took the readers' expectations into consideration, which made his translations acceptable. In the meantime, he broadened the horizon of his readers and narrowed the gaps between Chinese and Western culture.

III Alteration

Due to the social and cultural differences between the source and target languages, alterations are inevitable. In addition, on account of the readers, the translator has to make some compensation or replacement in his translation. In the process of translation, Lin Shu always made some changes. For example:

The slanting light of the setting sun quivers on the sea-like expanse of the river; the shivery canes, and the tall, dark cypress, hung with wreaths of dark, funeral moss, glow in the golden ray. (Harriet Beecher Stowe: *Uncle Tom's Cabin*)

日脚斜穿云罅而出，直射江上芦港。芦叶倒影，万绿荡漾于风漪之内，景物奇丽，江光如拭。(Lin's version)

Lin Shu made the alteration considering the Chinese reader's aesthetic tendencies. Although Lin Shu changed the word order of the original, the style and the literary effect of the original are reproduced.

IV Adaptation

On which Mr. Micawber delivered an eulogium on Mrs. Micawber's character, and said she had ever been his guide, philosopher, and friend and that he would recommend me, when I came to marrying time of life, to marry such another woman, if such another woman could be found. (Charles Dickens: *David Copperfield*)

密考泊遂历称其妻嘉言懿行，为世贤女，能相夫教子，共处患难，且谓余曰："汝论娶者，所娶亦当如吾妻。惟不审闺秀中更有贤类吾妻否？"(Lin's version)

In Lin's time, the wife had a very low status. For her, the most important responsibility was to take care of the husband and rear the children. So here in Lin's version, it was rewritten according to the feudal Chinese ethics.

④ Criticism of Lin Shu's Translations

Lin Shu was severely criticized during heated debates with younger intellectuals during the 1917–1919 New Culture and May Fourth movements and his popularity suffered badly. Many studies considered Lin Shu as an unfaithful translator and there is the problem of non-correspondence between Lin Shu's translations and their sources.

I The Choice of the Source Text

Lin Shu's translations cover a wide range of titles, from the novels of famous writers like Dickens and Scott to the mysteries of Nick Carter and even the exotic African tales of H. Rider Haggard. Only about a quarter of Lin's translations can represent the generally recognized classics of Western literature. Liang Qichao criticized Lin Shu as a translator who rendered "second and third-rate Western writers." Actually, almost 100 of Lin's translations were works by authors of little literary consequence, and about 30 more were adventure or detective stories by H. Rider Haggard or Arthur Conan Coyle.

Liang's criticism has been repeated again and again by other scholars, especially the generation followed them. The blames for the poor choices could be found in the diaries and personal reminiscences of a later generation, such as Lu Xun, Guo Moruo, Mao Dun et al.

However, some scholars harbor different ideas. According to Zheng Zhenduo, the poor choices of works are due to the irresponsibility or incapability of the collaborator. "Because he did not understand any foreign language, the selection of original works was completely in the hands of the oral collaborators with whom he worked; if the oral collaborator was comparatively knowledgeable regarding literature, the works selected by him were comparatively important. If the oral collaborator

had not much knowledge, what he selected would be worthless second-and third-rate work, completely without value. Lin suffered a great deal from their deficiencies; much of his precious effort he wasted. This is truly lamentable."

Anyway, no one was solely responsible for the poor selection of works. The collaborators' knowledge and taste in literature did influence the selection of the works.

II Mistranslation and Incorrect Omission

Lin Shu describes how he cooperates with his cotranslator in an article.

"I know no foreign languages. I cannot pass for a translator without the aid of several gentlemen, who interpret the texts for me. They interpret, and I write down what they interpret. They stop, and I put down my pen. 6,000 words can be produced after a mere four hours' labor. I am most fortunate to have my error-plagued, rough translations kindly accepted by the learned." (予不审西文，其勉强厕身于译界者，恃二三君子，为余口述其词，余耳受而手追之，声已笔止，日区四小时，得文字六千言。其间疵谬百出，乃蒙海内名公，不鄙秽其径率而收之，此予之大幸也。) It seems quite ridiculous for a person who knows no foreign languages to do translation. However, it is quite common in Chinese translation history, especially in the translation of the Buddhist Scripture. Lin and his cotranslator work with great efficiency. They can produce 6,000 words in four hours, which is incredible even to a professional translator. Anyway, mistranslations are inevitable if they work in a rush. Actually, Lin Shu also realized the criticism of the contemporaries and once defended him in the postscript of a novel.

"Recently my close friends from within the seas wrote to me. In the letters they listed mistakes in my translation for my review. I really appreciate it! However, I don't know any Western languages. What I did was just writing down the oral renditions [made by my collaborators]. Even if there were mistakes, I didn't know." (近有海内知交，投书举鄙人谬误之处见箴，心甚感之。惟鄙人不审西文，但能笔述，即有讹错，均出不知。) However, a number of persons and institutions were involved in the producing of the final version, such as the cotranslators, editors and publishers. This makes it quite difficult to determine who held what degree of responsibility for the final product.

Many scholars criticized Lin Shu because he deleted and edited the source texts at will. According to these scholars, the translator must abide by such principle as "faithfulness," meaning the target text must be faithful to the source text in translation. However, Lin Shu didn't follow the rule. "Lin seemed to have been more concerned about spinning his own yarn than acting as a faithful intermediary between the Western writer and his Chinese readers. Retelling the story in his own way, he often took liberties with the original, making changes and adaptations here and there to suit his purpose."

Arthur Waley regarded Lin Shu as one of the greatest early 19th century translators. In his view, Lin's translation is a means to re-revolutionize Chinese culture. In his "Notes on Translation," he gives an analysis of Lin's translation of Dickens:

"To put Dickens into classical Chinese would on the face of it seem to be a grotesque undertaking. But the results are not all grotesque. Dickens, inevitably, becomes a rather different and to my mind a better writer. All the over-elaboration, the overstatement and uncurbed garrulity disappear. The humor is there, but is transmuted by a precise, economical style; every point that Dickens spoils by uncontrolled exuberance, Lin Shu makes quietly and efficiently."

5 The Contribution of Lin's Translations

Zheng Zhenduo published "Mr. Lin Qinnan" in 1924 which was the first article discussing Lin Shu's contribution to translation and Chinese literature. In this article, he asked scholars not to underestimate Lin's achievements on translation. He said, "Perhaps there hasn't been a person who translated 40 world famous masterpieces till now in China."

I To Reconsider the Value of Fiction as a Genre

The oversea Chinese scholar Leo Ou-fan Lee (1965) studied Lin's translation and acclaimed him as one who "stands out as a pioneering genius who for the first time introduced a considerable volume of Western literature into China." In Lee's view, Lin not only urged the Chinese intellects to reconsider the value of fiction as a genre, but also opened the eyes of the Chinese readers to see the world.

In China, fiction was usually considered as a form of entertainment enjoyed by the lower class, and they were not serious literature. But by the end of the 18th century some intellects, such as Yan Fu and Liang Qichao, began to realize the importance of fiction as a medium for political propaganda, or a tool for social reform and education. They mentioned the role and influence of fiction in the West, and indicated that it could perform the same role in China. Due to the advocate of Liang Qichao and other scholars, many translations of Western fiction were published. Among these translators, Lin was the most productive one. If Liang Qichao is considered as an advocate of fiction as a genre, Lin Shu is by no means a prominent practitioner.

II To Change People's Disregard of Foreign Literature

Zheng Zhenduo mentioned in his article "Mr. Lin Qinnan," "At the time, in the eyes of the majority of intellectuals, China's backwardness was no more than the corrupt political structure. As to Chinese literature, it was still the most high-level and the most beautiful in the world. None of the Western literary works could compare with our Sima Qian, Li Bai and Du Fu's works. Until Lin Shu introduced a great number of Western Literary works into China, claiming that Scott's works were not inferior to Sima Qian's, they had not known that there was also so-called literature in Europe and America, where there were also writers who could compare favorably with our Sima Qian."

At the time when Lin Shu began his translation, the Chinese cultural superiority was still assumed in the realm of the arts and the humanities despite the failure of traditional Chinese beliefs in almost all other aspects of life. The Chinese intellects lacked interest to learn from the West or even thought that they had nothing to learn from the West in the areas of art and literature. Lin Shu was the first translator who introduced such famous writers as Shakespeare, Charles Dickens to the Chinese readers. From Lin's translations, the Chinese intellects and the younger generation began to eliminate their prejudice against the Western literature and realize its true value from an objective perspective. For instance, Lin's first translation *La Dame aux Camellias* has greatly influenced the Chinese readers, who began to realize that there were works in Western literature as touching as the Chinese classics *A Dream of Red Mansions* (《红楼梦》).

In the preface of the translation of *Uncle Tom's Cabin*, Lin Shu also compared the way of writing in *Uncle Tom's Cabin* with that of the classical Chinese, such as how to start, how to tell a story and how to end it. He proposed not to belittle Western literature.

"In its opening, unity, coherence, and conclusion, this book a chieves the purport and method of the ancient-style prose masters in every way. This shows that Chinese and Western styles of writing have similarities in their differences. The translators took the original writing and brought it into Chinese in the hope that those interested in Western learning will not dismiss Western books out of hand and say their style of writing is not equal to that of China." (是书开场、伏脉、接笋、结穴，处处均得古文家义法，可知中西文法，有不同而同者。译者就其原文，易以华语，所冀有志西学者，勿遽贬西书，谓其文境不如中国也。) Lin Shu eliminated people's prejudice on foreign literary works and since then more and more intellects were involved in translating foreign novels into China.

III To Exert a Tremendous Influence on Later Generation

Lin Shu's translation is a unique phenomenon in the history of Chinese translation. A Ying said, "Lin Shu brings Chinese intellectuals familiar with foreign literature, helping them know much about the first-class writers, and making them learn from foreign literature in order to improve the national literature." Actually, Lin's translations have exerted great

influence on the creation and translation of numerous writers such as Lu Xun, Mao Dun, Guo Moruo, et al.

Qian Zhongshu published *Lin Shu's Translation* (《林纾的翻译》) in 1979, which is the most influential essay to study the characteristics of Lin's translations. In this essay, Qian analyzed the conflicting nature of Lin Shu as a translator based on his reading experiences of Lin's translations. Lin's translation opened up a new world to the Chinese readers who knew nothing about the foreign languages and literatures.

6 Lin's Translation Practice

Two excerpts of Lin's translation of *Oliver Twist*

Each boy had one porringer, and no more-except on festival occasions, and then he had two ounces and a quarter of bread besides. The bowls never wanted washing. The boys polished them with their spoons till they shone again; and when they had performed this operation (which never took very long, the spoons being nearly as large as the bowls), they would sit staring at the copper with such eager eyes as if they could have devoured the very bricks of which it was composed: employing themselves, meanwhile, in sucking their fingers most assiduously, with the view of catching up any stray splashes of gruel that might have been cast thereon.

每人一杓，适满其碗。或佳节令辰，则每人予面包二两。碗亦不涤，以群儿饥，恒以舌舔碗如濯。既已，则执碗于手，引目视灶，几欲并吞其甃。人人既不得食，则自吮其指。见案上有剩浆，亦立舔之。

In depicting the experience of Oliver, a vivid scene that Noah teased Oliver's mother was completely revealed through Lin's translation.

Oliver, being left to himself in the undertaker's shop, set the lamp down on a workman's bench, and gazed timidly about him with a feeling of awe and dread, which many people a good deal older than he, will be at no loss to understand. An unfinished coffin on black trestles, which stood in the middle of the shop, looked so gloomy and death-like that a cold tremble came over him, every time his eyes wandered in the direction of the dismal object, from which he almost expected to see some frightful form slowly rear its head, to drive him mad with terror. Against the wall were ranged, in regular array, a long row of elm boards cut into the same shape: looking in the dim light, like high-shouldered ghosts with their hands in their breeches pockets

倭利物既至卧处，以二灯置诸板上。四周环瞩，皆死人所需物。年少不能无惧。左侧有未成之樐，则不敢引目左视，防是中预有鬼物凭附，夜来扑人。尤有棺片倚诸墙隅，在黑影中，似皆鬼魅离立。屋既褊狭，油腥触人，均作尸夗之气。

Through this excerpt, we can notice a conspicous feature of Lin's translation: he was good at retaining the surroundings and environment of original text, which was rarely seen in other translation works of that time.

One excerpt of Lin's translation of *Joan Haste*

Thus thought Joan; then, wear of the subject, she dismissed it from her mind for a while, and lying back upon the grass in idles contentment, watched the little clouds float across the sky till, far out to sea, they melted into the blue of the horizon. It was a perfect afternoon, and she would enjoy what was left of it before she returned to Bradmouth to face Samuel Rock and all her other worries. Grasshoppers chirped in the flowers at her feet, a beautiful butterfly flitted from tombstone to grey tombstone, sunning itself on each, and high over her head flew the jackdaws, taking food to their young in the crumbling tower over.

思极仰卧地上。观天际飞云，片片相逐，直至海上，与水云合，蔚蓝一色，气极清明。自念骤归见窘于阿姨，不如偷间斯须，以吸清空之气，较为幽静。时草虫嘶咽，野蝶群飞，仰见古塔之上，老鸦哺儿，声牙牙然。

In this excerpt, we can feel the attractive and graceful language of Lin's translation. Lin not only remain the beautiful scenery of the original, but also conforms to the classical habit of Chinese expression.

 Exercises

> **Translate the following paragraph into Chinese and compare your translation with Lin's translation and summarize the differences.**

Late in the afternoon of a chilly day in February, two gentlemen were sitting alone over their wine, in a well-furnished dining parlor, in the town of P-, in Kentucky. There were no servants present, and the gentlemen, with chairs closely approaching, seemed to be discussing some subject with great earnestness.

For convenience sake, we have said, hitherto, two gentlemen. One of the parties, however, when critically examined, did not seem, strictly speaking, to come under the species. He was a short, thick-set man, with coarse, commonplace features, and that swaggering air of pretension which marks a low man who is trying to elbow his way upward in the world. He was much over-dressed, in a gaudy vest of many colors, a blue neckerchief, bedropped gayly with yellow spots, and arranged with a flaunting tie, quite in keeping with the general air of the man. His hands, large and coarse, were plentifully bedecked with rings; and he wore a heavy gold watch-chain, with a bundle of seals of portentous size, and a great variety of colors, attached to it, — which, in the ardor of conversation, he was in the habit of flourishing and jingling with evident satisfaction. His conversation was in free and easy defiance of Murray's *Grammar*, and was garnished at convenient intervals with various profane expressions, which not even the desire to be graphic in our account shall induce us to transcribe. His companion, Mr. Shelby, had the appearance of a gentleman; and the arrangements of the house, and the general air of the housekeeping, indicated easy, and even opulent circumstances. As we before stated, the two were in the midst of an earnest conversation. (Harriet Beecher Stowe: *Uncle Tom's Cabin*)

(Lin's version: 美国砭脱沟省交春垂二月，犹阴寒逼人。时有二人对酌，旁无僮厮杂侍。此二人者，性情相貌大复不类。其一人狞丑，名曰海留，衣服华好，御金戒指一，镶以精钻，又佩一金表。状似素封，而谈吐鄙秽，近于伧荒。其一人文秀，家亦少康，名解而培。)

8 References and Further Readings

(1) LEE L O. Lin Shu and His Translations: Western Fiction in Chinese Perspective [J]. Papers on China, 1965(19): 159-193.

(2) GAO W. Recasting Lin Shu: A Cultural Approach to Literary Translation [D]. Brisbane: Griffith University, 2003.

(3) 韩洪举. 林译小说研究[M]. 北京: 中国社会科学出版社, 2005.

(4) 钱锺书. 林纾的翻译[M] //翻译研究论文集. 北京: 外语教学与研究出版社, 1984.

Chapter Six

Hu Shi's Translation Theory and Practice

Hu Shi (1891–1962) was one of the greatest Chinese philosopher and essayist. His courtesy name was Shi–zhi. Hu is widely recognized today as a key contributor to Chinese liberalism and language reform in his advocacy for the use of vernacular Chinese. He was also an influential Redology scholar as well as a translator.

① An Introduction to Hu Shi

In 1910, Hu Shi was sent to study agriculture at Cornell University in the United States. In 1912, he changed his major to philosophy and literature. After receiving his undergraduate degree, he went to Columbia University to study philosophy. At Columbia, he was greatly influenced by his professor, John Dewey, and Hu became Dewey's translator and a lifelong advocate of pragmatic evolutionary change. He returned to lecture in Peking University and soon became one of the leading and influential intellectuals during the May Fourth Movement and later the New Culture Movement. His most important contribution was the promotion of vernacular Chinese in literature to replace classical Chinese, which ideally made it easier for the ordinary person to read.

In an article originally published in *New Youth* in January 1917 entitled *A Preliminary Discussion of Literature Reform*, Hu originally emphasized eight guidelines that all Chinese writers should take to heart in writing:

(1) Write with substance. By this, Hu meant that literature should contain real feeling and

human thought. This was intended to be a contrast to the poetry with rhymes and phrases that Hu saw as being empty.

(2) Do not imitate the ancients. Literature should not be written in the styles of long ago, but rather in the modern style of the present era.

(3) Respect grammar. Hu did not elaborate at length on this point, merely stating that some recent forms of poetry had neglected proper grammar.

(4) Reject melancholy. Recent young authors often chose grave pen names, and wrote on such topics as death. Hu rejected this way of thinking as being unproductive in solving modern problems.

(5) Eliminate old clichés. The Chinese language has always had numerous four-character sayings and phrases used to describe events. Hu implored writers to use their own words in descriptions, and deplored those who did not.

(6) Do not use allusions. By this, Hu was referring to the practice of comparing present events with historical events even when there is no meaningful analogy.

(7) Do not use couplets or parallelism. Though earlier writers had pursued these forms, Hu believed that modern writers first needed to learn the basics of substance and quality, before returning to these matters of subtlety and delicacy.

(8) Do not avoid popular expressions or forms of characters. This rule, perhaps the most well-known, ties in directly with Hu's belief that modern literature should be written in the vernacular, rather than in classical Chinese. He believed that this practice had historical precedents, and led to greater understanding of important texts.

Hu's literary revolution began with a poetic revolution, but quickly extended to literature in general, and then to expression of new ideas in all fields. Hu's program offered a pragmatic means of improving communication, fostering social criticism, and reevaluating the importance of popular Chinese novels from past centuries.

2 Hu's Translation Ideas

Hu Shi's introduction and translation of foreign literature can be divided into three periods. The first period was from 1906 to 1909 when he studied in Public School of China (中国公学). He practiced to translate from English to Chinese and vice versa during this period. Hu

Shi translated *The Soldier's Dream* written by Thomas Compbell and *Song of the Shirt* by Thomas Hood. For this period, Hu Shi used classical Chinese as his literary language and his poems were written strictly with five or seven Chinese characters in each line. The second period went from 1909 to 1917 when he was studying in America. In 1912, he translated *La Derniere Classe* by a French novelist Alphonse Daudet. This translation brought him great success and later was selected into the textbook for high school students. This attempt of translation again demonstrated Hu Shi's translating competence and his command of vernacular Chinese. The third period was from 1917 to 1940. In 1917, after graduation from Columbia University, Hu Shi came back to Peking University on the invitation of the translation practice serving the New Cultural Movement. He thought that we should create a new literary language by means of introducing Western classic works, which could provide a good example for imitation and at last, our countrymen will create our new literature. He believed that Western literature had many advantages that could be provided as good examples for our creation of new literature. What's more, introducing Western literature was an effective way to introduce new literature in genre and in new thoughts. For this period, his translated works of short stories included *Miggies* and *The Outcasts of Poker Flat* by Francis Bret Harte. His literary language was totally in vernacular Chinese, providing good examples for literary revolution.

His article *On Constructive Literary Revolution*, which appeared in New Youth in1917, was the first proclamation of constructing new literature in China. He thus was the first to propose reforming Chinese literature through the translation of foreign literary masterpieces. He pointed out in this article that "to create new literature, what we need first is a tool, and second is a method… we should immediately start to translate Western masterpieces so that we have models to follow if we are to explore methods of literature." (创造新文学的第一步是工具，第二步是方法……我们如果要研究文学的方法，不可不赶紧译西洋的文学名著，做我们的模范。) He thought that the ineffectiveness of present situation was due to the improper translation methods adopted by translators. He suggested in the same articles that translators should:

(1) Choose those masterpieces of famous writers only, rather than those second-class works. He organized a meeting to select first-class foreign literary works and planned to organize other translators to render and publish about one hundred novels, five hundred short stories, three hundred plays, and prose of fifty writers within five years.

(2) Adopt a vernacular prose style in the translation of those dramas of a verse style. He criticized Lin Shu's translation, as he believed that classical Chinese in our translation would definitely cause a great loss of the spirit of the original. (用古文译书，必失原文的好处。) The standard he adopted in translation was a unity of faithfulness and expressiveness. He once used a word to depict his translation standard, that is "good," by which he meant that a translated version

should bring pleasure to readers. By faithfulness, he meant that the translation should be faithful to the original spirit. Hu Shi held that a translator should first be responsible for the author to keep the spirit of the original; and secondly he should be responsible for the readers and make his version intelligible. (译书第一要对原作者负责，求不失原意；第二要对读者负责，求他们能懂，) In the preface to his second anthology of short story translations, he remarked that the literary works that were hard to understand could never succeed in educating people, and thus clearness in meaning is of primary importance in literary translation. (决没有叫人读不懂看不下去的文学书而能收教训与宣传的功效的。所以文学作品的翻译更应该努力做到明白晓畅的基本条件。)

Hu Shi valued high the cultural significance of translation. In his article "Translated Literature of Buddhism," he mentioned Kumarajiva, one of the noteworthy translators of Buddhist Scripture, as he thought Kumarajiva was a man gifted with the ability of literary appreciation. "Kumarajiva was against literal translation"; "He could translate Buddhist Scripture into good Chinese"; "As far as the translation of Buddhist Scripture is concerned, though Xuanzang's translation was very faithful, however, what became the literary masterpiece in history was that of Kumarajiva." He argued that the translation of Buddhist Scripture enriched Chinese literature. With the introduction of Buddhist classics into the Chinese literature which was commonly criticized as lacking imagination; Chinese literature went through its first flourish.

Hu Shi's greatest contribution to translation history was that he pioneered a road to translating foreign masterpieces in vernacular Chinese. He had a good understanding of the function of translation and regarded those translations understandable and enjoyable for readers as most successful. He criticized Lin Shu and Yan Fu by saying that, as they employed classical Chinese in their translations, they failed to meet the demand of the time to introduce new objects and new thoughts through translation. "Classical Chinese is a dead language which can not go far and disseminate among common people no matter how skillfully one can handle it, for it only can be appreciated by a small group of people." ("古文究竟是已死的文字，无论你怎样做得好，究竟只够供少数人的赏玩，不能行远，不能普及。") In his opinion, each historical period had its own language in literature. What he pursued to create was a kind of vernacular language, neither inherited from tradition nor borrowed from the West. It was designed to meet the demand of that special period and belonged to the common people of that time.

3 Case Studies of His Translation Practice

Interestingly, American female poet Sara Teasdale's poem *Over the Roofs* was translated by Hu Shi in 1919 as 《关不住了》, and was included in his own poem collection *Book of Experiments*

(《尝试集》). Hu explained in the preface to the collection that he considered his translation of Teasdale's poem to be a "new era of success" in his "attempt at new poetry." Hu Shi did not simply take 《关不住了》 as a translation of *Over the Roofs* but a creation and also a reflection of the thoughts of the author.

The original text:

Over the Roofs

I said, "I have shut my heart

    As one shuts an open door,

    That Love may starve therein

    And trouble me no more."

    But over the roofs there came,

    The wet new wind of May,

    And a tune blew up from the curb

    Where the street-pianos play.

    My room was white with the sun,

    And Love cried out to me,

    "I am strong; I will break your heart

    Unless you set me free."

    And Hu's version is as follows:

我说："我把我的心收起，

    像人家把门关了，

    叫爱情生生的饿死，

    也许不再和我为难了。"

    但是屋顶上吹来，

    一阵阵五月的湿风，

    更有那街心琴调，

    一阵阵的吹到房中。

    一屋里都是太阳光，

    这时候爱情有点醉了。

他说："我是关不住的，

    我要把你的心打碎了！"

From the translation of *Over the Roofs*, we could notice that Hu Shi began to focus on both content and form in translation. The translated version is divided into three stanzas and every stanza contains four lines. The Chinese version has the same ABCB rhyme scheme with the original. The arrangement of rhyme scheme in Chinese version was in accordance with its English version in the even lines, and rhyme was attempted in the Chinese version. He tried to provide models for new literature.

He also rendered two poems in Edward Fitzgerald's translation of *The Rubáiyát* and included them in his *Book of Experiments*. The original poems are as follows:

No. 7

Come, fill the Cup, and in the Fire of Spring

The Winter Garment of Repentance fling:

The Bird of Time has but a little way

To fly — and Lo! The Bird is on the Wing.

No. 99

Ah, Love! Could you and I with Fate Conspire?

To grasp this sorry Scheme of Things entire,

Would not we shatter it to bits — and then

Re-mould it nearer to the Heart's Desire!

For the first one, Hu Shi translated like this:

来！
斟满了这一杯！
让春天的火焰烧了你冬天的忏悔！
青春有限，飞去不飞回。——
痛饮莫迟挨！

So in the translation, some original images were omitted, for example, bird. But the basic tone is preserved and even more strongly reflected in the final exclamation: 痛饮莫迟挨！(Drink, otherwise it is too late!) This chimes with Omar Khayyám's philosophy of enjoying life and pleasure.

The second one is included in *Book of Experiments* and even given a title "Hope"("希望") like the following:

要是天公换了卿和我，
该把这糊涂世界一齐都打破，
要再磨再炼再调和，
好依着你我的安排，把世界重新造过！

As to this translation, Hu's friend Xu Zhimo made a comment that it has high readability, but that is Hu Shi, not Omar. Ironically, the poem at Omar's hand is not a poem of love (the first word "love" of the poem was added by the English translator Edward Fitzgerald); rather, it is a poem of resistance against evil force and pursues independence. In this sense, it is Hu Shi's version that is to the point of Omar's original idea.

Despite his strong objection of classic Chinese literature, Hu Shi actually is skillful of integrating some positive elements in classic literature in his translation. For example, it is not difficult to find the connections between Hu's translations with a poem written by a late Song poet Guan Daosheng.

> 你侬我侬，忒煞情多；情多处，热如火；把一块泥，捻一个你，塑一个我，将咱两个一齐打碎，用水调和；再捻一个你，再塑一个我。我泥中有你，你泥中有我；我与你生同一个衾，死同一个椁。

The third case is an excerpt from Hu's translation of a short story. The following is the original text and his translation. From this example, we can also see Hu's ideas in translation.

The meal was a culinary success. But more, it was a social triumph-chiefly, I think, owing to the rare tact of Miggles in guiding the conversation, asking all the questions herself, yet bearing throughout a frankness that rejected the idea of any concealment on her own part, so that we talked of ourselves, of our prospects, of the journey, of the weather, of each other — of everything but our host and hostess. It must be confessed that Miggles's conversation was never elegant, rarely grammatical, and that at times she employed expletives the use of which had generally been yielded to our sex. But they were delivered with such lighting — up of teeth and eyes, and were usually followed by a laugh — a laugh peculiar to Miggles — so frank and honest that it seemed to clear the moral atmosphere.

> 这一餐饭,在滋味上固然是大成功,在社交上尤是大胜利。这不能不归功于米格儿领导谈话的过人本领。她会问话，问时的态度非常坦白，使人不好隐藏掩饰。于是我们大谈我们自己，谈我们的志望，谈我们路上的事，谈天气——什么都谈，只不谈：我们的主人和女主人。米格儿的谈话是不文雅的，往往不免文法上的错误，有时她还用几个发咒的字，平常是只许我们男人用的。但她说话时，牙齿一露，眼光一闪，说完总带一笑——米格儿的特别一笑——又坦白，又诚恳，自然使人心里爽快。

④ Exercises

(1) Read Hu Shi's poem collection *Book of Experiments*, and tries to analyze the inaction between his translation and writing.

(2) Try to illustrate the influence of Hu Shi's poetry translation practice in the construction of Chinese new poetry.

⑤ References and Further Readings

(1) 廖七一. 胡适诗歌翻译研究[M]. 北京: 清华大学出版社, 2006.

(2) 郭著章. 翻译名家研究[M]. 武汉: 湖北教育出版社, 1999.

Chapter Seven

Lu Xun's Translation Theory and Practice

① An Introduction to Lu Xun

Lu Xun was the pen name of Zhou Shuren (1881–1936). He was one of the greatest Chinese writers of the 20th century. Considered the founder of modern vernacular literature, Lu Xun was a short story writer, editor, critic and essayist. Additionally, Lu Xun was also a prolific translator and introducer of foreign literature and literary theories. Creative writing and translation were of equal importance to Lu Xun in contributing to the creation of a new and progressive China by means of enlightening the people and "changing their minds."

Born in Shaoxing, Zhejiang province, Lu Xun was named Zhou Zhangshou (周樟寿) with his style name Yucai (豫才). Lu Xun was educated at Jiangnan Naval Academy (江南水师学堂) (1898–1899), and later transferred to Jiangnan Military Academy (江南陆师学堂). It was there Lu Xun had his first contacts with Western learning, especially the sciences; he studied some German and English, reading, amongst some translated books, Huxley's *Evolution and Ethics*, J. S. Mill's *On Liberty*, as well as novels like *Ivanhoe and Uncle Tom's Cabin*.

Moving to Tokyo in spring 1906, he came under the influence of scholar and philologist Zhang Taiyan and with his brother Zuoren, also on scholarship, published a translation of some East European and Russian Slavic short stories. In 1906 he stopped medical study to devote himself entirely to writing. His decision to take up writing instead of becoming a doctor was primarily due to his encounter of a slides show about a Chinese man who was beheaded by Japanese troops for spying during the Russo-Japanese War of 1904–1905. The lack of spirit and numbness of the Chinese audience evoked him. In his "Preface to *Call to Arms*" he stated "the best way to effect a spiritual transformation—or so I thought at the time—would be through literature and art." Such decisiveness showed

Lu Xun's revolutionary ability. His sensitivity as a Chinese towards his own country's political, literal, cultural aspects determined his controversial approaches throughout his entire life. He spent the next three years in Tokyo writing and translating the literature of those countries into Chinese. His translations are around 20 volumes or more—notably from Russian (he particularly admired Nikolai Gogol and made a translation of *Dead Souls*, and many other works such as prose essays).

② Lu Xun's Translation Ideas

Lu Xun read many translations by Yan Fu and Lin Shu in the beginning and was greatly influenced by them. However, he soon became critical of them. Although Lu Xun was interested in Yan Fu's *Evolution and Ethics*, Yan's later translations didn't interest him. In the meanwhile, he thought Lin Shu's translations were often of inferior quality and contained many mistranslations. That was the reason why he started to translate. Lu Xun felt that the Chinese custom of free translations had become a bad habit which is still lingering on and had to be fought. Carefulness and respect for the original text were Lu Xun's main demands on a translation.

There is little doubt that Lu Xun stood at the center of the debates on translation in the late 1920s and early 1930s; in more ways than one he can also be considered the first modern translation theorist in China.

In Chinese translation history, over the time Chinese scholars have never stopped experimenting different strategies in literary translation. Straightforward translation (直译) or literal translation, sense-for-sense translation (意译) and free translation (自由译) were summarized as follows:

直译	意译
straightforward translation / direct translation	sense-for-sense translation / sense translation
formal correspondence	semantic correspondence
word-to-word translation (逐字译)	free translation (自由译)
stiff translation (硬译)(Lu Xun)	distorted translation (歪译)(Lin Shu)

Lu Xun's translation works amounted to about 200. In contrast to his achievement and recognition in the history of modern Chinese literature, his translation works generated little attention. Lu Xun was viewed by some later theorists as the pioneer of foreignization method from his stiff translation in China. (He insisted that "he would rather be faithful to the original than be fluent to the translation (宁信而不顺)." In other words, stiff translation refers to the translated texts that follow the originals very closely and are sometimes "translated nearly word by word." They often deliberately go against the Chinese language habits and avoid Chinese idiomatic expressions, or even break the Chinese grammatical rules. In many cases, they may be quite difficult to understand. In several articles, Lu Xun attacks the concept of "fluency(顺)." According to Lu Xun, a hard translation, although not desirable, could keep the original ways of expression, and only in this way the Chinese language could develop. What is "stiff" today will be "fluent" tomorrow. Some of the "stiff" expressions will be discarded and fall into disuse because they are not good enough or not necessary. It is crucial, however, to revisit the paths and thoughts he experienced as a prominent writer who brought in foreign knowledge via translation to China. It is also important to point out that Lu Xun initially did not choose the foreignizing over the domesticating method; rather it was "at least a combination of both methods."

Lu Xun put forth an explanation for his preference for extreme literalism; he went beyond the choice of a translation method and gave a "political" explanation. Lu Xun stressed that it was a special class of readers that his translations were intended for — the proletariat literary critics who had special class interests to champion. Extreme faithfulness to the original was a way of ensuring that "true" Marxist literary thought be presented to those who wanted the facts as they were. What's more, translation — in addition to introducing the content of the original to Chinese readers -- has another important function, that is, helping us create a new modern Chinese language. There was a popular misunderstanding that Chinese language is inferior to the Western languages. Many intellectuals, with Lu Xun and Qu Qiubai as representatives, at that time believed that the Chinese language (as well as its writing system) is so deficient that it lacks names for many everyday objects. Indeed it has not developed completely beyond the stage of "sign language" — everyday conversation almost can't do without the help of "gestures." There is almost a complete absence of all those adjectives, verbs and prepositions that express subtle differences and complex relationships. Lu Xun said in 1931, "The Chinese language is just too imprecise" and that "to cure this ailment, I believe we have to suffer some more pain and embody our thought in wayward syntactical structures — ancient, dialectal, as well as foreign — so that one day these structures can become our own."

According to Lu Xun, introducing western literature was a very serious thing. It was not only a question of introducing literature, but above all one of introducing new thoughts, new ways of thinking to pave the way for a reform of the Chinese society.

Apart from the demand for faithfulness, Lu Xun also mentioned other questions. He criticized a tendency among the critics to point out only the faults, saying that critics should "point out what is bad and praise what is good, and if nothing is good he should praise what is rather good (指出坏的，奖励好的，倘没有，则较好的也可以)."

In addition, Lu Xun mentioned that a translation directly translated from the original is better than an indirect one, but one cannot demand only direct translations. Otherwise, one would get only works from the Anglo-Saxon world and from Japan, and China would not have met Ibsen, Ibáñez, H. C. Andersen or Cervantes. (中国人所懂的外国文，恐怕是英文最多，日文次之，倘不重译，我们将只能看见许多英美和日本的文学作品，不但没有伊卜生，没有伊本涅支，连极通行的安徒生的童话，西万提司的《吉河德先生》，也无从看见了。)

③ Lu Xun's Translation Practice

At the very beginning, Lu Xun was greatly influenced by Lin Shu and Yan Fu and mainly focused on the translation of English, French and American literature from Japanese. In his early years, he resorted to science fiction to save the declining China out of dilemma. In order to enlighten people's mind, Lu Xun translated western fictions written by *Jules Gabriel Verne* and *Hugo* et al.

Lu Xun's translation works ranged from science fiction to novels and criticism. His translation style varied over the time. Researchers tend to focus on his preference for extreme literalism towards Russian literary works and Marxist literary critics. Yet, his early translation works represent a quite different style.

Let us start with one of his earlier works to allocate his clear "domesticating" strategy. Example is chosen from a French author Jules Verne's "*From the Earth to the Moon in 97 hours 12 minutes*," which Lu Xun translated from its Japanese translation in 1903.

In his preface, Lu Xun stated that he had altered the original 28 chapters of the novel into 14. He also used a combination of classical/formal language and vernacular language to achieve both readability and simplicity towards the readership. He did not mention "faithfulness." What concerned him was how his readers would perceive this "new" fiction. His decision of "leave the reader in peace, as much as possible, and move the author towards him" illustrated Lu Xun's initial belief of producing a fluent/transparent translation.

Lu Xun strictly chose to inherit the traditional style in classical Chinese novels to create new titles for each section. For example, his first section title was written as:

第一回 悲太平会员怀旧 破寥寂社长贻书

In English version's first two chapters' titles were:

Chapter I The Gun Club

Chapter II President Barbicane's Communication.

A possible Chinese translation may be like this:

第一章 枪械俱乐部

第二章 巴比肯主席的交流

It is obvious that Lu Xun gave a great deal of extra information in the title to readers. The title almost served as a summary of the two chapters. He deliberately omitted words like "gun" and "Barbicane" in the title to minimize the "foreignness" to target — culture. In order to make the title more Chinese, he even tried to echo the words in the title: 悲 (*v.* "moan") echoes with 破 (*v.* "break"); 太平 (*n.* "peace") with 寥寂 (*n.* "loneliness"); 会员 (*n.* "members") with 社长 (*n.* "chief"); 怀旧 (*v.* phrase "chat about old times") with 贻书 (*v.* phrase "resigned from the post"). He rewrote the titles of the novel to serve the only purpose of familiarizing his readers of the story environment.

Let's continue with the first sentence from the novel's English version:

During the War of the Rebellion, a new and influential club was established in the city of Baltimore in the State of Maryland.

A possible Chinese translation may be like this:

> 在独立战争期间，马里兰州的巴尔的莫市中成立了一所全新的并具有影响力的绅士俱乐部。

Lu Xun's approach, however, was very different.

> 凡读过世界地理同历史的，都晓得有个亚美利加的地方。至于亚美利加独立战争一事，连孩子也晓得是惊天动地；应该时时记得，永远不忘的。今且不说，单说那独立战争时，合众国中，有一个麦烈兰国，其首府名曰拔尔地摩，是个有名街市。真是行人接踵，车马如云。这府中有一所会社，壮大是不消说，一见他国旗高挑，随风飞舞，就令人起一种肃然致敬的光景。

Without difficulty, one can tell that Lu Xun's translation is at least four times longer than the possible Chinese translation.

A simple introductory sentence was manipulated into a paragraph with a combination of

background information, situation describing and introduction. Lu Xun added his own opinion and knowledge towards certain facts and events. He created an environment which involved the reader. Sometimes, he even faked some facts either due to his limited knowledge or purely to achieve the easiness of reading. Considering his written style, it is obvious that he still followed the traditional way of Chinese storytelling by creating lots of situational information which did not exist in the source text. And it is obvious that he almost "forgot" that he was translating from someone else's work. He could be so involved that he would "rewrite" the whole thing. Lefevere said "rewriting manipulates, and it is effective." It seems Lu Xun recognized this power early. In the translation's preface, Lu Xun stressed that the lack of scientific novels in China during that period (presumably early 20th century) had caused the stupidity of the Chinese people. Because a good scientific novel can help the reader learn new knowledge unconsciously, therefore he or she would be able to challenge the traditional non-sense way of approach, revolutionize the way of thinking and achieve a pure material civilization. His idea was to use this new type of literature to smoothly introduce a revolution to the long sleeping China. To achieve such smoothness, he chose to domesticate his translation. Lu Xun believed by introducing science into imperial China, ordinary people would start to think and to explore themselves of the real world. He obviously believed that the best way to bring such alien to them was to make it look as familiar to others as possible.

Later, Lu Xun shifted his attention to the translation of literature and theories of literature and art. In this period, Lu Xun translated over 100 foreign literary works, with Japan's literary works as its majority. He also translated the short stories of Eastern Europe and children's literature and foreign arts. In this period, literal translation was mainly used by Lu Xun. In the third period (1928-1936), also the prime years of Lu Xun's translation, Lu Xun gave priority to the literature reflecting revolutionary thoughts. He translated many Russian literary works and Marxist literary theories.

In 1909, Lu Xun published *Stories from Abroad* (《域外小说集》) in Japan, a collection of short stories from Eastern Europe. It was a series of books co-translated by Lu Xun and Zhou Zuoren. Among the two volumes of the collection, Lu Xun himself only translated three stories. But this co-translated *Stories from Abroad* witnessed the turning point on Lu Xun's transformation of translation strategies, in which Lu Xun challenged the unfaithfulness and arbitrary alteration to the original texts by applying literal translation. Lu Xun mentioned this in a letter to a friend, "it's been too late to regret not having adopted literal translation when I was young, fancying me smart (年少时自作聪明，不肯直译，回想起来真是悔之晚矣)." In translating these short stories, Lu showed a quite distinctive style. He tried to keep the word order and the sentence order of the original, although it sometimes became awkward. In other words, he began to advocate strict literal translation which was rare in China at that time.

Since his encounter with Russian literature in the early 1920s, especially with works produced by "the fellow travellers" of revolution from early 1900s, Communism and Marxism started to make impact on his ideology. His written works focused on those poor people from the very bottom of the society struggling with their life. His choice of translation also switched to the similar area. He realized to truly wake up the sleeping majority by using literature, one must start to reflect the real life of those who suffered the most. He was not alone on this, the May Fourth Movement supported and fought with him. However, we shall leave this aside and focus on his translation work during this period (1920s–1930s). Has his ideological change made any influence over his translation strategy and how significant was the impact? The example below is chosen from a short story collection named "The Harp" (竖琴). In it, I chose Lu Xun's translation of a Russian writer Evgeni Zamyatin's "The Cave." The English translation of the same story is from an American writer Clarence Brown.

> 冰河，猛犸，旷野。不知什么地方好象人家的夜的岩石，岩石上有着洞穴。可不知道是谁，在夜的岩石的小路上，吹着角笛，用鼻子嗅出路来，一面喷起白白的粉雪。
>
> （Lu Xun's version）

We are lost in Lu Xun's words at first glance. The awkwardness derived from the twisted grammar and the meaning was distorted, particularly those in bold fonts.

The following is the English translation by Brown.

> Glaciers, mammoths, wastes. Black, nocturnal cliffs, vaguely like houses; in the cliffs — caves. And there is no telling what creature trumpets at night on the rocky path among the cliffs and, sniffing the path, raises clouds of powdered snow.

The English versions contain almost exactly the same lexical units. Equivalence can also be located down to word level. However, in Lu Xun's work, he did not even make any linguistic adaptation, let alone cultural integration. Opposite to his early method, Lu Xun deliberately chose to use stiff translation to maintain the foreignness of the target text.

To what extent does Lu Xun's translation illustrate such foreignness? From a cultural point of view, both "glacier" and "mammoths" are alien concepts for the target readership at that time due to limited travelling and scientific reading. A "domesticated" translator probably would replace them by something familiar to Chinese such as "frozen lake" and "dragon." On linguistic level, the resistance became much harder. Lu Xun refused to make any grammatical change to make the text more readable. The cohesion at both lexical and grammatical level is very loose, sometimes even wrong. For example, in Chinese, if one uses a noun to modify another noun it creates a subordinate relationship with a reasonable dependence. Here, Lu Xun used three nouns: "人家" (someone's house), "夜" (night) and "岩石" (rocks) to modify one after another. It created a chaotic grammar, a reader would not be able to understand which belongs to which. It is grammatically wrong. Little reference or other cohesive devices can be located in these three short sentences. Not one native Chinese could understand the text by reading it once. This certainly produced a strong resistancy in the target language culture because it challenged every angle of it as Venuti suggested that "foreignizing translation signifies the difference of the foreign text…by disrupting the cultural codes that prevail in the target language." Lu Xun reached almost full extent of 'foreignizing' in this translation.

③ Exercises

(1) Try to illustrate the interactions between Lu Xun's translations and their writings.

(2) Analyze the reasons of the change of Lu Xun's translation ideas, from domestication to foreignization.

④ References and Further Readings

(1) CHAN T L. Twentieth-Century Chinese Translation Theory: Modes, Issues and Debates [M]. Amsterdam: John Benjamins, 2004.

(2) LUNDBERG L. Lu Xun as a Translator: Lu Xun's Translation and Introduction of Literature and Literary Theory, 1903–1936 [M]. Stockholm: Orientaliska Studier, 1989.

(3) 王友贵. 翻译家鲁迅[M]. 天津: 南开大学出版社, 2005.

Chapter Eight

Liang Shiqiu's Translation Theory and His Disputes with Lu Xun

① An Introduction to Liang Shiqiu

Liang Shiqiu (1903–1987) was a renowned educator, writer, translator, literary theorist and lexicographer. Liang was born in Beijing in 1903 and was educated at Tsinghua College in Beijing from 1915 to 1923. He went on to study at Colorado College and later pursued his graduate studies at Harvard and Columbia Universities. At Harvard, he studied literary criticism under Irving Babbitt, whose New Humanism helped shape his conservative literary tenets.

After his return to China in 1926, he began a long career as a professor of English at several universities, including Peking University, Qingdao University, and Jinan University. He also served as the editor of a succession of literary supplements and periodicals, including the famous *Crescent Moon Monthly* (1928–1933). During this period, he published a number of literary treatises that showed the strong influence of Babbitt and demonstrated his belief that human life and human nature are the only proper subjects for literature.

His major works as a translator included James Barrie's *Peter Pan* (《潘彼得》), George Eliot's *Silas Marner* (《职工马南传》) and Mr. Gilfil's *Love Story* (《情史》), and Emily Brontë's *Wuthering Heights* (《咆哮山庄》). His translation works included George Orwell's *Animal Farm* (《百兽图》) and Marcus Aurelius' *Meditations* (《沉思录》). However, he is now remembered chiefly as the first Chinese scholar who has single-handedly translated the complete works of Shakespeare into Chinese. This project, first conceived in 1930, was completed in 1968. In 1949, Liang went to Taiwan where he taught at Taiwan Normal University until his retirement in 1966. During this period, he established himself as a lexicographer by bringing out a series of English-Chinese and Chinese-English dictionaries. Liang's literary fame rests, first and foremost, on the hundreds of short essays on familiar topics, especially those written over a span of more than four decades (1940–1986) and collected under the general title of 《雅舍小品》, now available in English translation under the title *From a Cottager's Sketchbook*.

② Liang Shiqiu's Translation Ideas

The decades of the 1920s and 1930s witnessed the translation controversy between Lu Xun and Liang Shiqiu. The controversy lasted for nearly eight years, and its effect in severity of eloquence has since then remained unprecedented in the history of Chinese literature. The cause of the controversy was Liang's article "On Lu Xun's Stiff Translation"(《论鲁迅先生的"硬译"》) published in 1929. To him, Lu Xun had followed the original text too closely and ended up with syntax much too convoluted to understand. Reading Lu's translations were, consequently, like "reading a map and trying to locate places with one's fingers." Liang averred that they were more than just "stiff translations"; they were "dead translations" (死译). The followings are excerpts:

Personally speaking, I always feel that the first requirement of having a book translated is to make it comprehensible; or else, would it not be a sheer waste of the reader's time and effort? Mistranslation is indeed unacceptable, for it would be altogether too unfaithful to the original text and turn cream into dregs. However, it is impossible not to mistranslate an entire book from beginning to end. Even if there are a few distorted instances found on the same page, there must nevertheless be parts remaining that are not mistranslated.

Furthermore, even though partial mistranslations are mistakes, and even though the mistakes may really be endlessly harmful, you have nevertheless enjoyed reading them. Dead translation, on the other hand, is very different. Dead translation is bound to be dead from beginning to end and it makes no difference whether it is read or not, except that reading it would mean spending time and energy in vain. Besides, while committing the error of distorted translation could not possibly coincide with making dead translation at the same time, dead translation might as well involve distorted translation. Therefore, I think it goes without saying that we certainly abhor distorted translation, but the trend of dead translation, above all, must be halted.

What is dead translation? "Dead translation is," said Chen Xiying, "not only putting every word and every sentence in the same order as the original, but also not allowing the addition of a single word or even the change of the order of any words. Nominally it is translation, but such translation is worse than non-translation (非但字比句次，而且一字不可增，一字不可先，一字不可后，名曰

翻译：而"译犹不译")." Even Mr. Zhou Zuoren, who advocated literal translation, had named such translation "dead translation." It is he, most probably, who had coined the term.

> 这意义，不仅在说，凡观念形态，是从现实社会受了那唯一可能的材料，而这现实社会的实际形态，则支配着即被组织在它里面的思想，或观念者的直观而已，在这观念者不能离去一定的社会底兴味这一层意义上，观念形态也便是现实社会的所产。

There are many examples of dead translation. Let me cite now only Mr. Lu Xun's translations as an example, because everybody knows how tersely and wields his pen in his short stories and essays and no one would say that his pen is inadequate. However, his translation is not far from "dead translation." Now, in order to show how even Lu Xun, despite his agile pen, cannot escape "dead translation," I am going to pick at random a few extremely esoteric sentences from one of his latest translations, namely, *On Art* by Lunacharsky.

Although the fact that the passages above are excerpts from the translations and removing the context has probably made them quite incomprehensible, linguistically speaking, nevertheless, one would wonder who could ever understand their very odd syntax. When I read these two books, I found the language really very difficult. Reading such books is like reading a map, and one would have to have one's finger on it to trace the clues to the sentence structures.

According to Lu Xun, "the inherent deficiency of the Chinese language" is one of the two reasons why his translation is incomprehensible. If it is so, as long as the Chinese language is not reformed, there is no chance but for translated works to become fifty per cent abstruse. Chinese is different from foreign languages, for some sentence structures of which simply do not exist in Chinese, and this is exactly why translation is difficult. If the grammar, syntax and lexis of a language pair are identical, what task is there for the translator? We cannot force the reader to 'grind through' the text, regardless of its obscurity, simply on the ground that Chinese has its inherent deficiency."

It would not do any harm to modify the syntax somewhat and to make it peremptory so that the text becomes intelligible to the reader, because it is no pleasure to "grind through" a text. There is no evidence either that stiff translation can preserve "the original tone of terseness and conciseness." And if even stiff translation could preserve "the original tone of terseness and conciseness," then it would be a miracle. How then can we ever say that Chinese has its "deficiency?"

However, in Lu Xun's response to Liang in his essay "'Stiff Translation' and the 'Class Nature of Literature'"(《"硬译"与"文学的阶级性"》, 1930), Lu Xun put forth an explanation for his preference for extreme literalism; he went beyond the choice of a translation method and gave a "political" explanation. After saying that his translations did convey the tone of their originals, Lu

Xun stressed that it was a special class of readers whom his translations were intended for -- the proletariat literary critics who had special class interests to champion. Extreme faithfulness to the original was a way of ensuring that "true" Marxist literary thought be presented to those who wanted the facts as they were. Naturally, Critics had not been taken in by Lu's rationale. David Pollard, for one, has argued, "There is something not quite right in the head of a translator who would say that his translations were not intended to please the reader, but to make him uncomfortable." In any case, the asserted link between accuracy and literalism is extremely tenuous — one can be inaccurate even though one stays very close to the original. The fact that Lu Xun resorts to a variety of arguments (political, aesthetic, linguistic) to justify his method only shows an irrational obsession with literalism on his part.

③　Liang Shiqiu's Translation Practice

(1) *Wuthering Heights* is the name of Mr. Heathcliff's dwelling, "wuthering" being a significant provincial adjective, descriptive of the atmospheric tumult to which its station is exposed in stormy weather. Pure, bracing ventilation they must have up there at all times, indeed. One may guess the power of the north wind blowing over the edge by the excessive slant of a few stunted firs at the end of the house, and by a range of gaunt thorns all stretching their limbs one way, as if craving alms of the sun. (Emily Bronte: *Wuthering Heights*)

> 希兹克利夫先生的住处名叫咆哮山庄。"咆哮"是当地的一个很有意义的形容词，描写在风暴的天气里此地所感受的气象的骚动。纯洁兴奋的空气，他们这里当然是随时都有；屋的尽头处几棵发育不全的枞树之过度倾斜，以及一排茁壮的荆棘之向着一个方向的伸展四肢，好像是向太阳乞讨，这都能使我们猜想到吹过篱笆的北风的威力。
>
> (Liang's version)

(2) To see the world in a grain of sand,

And a heaven in a wild flower,

Hold infinity in the palm of your hand,

And eternity in an hour. (William Blake: *Auguries of Innocence*)

> 一颗沙里看出一个世界，
>
> 一朵野花里看出一个天堂，
>
> 把无限抓在你的手掌里，
>
> 把永恒放进一刹那的时光。 (Liang's version)

(3) John Anderson my Jo, John,

When we were first acquent;

Your locks were like the raven,

Your bony brow was brent;

But now your brow is beld, John,

Your locks are like the snow;

But blessings on your frosty pow,

John Anderson my Jo.

John Anderson my Jo, John,

We climb the hill thegither;

And mony a canty day, John,

We've had wi' anc anither:

Now we maun totter down, John,

And hand in hand we'll go;

And sleep thegither at the foot,

John Anderson my Jo. (Robert Burns: *John Anderson My Jo*)

约翰安德森我的心肝，约翰，

想当初我们俩刚刚相识的时候，

你的头发黑的象是乌鸦一般，

你的美丽的前额光光溜溜，

但是如今你的头秃了，

约翰，你的头发白得象雪一般，

但愿上天降福在你的白头上面，

约翰安德森我的心肝！

约翰安德森我的心肝，约翰，

我们俩一同爬上山去，

很多快乐的日子，

约翰，我们是在一起过的：

如今我们必须蹒跚的下去，

约翰，我们要手拉着手的走下山去，

在山脚下长眠在一起，

约翰安德森我的心肝。(Liang's version)

(4) Liang Shiqiu was the only Chinese who single-handedly finished rendering Shakespeare's complete dramas, and began his translation in 1931 at Hu Shi's invitation of himself and four others to embark on the project of translating the complete plays. The retreat of the other four from the ambitious plan was due to different reasons, for example, Xu Zhimo died as a result of an air crash in the same year. When he was still in Chinese mainland, Liang Shiqiu translated eight plays in this decade, namely, *The Merchant of Venice* (1936), *All's Well That Ends Well* (1936), *Macbeth* (1936), *King Lear* (1936), *Othello* (1936), *The Tempest* (1937), *Twelfth Night* (1938), and *Hamlet* (1938). He did not fulfill his dream of finishing his translations within five or ten years, or exactly speaking, Hu Shi's, until 1967, eighteen years after he moved to Taiwan. The same year saw the publication of his translations of Shakespeare's thirty-seven plays printed by the Taipei Far East Publishing House. Liang Shiqiu's *The Complete Plays of Shakespeare* was for the first time introduced to Chinese mainland as late as in 1996.

While Liang Shiqiu mainly translated the playwright's original blank verse and prose into vernacular Chinese prose, verse did appear in his rendition when Shakespeare let his actors speak in rhymed verse, as Zhou Zhaoxiang says of Liang: "The original blank verse and prose have been translated into vernacular Chinese prose, whereas rhyme and interlude all into verse." ("用白话散文译原文的无韵诗和散文，但原文的押韵处和插曲等一律译做韵语。") Take his translation of Shakespeare's rhymed couplets as an example.

I'll have grounds

More relative than this. The play's the thing

Wherein I'll catch the conscience of the King. (*Hamlet*, Act 2 Scene 2)

> 我要有比这更确切的证据。
> 演戏是唯一的手段
> 把国王的内心来试探。(Liang's version)

In contrast to his normal prose translation, Liang used the same rhyme of "an" at the end of the last two sentences, "duan" and "tan" respectively, in retaining Shakespeare's rhyme of "ing." What is more, Liang divided his translation into lines in order to emphasize his similarity in form with Shakespeare's verse.

Below are two excerpts from *Venice Merchants*. The two translation versions offered by Liang and Zhu are also given below.

BASSANIO Antonio, I am married to a wife

Which is as dear to me as life itself;

But life itself, my wife, and all the world,

Are not with me esteem'd above thy life;

I would lose all, ay, sacrifice them all

Here to this devil, to deliver you.

安图尼欧，我娶了一个妻，我爱她如命；但是我的命，我的妻，再加上全世界，我觉得不及你的性命之可贵：我愿损失一切：牺牲一切给这恶魔，来救你。(Liang's version)

安东尼奥，我爱我的妻子，就像我自己的生命一样；可是我的生命、我的妻子以及整个的世界，在我的眼中都不比你的生命更为贵重；我愿意丧失一切，把它们献给这恶魔做牺牲，来救出你的生命。(Zhu's version)

Tell me where is fancy bred,

Or in the heart, or in the head?

How begot, how nourished?

Reply, reply.

It is engender'd in the eyes,

With gazing fed; and fancy dies

In the cradle where it lies.

Let us all ring fancy's knell

I'll begin it, — Ding, dong, bell.

Ding, dong, bell.

告诉我爱情生自何方，

是在心里，是在头上？

怎样的生，怎样的长？

你说，你说。

爱情是诞生在眼睛里，

靠了凝视才得长大的；

结果还是死在摇篮里。

我们来给爱情敲丧钟：

我先敲。——叮，当，咚。(Liang's version)

告诉我爱情生长在何方？

还是在脑海？还是在心房？

它怎样发生？它怎样成长？

回答我，回答我。

爱情的火在眼睛里点亮，

凝视是爱情生活的滋养，

它的摇篮便是它的坟堂。

让我们把爱的丧钟鸣响，

叮当！叮当！   (Zhu's version)

④ Exercises

(1) Try to compare Liang Shiqiu's translation of *Wuthering Heights* with Yang Yi's.

(2) What is the significance of Lu and Liang's debate on stiff translation?

(3) Try to summarize Liang's contribution to the translation of Shakespeare.

⑤ References and Further Readings

(1) BAI L. Translator Studies: Liang Shiqiu's Discourse on Translation [J]. Across Languages and Cultures, 2011, 12(1): 71-94.

(2) CHAN L T. What's Modern in Chinese Translation Theory? Lu Xun and the Debates on Literalism and Foreignization in the May Fourth Period [J]. TTR: Traduction, Terminologie, Rédaction, 2001, 14(2): 195-223.

(3) YANG X. Studies of Liang Shiqiu's Translation Thought [D]. Hangzhou: MA Thesis, Zhejiang University of Finance and Economics, 2009.

Chapter Nine

Lin Yutang's Translation Theory and Practice

① An Introduction to Lin Yutang

Lin Yutang (1895–1976) was a major figure of 20th century Chinese intellectual and literary history. He was a well-known writer as well as a prominent translator. His informal but polished style in both Chinese and English made him one of the most influential writers of his generation, and his compilation and translations of classical Chinese texts into English were bestsellers in the West.

Lin Yutang was born in a mountain village in Xiamen, Fujian Province. His father was a Christian pastor, so Lin Yutang attended mission school. In 1911, Lin went to St. John's University in Shanghai for his bachelor's degree, and then he received a half-scholarship to continue study for a doctoral degree at Harvard University. Later, he left Harvard early to France and eventually to Germany to complete his requirements for a doctoral degree at the University of Leipzig. In 1923, Lin returned to China and became a professor in Peking University. In 1928, Lin moved to Shanghai and began to make his reputation as a literary figure. He achieved great popular success in the 1930s when he proposed "humor" in China and was known as China's "Master of Humor." He advocated humor, leisure (闲适) and self-expressiveness (性灵). In 1936, Lin left China to America where he wrote his works in English and became widely read. His book *Moment in Peking* was an immediate success and won him international reputation. In the meantime, he was also an outstanding translator and critic of the Chinese culture, attempting to bridge the cultural gap between the West and the East.

Lin Yutang translated many works. Translation constituted a large part of his production. His masterpiece of translation was *Six Chapters of a Floating Life* by Shen Fu, a scholar in the Qing Dynasty. According to Guo Zhuzhang, Lin's translations are as follows.

English-Chinese Translations:

(1) *The Chinese Puzzle* by Arthur Ransome as 《国民革命外纪》, 1928;

(2) *Women and Knowledge* by Mrs. Russel as 《女子与知识》, 1928;

(3) *Biography of Ibsen and His Love Letters* by Georg Randes as 《易卜生评传及其情书》, 1929;

(4) *Pygmalion* by George Bernard Shaw as 《卖花女》, 1929.

Chinese-English Translations:

(1) 《浮生六记》 by Shen Fu (沈复) as *Six Chapters of a Floating Life*, 1939;

(2) 《冥寥子游》 by Tu Long (屠龙) as *The Travels of Mingliaotse*, 1940;

(3) 《庄子》 as *Chuangtse*, 1957.

(4) 《红楼梦》 by Cao Xueqin(曹雪芹) as *A Dearm of the Red Mansions* (unpublished)

Lin was a bilingual writer. Many of his English works were mingled with translation. Besides the translations mentioned above, he also edited and rewrote many Chinese works into English, of which the most influential ones are:

(1) *The Wisdom of Confucius*, 1938;

(2) *The Wisdom of China and India*, 1942;

(3) *The Wisdom of Laotse*, 1948;

(4) *The Chinese Theory of Art: Translation from the Master of Chinese Art*, 1967.

Lin Yutang wrote in English and translated for almost 30 years in the USA. He conquered the Western readers by introducing the Chinese culture to them. In the meanwhile his master of English language is admired and praised. In 1940, when he was awarded the honorary doctorate degree by Elmira College, he was highly praised by the president of the college.

"Lin Yutang — philosopher, writer and wit-patriotic and yet a citizen of the world: by the magic of your pen, you have portrayed the soul of your great people to the people of the English speaking world in a way no person has ever done before. In doing so, you have spoken to the people of the English speaking world in their own language with an artistry that is at once their envy, admiration, and despair."

2 Lin Yutang's Translation Theory

Lin Yutang devoted his life to the introduction of the Chinese culture to the Western readers. During his translation practice, he proposed his own translation theories. The most systemic articles on translation theory are *On Translation* (《论翻译》) and *On Poetry Translation* (《论译诗》). In his famous article *On Translation*, Lin pointed out that "translation is an art"(翻译是一种艺术). Lin pointed out three "responsibilities" and explained the implications of the three "responsibilities" in detail. He also proposed three criteria for translation — "faithfulness," "fluency" and "beauty." (忠实、通顺和美)

I Three Responsibilities

According to Lin, a successful translation asks three requirements for translators.

(a) The translator should have a complete understanding of the language and contents of the source text (第一是译者对于原文文字上及内容上透彻的了解).

(b) The translator should have a good command of Chinese so that he can produce a smooth and expressive version (第二是译者有相当的国文程度，能写清顺畅达的中文).

(c) The translator should be trained properly to hold proper opinions on the standards and techniques of translation (第三是译事上的训练，译者对于翻译标准及技术的问题有正当的见解).

Lin's requirements for translators are prerequisites for them before they start to work on any translation.

II Three Criteria

Lin Yutang proposes three criteria for translation, "faithfulness," "fluency" and "beauty"(忠实、通顺和美), with the first two similar to the criteria ("faithfulness, fluency and elegance", 信、达、雅) put forward by Yan Fu. Lin further explained his own translation criteria: faithfulness (忠实), fluency (通顺), aesthetic quality (美). Then, Lin Yutang put emphasis on "faithfulness."

1) Faithfulness

Faithfulness does not mean a word-for-word translation.

"Faithfulness" is "the very first responsibility for the translators to fulfill."(译者的第一责任)" Faithfulness indicates that the translator should be responsible to the original work and the original

writer."

According to Lin, faithfulness doesn't mean a word-for-word translation (忠实非字字对译之谓). At Lin's time, there was a heated debate on "literal translation" and "free translation" in China, especially between Lu Xun and Liang Shiqiu and Zhao Jingshen. Lu Xun was a typical representative of "literal translation," he even proposed *stiff translation* (硬译) and "rather to be faithful than smooth" (宁信而不顺) in opposition to "rather to be smooth than faithful" (宁顺而不信) put forward by Zhao Jingshen. Since both sides insisted on their own translation criteria, the debate lasted for a long period of time and many scholars were involved in. Lin Yutang also introduced his ideas on "literal translation" and "free translation."

He assumed four types of translation concerning the degree of faithfulness, i.e., literal translation, dead translation, free translation and random translation. Dead translation and free translation are the extremes of literal translation and random translation. In order to keep the exotic flavor of the original work or to make the version fluent and elegant, the translator may resort to the dead translation and random translation. He also listed examples of dead translation:

"The apple of my eye" was translated into "我目的苹果";

"嫁祸他人" was translated into "marry the misfortune to others."

Also, he criticized Yan Fu and Lin Shu for their random translation. In Lin's opinion, both random translation and dead translation should be avoided. However, he disagreed with the naming of "literal translation" and "free translation." He thought, "The naming is convenient to the users, but impertinent to the attitudes of the translator for it does not reveal the translation process, rather it would be misinterpreted."

"A faithful version will not only convey the meaning of the source text, but also its spirit. The version should be faithful to the spirit of the words and their implications. It is not possible to achieve absolute faithfulness. " (译者不但须求达意，而且须以传神为目的。译文须忠实于原文之字神句气与言外之意。绝对忠实不可能。)

"Words of each language have the beauty of sound, meaning, spirit, form, literary style and literary form. When translating the literary works, the translator may get the meaning and forget the spirit or get the spirit and forge the style. It is no easy work for the translator to keep the meaning, spirit, style and sound of a word at the same time in his translation. Each word has its unique features. Thus, it is not possible to find a word which is exactly the same as the word but a similar one." (凡文字有声音之美，有意义之美，有传神之美，有文气文体形式之美，译者或顾其意

而忘其神，或得其神而忘其体，决不能把文意文神文体及声音之美完全同时译出。一字有一字的个性，在他国语言中觅一比较最近之字则有，欲觅一意义色彩个性完全相等的字就没有。）

Take Lin's translation of Li Qingzhao's poem as an example.

寻寻觅觅，冷冷清清，凄凄惨惨戚戚。（李清照《声声慢》）

> So dim, so dark,
>
> So dense, so dull,
>
> So damp, so dank,
>
> So dead! (Lin's translation)

In this example, Lin restructured the original poem. He repeated the word "so" and employed seven adjectives beginning with the letter "d," which successfully transplanted the beauty of the sound and the form of the original poem. However, Lin also expressed the difficulty of translating this poem. According to him, the most difficult part was how to translate the 14 overlapping words and how to keep the artistic conception of the poem. Therefore, in his version, Lin adopted alliteration to translate the Chinese overlapping words. In this way, the version achieved the beauty of both form and sound.

2) Fluency

According to Lin Yutang, fluency was about how to render the Western ideas into Chinese. He mentioned that the translated work should follow the norms of the Chinese language. In the meantime, the translator would inevitably be influenced by the source language norms during his practice. If the translator overlooked the differences between Chinese and Western ways of thinking and translated literally, it will result in "chinglish" or "Non-Chinese." The violation of the norms was also the violation of fluency even if there was no grammatical mistakes. In Lin Yutang's view, a faithful version must be fluent. If a translation was not fluent, if could not be faithful to the source text. Faithfulness did not mean to closely follow the grammar of Western language, and express in unreadable Chinese. As a translator, he should be responsible for both the source text and the target readers. Therefore, the version should be both faithful and smooth. Lin proposed that a fluent translation should be based on sentence-to-sentence translation rather than word-for-word translation. The translator should figure out the exact meaning of a sentence in the source text and reproduce it in the target text following the usage and grammar of the target language. He was opposed to the Europeanized sentences. In his opinion, Europeanization was done on lexical level rather than on syntactical level.

3) Beauty

"Apart from utility, the beauty of a translation should also be given consideration. An ideal translator should regard translation as an art. He should make translation a fine art, love it as loving art, and be conscientious with it as with art. When translating the literary works from abroad, especially poetry and novels, the translator should pay enough attention to the criterion of 'beauty'." (According to Lin Yutang, translation is an art and an ideal translator should make translation a fine art. (使翻译成为美术之一种。) So when we translate the Western literary text, such as poetry and fiction into Chinese, we have to take its aesthetic value into consideration.

To sum up, Lin Yutang is both a translator and a translation theorist. He proposed his own opinions on translation criteria, especially his illustration of "faithfulness," the responsibilities of the translator and the translation of poetry.

③ Lin Yutang's Translation Practice

Lin Yutang published more than 50 translated essays, poems and other works, either from Chinese into English or from English to Chinese. Of those works, the most famous one is his translation of Shen Fu's *Six Chapters of a Floating Life* (《浮生六记》).

(1) 乘骑至华阴庙。过华封里，即尧时三祝处。庙内多秦槐汉柏，大皆三四抱，有槐中抱柏而生者，柏中抱槐而生者。殿廷古碑甚多。内有陈希夷书"福"、"寿"字。华山之脚有玉泉院，即希夷先生化形蜕骨处。有石洞如斗室，塑先生卧像于石床。其地水净沙明，草多绛色，泉流甚急，修竹绕之。洞外一方亭，额曰"无忧亭"。旁有古树三株，纹如裂炭，叶似槐而色深，不知其名，土人即呼曰"无忧树"。

太华之高不知几千仞，惜未能裹粮往登焉。归途见林柿正黄，就马上摘食之。土人呼止，弗听，嚼之，涩甚，急吐去。下骑觅泉漱口，始能言。土人大笑。盖柿须摘下，煮一沸始去其涩，余不知也。（沈复 《浮生六记》）

One day we went on horseback to the Huayin Temple, passing through the Huafeng Village, the place where old Emperor Yao prayed three times for his people. There were at the Temple many locust trees dating back to the Ch'in Dynasty and cypress trees of the Han Dynasty, mostly three or four fathoms in circumference, some locust trees growing inside a cypress, and some cypresses growing inside a locust tree. There were any number of old stone inscriptions in the different courtyards, with two in particular consisting of the two characters for "Good Fortune" and "Longevity" respectively written by Ch'en Hsiyi. There was a Jade Fountain Court at the foot of the Huashan Mountains, where Ch'en had departed from this earth as a Taoist fairy. His image, in a couching position, lay on a stone bed in a very small cave. At this place, the water was very clear and the sands nice and clean; most of the vegetation was of a deep red color and there was a very rapid mountain stream flowing through a thick bamboo grove. A square pavilion stood outside the cave with the signboard:

"Carefree Pavilion." By its side were three old trees, whose barks were cracked like broken coal and whose leaves resembled those of the locust tree, but were of a deeper color. I did not know their name, but the natives aptly and conveniently called them "care-free trees."

I have no idea how many thousand feet high the Huashan Mountains are and regret very much not having been able to pack up some dry provisions and go exploring them for a few days. On my way back I saw some wild persimmons, which were of a ripe color. I picked one from the tree while on horseback, and was going to eat it then and there. The native people tried to stop me, but I wouldn't listen to them. Only after taking a bite did I find it to have a very harsh flavor. So much so that I quickly spat it out and had to come down from horseback and rinse my mouth at a spring before I could speak, to the great merriment of my native advisers. For persimmons should be boiled in order to take away their harsh flavor, but I learnt this a little too late. (Lin's version)

(2) 水光潋滟晴方好；

山色空蒙雨亦奇。

欲把西湖比西子；

浓妆艳抹总相宜。　　（林语堂《东坡诗文选》）

The light of water sparkles on a sunny day;

And misty mountains lend excitement to the rain.

I like to compare the West Lake to "Miss West,"

Pretty in a gay dress and pretty in simple again. (Lin's version)

(3) 满纸荒唐言，

一把辛酸泪。

都云作者痴，

谁解其中味?

These pages tell of babbling nonsense,

A string of sad tears they conceal.

They all laugh at the author's folly;

But who could know its magic appeal? (Lin's version)

Pages full of fantastic talk

Penned with bitter tears;

All men call the author mad,

None his message hears. (Yang Hsianyi & Gladys Yang's version)

Pages full of idle words

Penned with hot and bitter tears:

All men call the author fool;

None his secret message hears. (David Hawkes's Version)

Paper full of wildly impossible stories.

A handful of hot bitter tears.

Everyone says that the author is crazy.

Who can explain its inner flavour? (Bonsall's Version)

4 Exercises

> **Translate the following paragraph into English and then compare your translation with Lin's translation and summarize the differences.**
>
> 笋为蔬中尤物；荔枝为果尤物；蟹为水族中尤物；酒为饮食中尤物；月为天文中尤物；西湖为山水中尤物；词曲为文字中尤物。（张潮《幽梦影》）

5 References and Further Readings

(1) 林语堂. 论翻译 [M] // 罗新璋. 翻译论集. 北京: 商务印书出版社, 1984: 60–63.

(2) 林语堂. 论译诗 [M] // 林语堂，梁实秋，居浩然，等. 翻译纵横谈. 香港: 香港辰冲图书公司, 1969.

(3) CHEN H. Literary Self-Translation: A Case Study of Lin Yutang's "Between Tears and Laughter" [D]. Hangzhou: MA Thesis, Zhejiang University of Finance and Economics, 2009.

Chapter Ten

Guo Moruo's Translation Theory and Practice

1 An Introduction to Guo Moruo

Guo Moruo (1892–1978), courtesy name Dingtang, was a famous poet, novelist, dramatist, historiographer, archaeologist and a distinguished translator enjoying a very high status in the history of translation in modern China.

Guo Moruo, originally named Guo Kaizhen, was born in the small town of Shawan and now is the central urban area of the prefecture level city of Leshan in Sichuan Province. The son of a wealthy merchant, Guo Moruo early manifested a stormy, unbridled temperament. After receiving a traditional education, he went to Japan to study medicine in 1913. There he began to devote himself to the study of foreign languages and literature, reading works by Spinoza, Goethe, the Bengali poet Rabindranath Tagore, and Walt Whitman. His own early poetry was highly emotional free verse reminiscent of Whitman and Percy Bysshe Shelley. The new-style poems that Guo published were later compiled into the anthology *Goddess* (《女神》, 1921). Its publication laid the first cornerstone for the development of new verse in China. In the same year, Guo, together with Cheng Fangwu, Yu Dafu, and Zhang Ziping, gave impetus to the establishment of the Creation Society, one of the most important literary societies during the May Fourth period in China.

As a writer, Guo was enormously prolific in every genre. Besides his poetry and fiction, his works include plays, nine autobiographical volumes, and numerous translations of the works of Goethe, Friedrich von Schiller, Ivan Turgenev, Tolstoy, Upton Sinclair, and other Western authors. After 1949, Guo held many important positions in the People's Republic of China. In 1978, he died in Beijing.

Most of Guo's translation works were published during the years from 1919 to 1949. Among these, the most famous books are:

Faust by Goethe as《浮士德》, 1919;

Immensee by Storm as《茵梦湖》, 1921;

The Sorrows of Young Werther by Goethe as《少年维特之烦恼》, 1922;

Rubáiyát of Omar Kháyyám by Omar Khayyám (translated from Fitzgerald's English version) as《鲁拜集》, 1924;

Social Organization and Social Revolution by Kashojo as《社会组织和社会革命》, 1925;

Shelly's Poems by Shelly as《雪莱诗选》, 1926;

The Jungle by Upton Sinclair as《屠场》, 1929;

War and Peace by L. Tolstol as《战争与和平》, 1931.

Guo Moruo had contributed much to the history of Chinese translation in both theory and practice. His translation practice went simultaneously with his creation. Guo was a productive and influential practitioner. It is estimated that he had translated more than a hundred works of over sixty writers or poets in ten countries with the total words of over three million. His translation works varies in genre and subject from poems, novels, drama to scientific works, historical works of archaeological discoveries and Marxist classical works. As Guo himself mentioned, "I do believe only a few translators could surpass me if considering the number of the words of translations."

② Guo Moruo's Translation Theory

In the course of his translation practice, Guo Moruo also expressed his special views on literary translation, especially on poetry translation. Like most of the translators in his time, Guo illustrated his ideas about translation in the articles on translation issues or in the prefaces or postscripts of the translation works. His viewpoints on translation can be found in the following articles: "Three Letters on Translation" (《论诗三札》), "On the Study and Introduction of Literature" (《论文学的研究与介绍》), "Remarks on the Movement of Annotation Movement and Others" (《讨论注释运动及其他》).

I On Poetry Translation

"I always believe that there is flavor translation besides literal translation and free translation.

A good translation takes into account the form, meaning and flavor of the original work. If a translated poem fails to follow the meaning of the original poem but keeps the flavor, it is still a good translation. However, if it is a literal translation or even dead translation, it does not deserve the name of translation at all." (我始终相信，译诗于直译，意译，之外，还有一种风韵译。字面，意义，风韵，三者均能兼顾，自是上乘。即使字义有失而风韵能传，尚不失为佳品。若是纯粹的直译死译，那只好屏诸艺坛之外了。)

Guo believed that an ideal translation does not distort the form, meaning and most important of all, the flavor. The translator may restructure the sentences to reproduce the flavor without damaging the meaning.

Moreover, Guo Moruo proposed that free translation is a better method in poetry translation. It is not possible to translate a poem if one employs literal translation.

"It is not possible to translate poems word-for-word like translating telegraph code. If this method is employed, the version cannot be called a poem unless the source language is identical to the target language. However, if they are identical, there is no necessity to do translation. Therefore, whatever other people may utter their viewpoints, poetry translation differs from translation of other literary genres. It should be the reproduction of the translator's feelings when he reads the original poems... Some translators insist that literal translation should be adopted in poetry translation and endeavor to impose their ideas on others. Therefore, a conclusion is drawn that poems are untranslatable. Friends! You may change your mind. Poems are untranslatable as long as they are translated literally." (诗的翻译，假使只是如象对翻电报号码一样，定要一字一句的逐译，这原是不可能的事情：因为这样逐译了出来，而译文又要完全是诗，这除非是两种绝对相同的语言不行，两种绝对相同的语言没有，有时亦无须乎翻译了。随你如何说，诗的翻译，绝不是那么一回事！诗的翻译应得是译者在原诗中所感得的情绪的复现……独于我们的译家定要主张直译，而又强人以必须直译，所得的结论当然是不能译。朋友们哟，你们的脑筋要改换过一次才行，诗不能译的话当得是诗不能直译呀！)

In Guo's opinion, if the original work is a poem or a work of art, the translation should also be a poem or work of art in the target language. The method of free translation ensures that the translation is also a work of art.

"A bottle of vodka cannot be changed into a bottle of water. It is better be changed into a bottle of *fenjiu* or *maotai*. However, it is worst if it is changed into a bottle of water with mud and sand in it." (一杯伏特加酒不能换成一杯白开水，总要还他一杯汾酒或茅台，才算尽了责，假使变成一杯白开水，里面还要夹杂些泥沙，那就不行了。)

Guo Moruo's translation reads very much like his writing, and it seems that there is no clear distinction between SL context and TL context for he emerged the inner essence into his translation.

In a word, he reproduced the original ideologically and artistically. He made a reproduction in his own language following the content of the SL text.

II Choice of Source Texts

"A marriage can take place between a man and a woman as long as they fall in love and have mutual understanding. I love Shelly. I can hear aspiration at the bottom of his heart. We share our thoughts, so we get married. We become one. Then his poem is just like my poem. Therefore, I translate his poems as if I were creating my own." (男女结婚要先有恋爱，先有共鸣，先有心声的交感。我爱雪莱，我能感听得他的心声，我能和他共鸣，我和他结婚了。—— 我和他合二为一了。他的诗便如像我自己的诗。我译他的诗，便如像我自己在创作的一样。)

In Guo Moruo's translation activates, he paid much attention to the selection of the source text which matched his own feelings and spirit of the time. His view on translation, especially on poetry translation, is very similar to that of Ezra Pound, who required that the translator should have spiritual empathy with the source language writer, and that only by penetrating into the source language writer's mind and soul and being his / her soul mate can the translators overcome the barriers of culture and languages in conveying the spirit and effect of the original poems.

Take Guo's translation of Goethe as an example. He loved Goethe very much and introduced many of Goethe's works to the Chinese. However, after he finished translating the first part of *Faust* in 1920, he departed Goethe for the moment for he could not understand the state of mind of elderly Goethe in the second part of *Faust*. In the 1940s, he began to translate the second part when he was similar to Goethe in age and experience. This time he was greatly touched by the second part of *Faust* and translated it like creating his own poems, finishing it in no more than one month.

III Requirements for an Ideal Translator

First, an ideal translator must have enough linguistic and cultural knowledge. (第一，译者的语学知识要丰富。)

Second, he must have a good understanding of the original work. (第二，对于原书要有理解。)

Third, he must study the original writer's life. (第三，对于作者要有研究。)

Fourth, he must have a good command of his mother tongue and manipulate it freely. (第四，对于本国文字要有自由操纵的能力。)

According to Guo, the translator must have a strong sense of responsibility. Those who translate widely and casually are irresponsible. He criticized the translators who earned a living and gained fame and wealth via translation.

IV Translation Vs Creation

"I think people lay too much emphasis on matchmakers, but too little on virgins; too much on translation, too little on creation…This phenomenon can be found in the arrangement of articles in newspapers and journals. The translated articles, good or bad, are put in prominent spaces, while the created ones are put in corners. " (我觉得国内的认识只注重媒婆，而不注重出自；只注重翻译，而不注重产生……而一般新闻杂志的体裁也默默地表示它差别的待遇。凡是外来的文艺，无论译得好坏，总要冠居上游；而创作的诗文，仅仅以之填补纸角。)

In "Three Letters on Translation", Guo compared creation to a maiden, and translation to a matchmaker. At the end of the article Guo Moruo concluded that the maiden should be respected and matchmaker be refrained. However, Guo was severely criticized for the derogatory metaphor "matchmaker," especially by Mao Dun, Zheng Zhenduo and Lu Xun. After the New Cultural Movement, scholars paid much attention to the introduction of foreign literature into China. Therefore, Guo's attitude towards translation irritated his contemporaries. They wrote many articles to criticize Guo and express their ideas about translation. Nevertheless, Guo did not give up his idea and maintained that translation is still a matchmaker. He defended himself by further explaining the term "matchmaker":

"However, translation is still a matchmaker, neither a flattering term nor a derogatory one. Since there is a good matchmaker or a bad one, 'matchmaker' is a neutral term. If the word is too vulgar and may offend the dignity of the translator, it can be replaced by '*hongye*' or '*jianxiu*' (both meaning 'matchmaker') or even a more modern on 'medium'." (但其实"翻译"依然是媒婆，这没有过分的"捧"，也没有过分的"骂"。"媒婆"有好的有不好的，翻译也有好的有不好的。要说"媒婆"二字太大众化了有损翻译家的尊严，那就美化一点，改为"红叶"，为"蹇修"，或新式一点，为"媒介"，想来是可以相安无事的吧。)

After many years of translation practice, Guo Moruo illustrated his views on translation and creation again in 1954. He maintained that a translator is not to parrot what the writer says. A good translation equals a creation.

"Translation is by no means an easy job. I not only treat translation activity with respect, but I clearly know how difficult it is. Each one involved in translation practice can experience it. As a creative work, a good translation equals creation or even surpasses translation. A writer must have life experience while a translator must experience the writer's life experience. In this sense, translation is even a harder job than creation. In a word, translation is not an ordinary job." (翻译是一项艰苦的工作，我不但尊重翻译工作，也深知翻译工作的甘苦。凡是从事翻译的人，大概都能体会到这一层。翻译是一种创作性的工作，好的翻译等于创作,甚至还可能超过创作，这不是一件平庸的工作。有时候翻译比创作还要困难。创作要有生活体验，翻译却要体验别人所体验的生活。)

3 Guo Moruo's Translation Practice

I If I Were a Dead Leaf thou Mightest Bear

If I were a swift cloud to fly with thee;

A wave to pant beneath thy power, and share

The impulse of thy strength, only less free

Than thou, O uncontrollable! If even

I were as in my boyhood, and could be

The comrade of thy wanderings over Heaven,

As then, when to outstrip thy skiey speed scarce

Seem'd a vision; I would ne'er have striven

As thus with thee in prayer in my sore need.

Oh, lift me as a wave, a leaf, a cloud!

I fall upon the thorns of life! I bleed!

A heavy weight of hours has chained and bowed

One too like thee: tameless, and swift, and proud.

(Percy Bysshe Shelly: *Ode to the West Wind*)

假如我是一篇败叶你能飘飏，

假使我是一片流云你能飞举，

假使我是在你威力之下喘息的波涛，

分享着你立波的灵动，

几乎和你一样的不羁；

假使我还在童年，

能为你漂泊太空的风云的伴侣，

那时我都幻想即使超过

你的神速！也觉不得稀奇；

我决不会如此地哀哀求你。

啊！你吹舞我如波如叶如云罢！

我生是创巨痛深，我是血流遍体！

时间的权威严锁了我，重压了我，

我个太浮，太傲，太和你一样不羁的。

(Guo Moruo's version)

II Spring

Little boy,	小童们，
Full of joy;	真高兴；
Little girl,	小姑娘们，
Sweet and small,	甜而嫩；
Cock does crow,	鸡在唱，
So do you;	人在吟；婴儿笑声，
Merry voice,	沁人心，
Infant noise,	多喜幸，
Merrily, merrily, to welcome in the year.	多喜幸，
(William Blake: *Spring*)	迎接新春。
	(Guo Moruo's translation)

 Exercises

> **Translate the following paragraph into Chinese, and then compare your translation with Guo Moruo's translation and summarize the differences.**
>
> The meat would be shoveled into carts, and the man who did the shoveling would not trouble to lift out a rat even when he saw one — there were things that went into the sausage in comparison with which a poisoned rat was a tidbit. There was no place for the men to wash their hands before they ate their dinner, and so they made a practice of washing them in the water that was to be ladled into the sausage. There were the butt-ends of smoked meat, and the scraps of cornered beef, and all the odds and ends of the waste of the plants, that would be dumped into old barrels in the cellar and left there. Under the system of rigid economy the packers enforced, there were some jobs that it only paid to do once in a long time, and among these was the cleaning out of the waste barrels. Every spring they did it; and in the barrels would be dirt and rust and old nails and stale water — and cartload after cartload of it would be taken up and dumped into the hoppers with fresh meat, and sent out to the public's breakfast…and for this they would charge two cents more a pound. (Epton Sinclair: *The Jungle*)

⑤ **References and Further Readings**

(1) 郭沫若.批判《意门湖》译本及其他 [J].创造季刊, 1922(1):2.

(2) 郭沫若.谈文学翻译工作 [M] // 罗新璋, 陈应年.翻译论集. 北京: 商务印书馆, 2009.

(3) 郭沫若.论诗三札 [M] // 罗新璋, 陈应年.翻译论集. 北京: 商务印书馆, 2009.

(4) 郭沫若.雪莱的诗 [M] // 罗新璋, 陈应年.翻译论集. 北京: 商务印书馆, 2009.

Chapter Eleven

Zhu Shenghao's Translation of Shakespeare

Zhu Shenghao (1912–1944) was a Chinese translator. Born in Jiaxing, Zhejiang Province, he was among the first few in China who translated the works of William Shakespeare's into Chinese language. His translation was of decent quality and style and honored by domestic and overseas scholars.

① An Introduction to Zhu Shenghao

Zhu Shenghao was born in a declining businessman's family in 1912. Since his childhood, he had been industrious in his studies. In his middle school he read a lot of classics including Shakespeare. And he had special interest in poetry and had read Shelley, Byron, John Keats, and Tennyson. This period of studies and reading laid a solid foundation of his language skills in Chinese and English. In 1929, he went to Zhijiang College to study Chinese Literature and chose English as his major. When he was a sophomore at university, he joined the "River Poetry Society", where his talent was recognized. The president of the society, professor Xia Chengdao (夏承焘), commented in his book *Diary of Learning Poetry at Wind Pavilion* (《天风阁学词日记》), "In reading Zhu Shenghao's seven essays on the Tang Dynasty poets, I found many opinions that had never been made before, with deep insight and incomparable sharpness. The talent and aptitude in him are between my teachers and my friends. I should not treat him as a student". In that beautiful campus, he read extensively in literary works. His love for poetry made him a well-known poet in Zhijiang College.

After graduation, he was recommended to work in the World Publishing House in Shanghai. Zhan Wenhu (詹文浒), who was in charge of the World Publishing House then, assigned the translation of Shakespeare's plays to him because of his extraordinary talent in both Chinese and English. Zhu Shenghao started with his ambitious plan to finish rendering the complete plays within two years in 1935. However, due to the Japanese invasion he failed to carry out his plan on schedule.

Unfortunately, he died of pulmonary tuberculosis at an early age of thirty-two after he had finished translating thirty-one and a half plays between 1935 and 1944. His early death resulted in publishing only twenty-seven of his translations under the title *The Complete Plays of Shakespeare* in three volumes by the Shanghai World Publishing House in 1947, which had originally planned to print his whole translations in four volumes.

Of more than twenty translators of Shakespeare, Zhu Shenghao deserves particular mention. Between 1935 and 1944, when life in China was profoundly disrupted by the Japanese invasion, Zhu Shenghao translated Shakespeare's plays, pressing on devotedly with this work despite suffering poverty and ill-health throughout his tragically short life. In order to adapt the plays to Chinese reading habits, Zhu did not adopt the chronological arrangement of the original Oxford Edition; instead, he divided these plays into four categories: comedy, tragedy, historical play, and miscellaneous. Until 2000, Zhu's work made up the core of the Chinese mainland version of *The Complete Works of Shakespeare*, and his translations have been the texts normally used for stage performances.

The first volume is made up of nine comedies: *A Midsummer Night's Dream*, *The Merchant of Venice*, *Much Ado About Nothing*, *All's Well That Ends Well*, *Twelfth Night*, *As You Like It*, *Measure for Measure*, *The Tempest*, and *Winter's Tale*. The second consists of eight tragedies: *Romeo and Juliet*, *Hamlet*, *Othello*, *King Lear*, *Macbeth*, *Coriolanus*, *Julius Caesar*, and *Antony and Cleopatra*. The last volume includes the rest that have not been collected in the first two volumes: *Love's Labours Lost*, *Two Gentlemen of Verona*, *The Comedy of Errors*, *Taming of the Shrew*, *The Merry Wives of Windsor*, *Titus Andronicus*, *Troilus and Cressida*, *Timon of Athens*, *Cymbeline*, *Pericles*, and *Prince of Tyre*.

Zhu's versions of the history plays were excluded from the collection because he finished only four and a half rather than ten. This regrettable fact, fortunately, was compensated with the publication of another collection under the same title *The Complete Plays of Shakespeare*, in which Zhu Shenghao's above-mentioned twenty-seven plays were collected together with Yu Erchang's (1904–1984) ten history plays, and was published by the Taiwan World Publishing House in 1957.

What was of great significance for the history of Shakespearean translation in Chinese mainland, and Chinese literature in particular was the publishing of *The Complete Works of*

Shakespeare by the People's Literature Press in 1978, for this marked the very beginning of Chinese translations of a foreign writer's complete works. This collection included a revised version of Zhu Shenghao's complete renditions of thirty-one plays, together with translations of the other six plays and of all Shakespearean poetry.

Even though Zhu Shenghao didn't see his translations published during his life, he enjoyed the highest honor and praise among all the translators. The popularity of his version and the elegance and maturity of his language prove that deserves this comment.

② Zhu Shenghao's Translation Ideas

Zhu Shenghao didn't write any translation theory works, but he certainly did have his own thinking about drama translation, particularly the translation of Shakespeare. His translation idea can be revealed from his self-preface of *The Complete Plays of Shakespeare.* With the limited text, this self-preface has clarified his translation ideas through his translation criteria, translation methods and translation attitude.

In the preface, Zhu Shenghao firstly mentioned his deep research on Shakespeare before translation and his motivation of this translation. He specially pointed out the significance of Shakespeare. "In the world history of literature, four figures of greatest significance are Homer in Greece, Dante in Italy, Shakespeare in Britain and Goethe in Germany. However, Homer, a hero in epics, is a little far from the present reality; Dante, while describing the world of heaven and hell, is contradictory with modern thought; Goethe is a good representative of modern spirit. However, Shakespeare achieved more compared with the above-mentioned three figures. Although Shakespeare told us the story of ancient aristocrats, what he tries to reveal is the universal characteristics for all the human beings, whether rich or poor, high or low-class. That's the reason his books were popular among the world, and his plays were performed on stage again and again. Just because he reveals the universality of human beings, his works can touch the human minds." He translated Shakespeare with another mission. In one of his letters to his wife, Zhu even anticipated himself to be a national hero after successfully translating the whole works of Shakespeare. Thus, his effort to translate Shakespeare's complete works was tinted with nationalism.

In addition, Zhu Shenghao described the situation then of Shakespeare translation in China. "Chinese readers have heard of Shakespeare for a

long time. Well-known writers also tried to publish their translations. But as I looked at the different translations available, I found a few of them to be rough and hasty, although most of them are too overcautious and rigid. Because of this rigidity, not only is the original allure completely lost but also the language is so obscure that it becomes almost unintelligible. It is impossible to grasp the meaning quickly. We cannot blame Shakespeare for this shortcoming; his translators are the ones responsible for this." Thus, in Zhu Shenghao's translation, what he proposed was "likeness in spirit" rather than "likeness in form."

Zhu Shenghao specially elaborated his method of translating Shakespeare. He explained, "I translate these works according to the following principles: first of all, I have tried as much as possible to capture the original appeal. Then, if I have no other choice, I look for clear and fluent expressions to preserve the charm of the original. But I do not agree with the rigid method of word-for-word translation. Whenever I run into something incompatible with Chinese grammar, I repeatedly and carefully go through the original words, sparing no effort to change entire sentence structures in order to make the original meaning as clear as the daylight, free from any obscure expressions. When I finish a paragraph, I transform myself into a reader, to examine if there is anything obscure." Meanwhile, he also kept in mind an imaginary stage: "I would also play the role of an actor on stage in order to detect whether the intonation was fluent or whether the rhythm was in harmony. If I was not satisfied with one word or one sentence, I often spent several days continually thinking about it."

Besides, Zhu Shenghao also described his experience of translating Shakespeare and hardship involved in this process. "However, my translation still leaves too much to be desired, partly due to my limited abilities/skills, partly due to the unfavorable circumstances in a remote village, with neither reference books to consult nor experts to get criticism from. As a result, there must be some mistakes or errors in my translation. If there are scholars willing to point out and correct them, it will be a blessing not only for me but also for all the Chinese readers."

In summary, his translation ideas can be concluded as follows.

Translation criterion: "preserve the original spirit as far as possible"

Translation method: "Whenever I run into something incompatible with Chinese grammar, I repeatedly and carefully go through the original words, sparing no effort to change entire sentence structures in order to make the original meaning as clear as the daylight, free from any obscure expressions."

Translation attitude: He devoted his whole life into the translation of Shakespeare's works.

3 Zhu Shenghao's Translation Practice

(1) Laer: I thank you; keep the door. O thou vile king,

Give me my father!

Queen: Calmly, good Laertes.

Laer: That drop of blood that's calm proclaims bastard,

Cries cuckold to my father, brands the harlot

Even here, between the chaste unsmireched brows

Of my true mother,

King: What is the cause, Laertes?

That thy rebellion looks so giant-like? (*Hamlet*: Act 4 Scene 5)

> 雷欧提斯：谢谢你们；把门看好了。啊，你这万恶的奸王！还我的父亲来！
>
> 王后：安静一点，好雷欧提斯。
>
> 雷欧提斯：我身上要是有一点血安静下来，我就是个野生的杂种，我的父亲是个王八，我的母亲的贞洁的额角上，也要雕上娼妓的恶名。
>
> 国王：雷欧提斯，你这样大张声势，兴兵犯上，究竟为了什么原因？(Zhu's version)

(2) Osw: What does thou know me for?

Kent: A knave' a rascal, an eater of broken meats; a base, proud, shallow, beggarly, three-suited, hundred-pound, filthy, worsted-stoking knave; a lily-livered, action-taking knave, whoreson, glass-gazing, superserviceable, finical rogue; one-trunk-inheriting slave; one that wouldst be a bawd in way of good service, and art nothing but the composition of a knave, beggar, coward, pander, and the son and heir of a mongrel bitch; one whom I will beat into clamorous whining, if thou deny'st the least syllable of thy addition. (*King Lear*: Act 2 Scene 1)

> 奥斯华德：你认识我是谁？肯特：一个无赖；一个恶棍；一个吃剩饭的家伙；一个下贱的、骄傲的、浅薄的、叫花子一样的、只有三身衣服、全部家私算起来不过一百磅的、卑鄙龌龊的、穿绒袜子的奴才；一个没有胆量的、靠着官府势力压人的奴才；一个婊子生的、顾影自怜的、奴颜婢膝的、涂脂抹粉的混帐东西；全部家私都在一只箱子里的下流胚，一个天生的王八胚子；又是奴才，又是叫花子，又是懦夫，又是忘八，又是一条杂种老母狗的儿子；要是你不承认这些头衔，我要把你打得放声大哭。(Zhu's version)

(3) As Caesar loved me, I weep for him; as he was fortunate, I rejoice at it; as he was valiant,

I honour him: but, as he was ambitious, I slew him. There is tears for his love; joy for his fortune; honour for his valour; and death for his ambition. (*The Life and Death of Julies Caesar*: Act 3 Scene 2)

> 因为凯撒爱我，所以我为他流泪；因为他是幸运的，所以我为他欣慰；因为他是勇敢的，所以我尊敬他；因为他有野心，所以我杀死他。我用眼泪报答他的友谊，用喜悦庆祝他的幸运，用尊敬崇扬他的勇敢，用死亡惩戒他的野心。(Zhu's version)

(4) Take, O, take those lips away,

That so sweetly were forsworn;

And those eyes, the break of day,

Lights that do mislead the morn:

But my kisses bring again, bring again;

Seals of love, but sealed in vain, sealed in vain. (*Measure for Measure*: Act 4 Scene 1)

> 莫以负心唇，
>
> 婉转弄辞巧；
>
> 莫以薄幸眼，
>
> 颠倒迷昏晓；
>
> 定情密吻乞君还，
>
> 当日深盟今已寒。(Zhu's version)

④ Exercises

(1) What is the uniqueness of drama translation compared with other genres of literature?

(2) Select some examples and compare Zhu Shenghao's translation of Shakespeare with Liang Shiqiu's and Bian Zhilin's.

(3) If possible, visit Zhu Shenghao's Former Residence in Jiaxing and do a fieldwork.

⑤ References and Further Readings

(1) HUANG A C Y. Chinese Shakespeares: Two Centuries of Cultural Exchange [M]. New York: Columbia University Press, 2009.

(2) 朱尚刚. 诗侣莎魂: 我的父母朱生豪宋清如[M]. 上海: 华东师范大学出版社, 1999.

(3) 朱安博. 朱生豪的文学翻译研究[M]. 北京: 国防工业出版社, 2014.

Chapter Twelve

Fu Lei's Translation Theory and Practice

① An Introduction to Fu Lei

Fu Lei (1908–1966) was born into a prosperous family near Shanghai and raised by his mother. He cried so loudly when he entered this world that his parents named him Lei, a Chinese word for "thunder." He was a famous translator and art critic. He studied art and art theory in France from 1928 until 1932. Upon his return to China, he taught in Shanghai and worked as a journalist and art critic until he took up translating. His translations, which remain highly regarded, include Voltaire, Balzac and Romain Rolland. He developed his own style, the "Fu Lei style," and his own translation theory. Though labeled a rightist in 1957, he persevered until 1966, when, at the start of the Cultural Revolution, he and his wife committed suicide. His letters to his son Fu Cong, a world-renowned pianist, were published posthumously and have become a bestseller in China.

Fu Lei was an outstanding translator, an artistic theoretician as well as a connoisseur of arts. He is one of the few modern writers who really master law of arts. His knowledge covered that of China and of foreign countries, of tradition and of modern times. Besides literature, he was excellent in painting and music, showing superb ability to appreciate them. His writing amounts to over one million words, which includes novels, prose, literary comments, prefaces, epilogues, reviews of his time, letters and works on fine arts and music.

In addition, Fu Lei translated over thirty literary works, most of which are French ones. His translation amounts to about 5 million words. Some of his translations are listed as follows.

(1) *Rodin L'Art* by Paul Gsell as《罗丹艺术论》, 1932;

(2) *Vie de Tolstoi* by Rolland as《托尔斯泰传》, 1934;

(3) *Vie de Michel- Ange* by Rolland as《米开朗琪罗传》, 1934;

(4) *Voltaire* by Maurois as《伏尔泰》, 1935;

(5) *Vie de Beethoven* by Rolland as《贝多芬传》, 1942;

(6) *Eugenie Grandet* by Balzac as《欧也妮•葛朗台》, 1949;

(7) *Le Père Goriot* by Balzac as《高老头》, 1950;

(8) *La Cousine Bette* by Balzac as《贝姨》, 1951;

(9) *Le Cousin Pons* by Balzac as《邦斯舅舅》, 1952;

(10) *Jean Christophe* by Rolland as《约翰•克里斯多夫》, 1953;

(11) *Philosophie de L'Art* by Taine Persondata as《艺术哲学》, 1963.

All his translations of 15 volumes had been published by Anhui People's Publishing House since 1981. Reading his writing, we got touched by his crystal thoughts and his noble personality, and understand his penetrating views on artists' personality, artistic theories, literary criticism, translation, etc.

② Fu Lei's Translation Ideas

I Spiritual Resemblance Theory

Spiritual resemblance theory is a very important part in Fu Lei's translation ideas, which can be mostly seen in his "Preface to the retranslation of *Le Père Goriot*" (1951). The following is an excerpt from this article.

In terms of effect, translation should be the same as copying painting, for what is searched for is spiritual similarity rather than formal similarity. However, when it comes to the practical work, translation is much more difficult than copying painting. The copied paintings employ the same materials (e.g. colors, canvas, paper or silk) and rules (e.g. chromatology, anatomy, perspective) as original ones, while the translated works and the original works are composed of different words and by different rules. Every language has its own characteristics governed by inviolable rules, with some imitable merits and some irremediable shortcomings as well. There are untranslatable points even between English, French and German, which are similar to each other in many ways. Therefore, in the case of translation between Chinese and Western languages, which are so much different and in conflict, it is far from enough to depend on dictionaries and follow the original grammars to convey the spirit and express the idea.

Translation literature of different countries varies a lot, and there is no English version of French style or French version of English style. Translation would be easy if breaking the structures and characteristics of the native language could convey the features of the foreign language and obtain the original spirit. Unfortunately, that kind of theory would mean to take measures without attending to the changes in circumstances, or to cut the feet to fit the shoes, causing losses on both sides. Different words and word classes, syntactic structures, grammar and conventions, rhetoric and poetic rules, and idioms of the two languages reflect different national ways of thinking, depth of perceptions, perspectives, customs and traditions, social backgrounds and ways of expressions. To convey in one language the peculiarities of another language, one has to "obtain the essence and leave the phenomenon, focus on the inside and forget the outside," just as Bo Le (the horse-judging master) appraised horses. Even for the most excellent translation, its charm may still be superior or inferior to the original. The distance should be shortened as much as possible, keeping the superiority or inferiority under control.

Some people may hold that the criteria for translation should not be so simple, and we may suppose the ideal translation is just like a text written by the original author in Chinese. The meaning and spirit of the original, the fluency and integrity of the translation could be combined in one. There should be no such flaws as to harming the meaning with diction or destroying the diction with the meaning.

II Translating as a Holy Career

Fu Lei regards translating as a holy career, and in his article "Fragments of My Translation Experience" (1957), he illustrated this point as follows:

Because I love literature and art, I regard literary work as a noble and sacred cause. Not only do I regard damaging artworks as serious as distorting the truth, but I also feel intolerable if someone introduces a piece of art and cannot return it to a piece of art, so my attitude and thinking toward it becomes unconsciously very solemn and conservative. If the translator does not deeply understand the original work, it will never be possible for the reader to understand it. To choose an original work is just like making friends with somebody: Some people are always at odds with me, so I do not force myself to be involved with them; some

people feels like we have known each other all along at our first sight, and even hate knowing each other so late. But even for the latter ones, it is not possible to truly understand them overnight. If I want to translate a work I like, I have to read it four times or five times, so that I can fully remember the plot and story and analyze it thoroughly, and the characters are vivid in my mind, and the subtle meanings hidden in the lines can be slowly figured out. But are the necessary conditions enough for translation after doing these preparations? The answer is definitely"No". Because translation works not only are about understanding and experiencing the original works, but also it needs to go further to express faithfully and touchingly what I know and experience from it. There are many examples of two people with opposite personalities becoming confidantes, and just like the old saying goes that certain opposite things can complement each other. It is also possible to love a work that is totally different from my own temperament, but to express such a work is equivalent to reborn and become a person who is different from my temperament, or another person who is actually the opposite to myself. If I knew that the author's temperament and mine went to extremes respectively, then it would be easier to handle it, because I will just choose not to translate it. However, in most cases, the spiritual distance between the two parties is not very clear. Whether my style can adapt to the style of the original work is not clear over a short time. It is hard to understand the author, but it is not easy to understand myself too. For example, I have a sense of humor, but never write humorous articles; I have a sense of justice, but never write dagger-like essays; faced with the pungent sentences and sharp words, but with the style being clean and elegant in Voltaire's allegorical novels. How can I not shrink from translating it, and try to translate first so that I know if I can manage it? The translation of Candide had been revised eight times, and I am still uncertain about how much the spirit of the original work is conveyed.

As far as literary genres are concerned, we should translate with a clear sense of our strengths and weaknesses. Those who are not proficient in theoretical arguments should not force themselves to translate books of theory. Those who are not poets should not translate poetry, for what they produce will not only be unpoetic; it will not be like prose either. To introduce literary works through a mirror of distortion makes one a literary culprit.

With regard to the different literary schools, we should know which school we fit best into: Romantic or Classicist, Realist or Modernist? Do we belong with certain writers of a particular school or write like certain works of a particular writer? Our limitations and ability to adapt will only be revealed in practice. We cannot force things. Even after translating several thousands of words of text, we may have to give up with regret. Even if we can adapt as appropriate, we still need to apply ourselves doubly hard. One measure of our adaptability is our enthusiasm about the original work, since emotional interest affects understanding, and vice versa. The other measure of our adaptability is our artistic insight. Without enough of it we may fool ourselves into believing that we are capable of such adaptation as is required when we are not.

Whatever the style of the original, it will always be unified and coherent. The translation, of course, should not be fragmented. But our language is still in its formative stage, unguided by specific, definite rules of usage. On the other hand, standardization is the staunch enemy of literary expressiveness. Sometimes we need to use classical literary Chinese, but whether it fits into the translated text is a problem. I retranslated *Jean Christoph* not just to correct my own errors; rather, the classical literary language used in my earlier translation creates a jarring hybridization of styles. Sometimes I need to use dialects, but using dialects with too strong a regional favor will tarnish the local coloring of the original. If I use simple Putonghua, the translation will be bland, uninteresting and aesthetically unsatisfying. We cannot reap immediate rewards by quickly rummaging through a great number of classical Chinese works or by familiarizing ourselves with a variety of dialects. These will only help us with our vocabulary and syntax. A coherent style can only be acquired after an extended period of artistic nurturing. As I said before, the language problem is, basically, one of aesthetic insight. To raise the standard of translations, we must first work out some objective criteria so that we can tell well from bad ones.

III Language of Translation

In the *Letter to Lin Yiliang on Translation* (1951), Fu Lei elaborated on the language of translation, the main idea of which is taken in the following:

As regards translation, I think the most difficult hurdles are actually the simplest, shortest and most easily understandable sentences in the original text, for example, *Elle est charmante* (*She Is Charming*). Anyone who has studied English and French for one to two months knows what that is. But translating it into Chinese, conveying the tone of the original text and reproducing the mood and atmosphere in the translation, is something I can hardly ever achieve. But this kind of sentence always serves as an important link between what goes before and what comes after in the original text. If this linkage cannot be transferred, the dazzling qualities of the text will be completely gone. The original text is like a cup of Longjing tea, with a lingering fresh taste, but the translation turns out to be a cup of insipid water. It is not easy even to bring out the simple and lively tone of *She Is Charming*. I do not mean to say that translating long sentences is not difficult, but that the difficulty lies not in conveying the spirit, but in focusing right. In a long sentence, there is always a very short and simple clause interspersed with three to four subordinate clauses, each of which contains other subordinate clauses introduced with participles. If all these clauses are broken down in the translation, then the balance is always lost, and the important can not be distinguished from the inconsequential.

In order to keep the core message intact, sometimes we cannot but put the subordinate clauses at the beginning, and translate the short main clauses at the end. But this approach has its own drawback as well: too many words get repeated.

Translating a single word is as difficult as translating a short sentence, and the easier or more common the word is, the more difficult it is to translate it well. Examples are "virtue," "spiritual," "moral," "sentiment," "noble," "saint" and "humble." Moreover, some abstract nouns simply do

not exist in Chinese. Take for example *La vraie grandeur d'ame* (*The Genuine Grandeur of the Soul*). If this phrase is translated into Chinese, it will still be fine if it stands alone, but not so if it is put into context, and the word order must be changed. By the way, another difficulty is that there are too many homophones in Chinese. If in one sentence the word *zhege* (this) is almost immediately followed by *gebie* (particular), then the repetition of two *ge*'s will not only be jarring to the ears, but also look rather awkward. This is because Chinese characters are monosyllabic. Every single word in a sentence is pronounced with the same force. It is different from foreign languages in which articles like "the" and "that" is unstressed — in French *ce* and *cette* are even less prominent. The articles and nouns in an English sentence are stressed quite differently, so what is important is distinguished from what is not. However, this does not work in the case of Chinese, which explains again why it is so difficult to get the emphasis right.

The above are practical problems of a trivial nature, now to a basic conceptual problem.

Vernacular Chinese is far inferior to foreign languages in terms of richness and variety. In this regard, classical Chinese has an edge. Zhou Zuoren has said, "If one translates in classical Chinese, which contains antithetical structures, the standard of the translation is to a certain extent guaranteed. The translation will be pleasing to the eyes, and its meaning will be close to that of the original." This is a very illuminating remark. Classical Chinese has its own rules and generic restrictions that cannot be changed at will; its vocabulary is very rich as well. By contrast, vernacular Chinese has been taken over from the general populace, and it has neither rules nor generic restrictions. Everyone gropes along, and ends up in great confusion.

Moreover, we cannot adopt a particular dialect as the basis for our vernacular Chinese. The language we now use is neither a northern nor a southern dialect, but a mixture of both. All the characteristics of the northern and southern dialects have been removed, giving us a language with skeletal elements that can be used to convey meanings but not feelings. As a result, stylistic qualities such as vividness, exquisiteness and profundity are totally gone.

The colloquial expressions in dialects are their life and soul. However, if they are deployed in translation, the local color of the original text will be erased and a foreigner will be turned into a Chinese person. Isn't that ridiculous?

However, if colloquial expressions are not used, the translation (or at least the conversations in it) will become lifeless and "artificially literary." Creative writers sometimes commit this mistake, because they worry that a pure dialect will obstruct readers' understanding. Hence, their work is written in Putonghua, which is actually very artificial. It is a language developed on the basis of the northern dialect, with all the colloquial elements removed. What aesthetic value can this kind of language have? Unfortunately, this is what we write now. I think the main reason that we cannot translate in good style is that our language is a "fake" language.

Furthermore, there is a great difference in mentality between ethnic groups. Foreign languages are analytical in nature; they are "prosaic." Chinese is synthetic in nature; it is "poetic." The different aesthetic qualities make it difficult to achieve semantic equivalence between Chinese and foreign languages. Actually, all translations are caught somewhere between "over-translating" and "under-translating," and the problem becomes more acute in translations into Chinese.

However, we are usually not bold enough when we translate; we are constrained by the words and syntax of the original text. To succeed, one has to read the original text thoroughly so as to fully grasp the nuances and the "spiritual resonance." Only by doing so can we be bold enough. It said, "The words in the dictionary are just like chemical symbols. Translating an English word into a Chinese one is like translating 'water' as 'H_2O'." That sounds fair enough. But we use "water," not "H_2O," in translation.

I do not mean that we can neglect the structures of the original sentences. On the contrary, we have to retain them as far as possible. However, no matter how novel these sentence structures are, the translation has to read like Chinese. This is certainly not easy to achieve, and only when the translator has very good taste can he exercise such judgements. Lao She is the only author in our country who writes long, Europeanized sentences that are still recognizably Chinese. I have mentioned all this because I do not wish merely to convey the spirit of the original text, but intend to create a new kind of Chinese language by introducing variations in syntax. There is room for exploration in this area. I have always held the opinion that this is precisely the job of translators. An author cannot persist in creating novel sentences. If he does so, the flow of his thoughts will be obstructed, and he ends up "seeing the wood for the trees." Paying too much attention to grammar, syntax and style is definitely not conducive to the creation of great works.

③ Fu Lei's Translation Practice

I Example 1

A cette nouvelle, il (Zadig) tomba sans conscience; sa douleur le mit au bord du tombeau.

–Etes-vous sujet a cette cruelle maladie?

–Elle me met quelquefois au bord du tombeau… (Voltair: *Zadig*)

> 听这消息，查弟格当场昏倒，痛苦得死去活来。
>
> "这种痛苦的病，你可是常发的？""有时候几乎把我命都送掉……" (Fu's version)

In example, the literal translation of the phrase "mettre qqn. au bord du tombea" is "将某人置于坟墓的边缘". Thus the above two sentences can be literally translated into "他的痛苦将其置于坟墓的边缘","它有时候将我置于坟墓的边缘". These translations sound unsmooth and Europeanized in standardized Chinese, which consequently results in the destroying of the smoothness and naturalness of the original style. Fu Lei's translations are free from the bound of any word or phrase and he translates the same phrase in different ways so that the translations sound smooth, natural and coherent.

II Example 2

In translating book titles, most of the literature translators in Chinese mainland like to adopt literal translation method. As far as the book title *Le Père Goriot* is concerned, the literal translation of "Goriot" into "高里奥", which is the first name of a person, is simple and undoubted. While how to translate "père" here? "Pere" means "father" in dictionaries. But once followed by a first name, it often refers to a person who is of an old age but does not deserve to be called "monsieur" because of his low social position. Thus "père" is exactly correspondent to the Chinese address "老头." Both the form and the content of the original should be considered in an ideal translation. But when the form and the content become contradictory and either one has to be sacrificed, we should put the content in the first place in order to achieve the "spiritual resemblance." Here *Le Père Goriot* shouldn't be literally translated into "高里奥爸爸," since the image of le père Goriot is by no means a Chinese old man. Instead, Fu Lei's translation of "高老头" achieves the "spiritual resemblance" with the original and leaves in Chinese readers' mind the image of an abject flour businessman in the 19th century in France.

III Example 3

In *Le Père Goriot*, the Chinese translation of the name Vautrin is the same worthy of being noticed. Vautrin is an escapee from the prison in the novel, who is with a personality of cruelty and coolness and hides himself in the Maison Vauquer. "伏脱冷," the Chinese translation of the name Vautrin by Fu Lei, not only takes consideration both the sound and the meaning, but also depicts wisely the personalities of this character. Mu Dan translates "Vautrin" into "吴特兰," which is of no special meaning. Chen Xuezhao's translation is "伏德昂." It seems improper to use the two Chinese characters "德" and "昂" in translating the name of a cruel and cool escapee.

④ Exercises

(1) Do you agree with Fu Lei's translation idea that resemblance in spirit weighs over that in form? Give examples to expound your understanding.

(2) "There is a great difference in mentality between ethnic groups. Foreign languages are analytical in nature; they are 'prosaic.' Chinese is synthetic in nature; it is 'poetic'." Fu Lei's analysis is incisive and illuminating. Give comments on this point.

⑤ References and Further Readings

(1) CHAN T L. Twentieth-Century Chinese Translation Theory: Modes, Issues and Debates [M]. Amsterdam: John Benjamins, 2004.

(2) 陈福康. 中国译学理论史稿[M]. 上海: 上海外语教育出版社, 2002.

(3) 文军. 中国翻译理论百年回眸[M]. 北京: 北京航空航天大学出版社, 2007.

(4) 傅敏. 傅雷谈艺录 (增订本)[M]. 北京: 生活·读书·新知三联书店, 2016.

Chapter Thirteen

Qian Zhongshu's Translation Theory and Practice

Qian Zhongshu (1910–1998) was a Chinese literary scholar and writer, known for his burning wit and formidable erudition. To the general public, he is best known for his satiric novel *Fortress Besieged*. His works of non-fiction are characterized by their large number of quotations in both Chinese and Western languages (including English, French, German, Italian, Spanish, and Latin). What's more, he is a great translator as well as a translation theorist. The translated passages in *On the Art of Poetry* (《谈艺录》) and *The Pipe-Awl Chapters* (《管锥编》) constitute a significant part of his full-length study. Moreover, he can be called a translation theorist in his own right, because he never fails to offer his views on the problem of translation. His most important and influential inquiry into translation is represented by his seminal essay "Lin Shu's Translations" (《林纾的翻译》), which was published in *Journal of Literary Studies* (《文学研究集刊》) in 1964.

① An Introduction to Qian Zhongshu

Born in Wuxi, Qian Zhongshu was the son of Qian Jibo, a conservative Confucian scholar. When he was one year old, according to a tradition practiced in many parts of China, he was given a few objects laid out in front of him for his "grabbing." He grabbed a book. His uncle then renamed him Zhongshu, literally "being fond of books."

During his primary school time, he began to get approach to Western literature. He loved two boxes of novels translated by Lin Shu and published by The Commercial Press, which differed from those Chinese novels he once read and thus led him to a totally new world. This experience advocated his interest to learn foreign languages. At that time, he began to think that if he could learn English well, he would read many interesting English novels. Despite failing in Mathematics, Qian was accepted into the Department of Foreign Languages of Tsinghua University in 1929 because of his excellent performance in Chinese and English languages. In 1935, Qian received government sponsorship to further his studies abroad. Qian headed for the University of Oxford. After spending two years at Exeter College, Oxford, he received a *Baccalaureus Litterarum* (Bachelor of Literature).

In 1949, Qian was appointed a professor in his alma mater. Four years later, an administrative adjustment saw Tsinghua changed into a science and technology-based institution, with its Arts departments merged into Peking University. Qian was relieved of teaching duties and worked entirely in the Institute of Literary Studies under PKU. He also worked in an agency in charge of the translation of Mao Zedong's works for a time.

A collection of short essays, *Marginalias of Life* (《写在人生边上》) was published in 1941. *On the Art of Poetry*, written in classical Chinese, was published in 1948. *The Selected and Annotated Song Dynasty Poetry* (《宋诗选注》) was published in 1958. *Seven Pieces Patched Together* (《七缀集》), a collection of seven pieces of literary criticism written (and revised) over years in vernacular Chinese, was published in 1984. The famous essay "Lin Shu's Translation" was included in the collection. Qian's five-volume 《管锥编》, literally "The Pipe-Awl Chapters" was translated into English as *Limited Views*. Begun in the 1980s and published in its current form in the mid-
1990s, it is an extensive collection of notes and short essays on poetics, semiotics, literary history and related topics written in classical Chinese.

Currently, there are no studies of Qian Zhongshu's translations and translation theory abroad, but in our country, both his translation theory and practice have been and are still very influential. His most important translation work, such as *Selected Works of Mao Zedong* (《毛泽东选集》), *Mao Zedong's Poems* (《毛泽东诗词》) and his innumerable translated quotations in *On the Art of Poetry* and *Limited Views* as well as his famous essay "Lin Shu's Translation" revealed his thoughts on translation and won great renown among Chinese scholars. In "Lin Shu's Translation", he proposed the famous translation theory of "realm of transformation" (化境), which later gained great prestige among Chinese translators.

② Qian Zhongshu's Translation Ideas

Qian Zhongshu's "realm of transformation" describes what an ideal translation is like, differentiates the good translation from the bad, and contains hidden echoes of similar terminology from traditional Chinese poetics and art criticism. Qian began by talking briefly about the etymological and semantic associations of the Chinese word "译" (to translate). Then he explained what he meant by "transformation":

The highest standard in literary translation is "化", transforming a work from the language of one country into that of another. If this could be done without betraying any evidence of artifice by virtue of divergences in language and speech habits, while at the same time preserving intact the flavor of the original, then we say that such a performance has attained the realm of transformation, "the ultimate of transmutation." This kind of achievement in language has been compared in the 17th century to the transmigration of souls, replacing of the external shell and retaining the inner spirit and style without the slightest deviation. In other words, a translation should cleave to the original with such fidelity that it would not read like a translation, for a literary work in its own language will never read as though it has been through a process of translation.

Nevertheless, there are inevitable gaps — between one national language and another, between the translator's comprehension and literary style and the form and substance of the original work, and frequently between the translator's appreciation of the work and his ability to express it. It is an arduous journey that takes off from one language, after inching its way and negotiating many gaps, arrives safely in the midst of another. One is bound to encounter obstacles in transit and suffer certain losses and damages. For this reason, translations cannot avoid being somewhat unfaithful, violating

or not exactly conforming to the original in meaning or tone. That is what we call "讹", "misrepresentation." There is a Western saying, "the translator is a traitor" (Traduttore, traditore). The Chinese ancients also said something to the effect that *fan* in *fanyi* (翻译, translation) amounts to *fan* (反), to turn over — as in turning a piece of embroidery inside out. The words transmit and entice explain, of course, how translation functions in cultural interchange; it acts as a middleman, a liaison, introducing foreign works to the readers and enticing them into a fondness for these works, as though playing the role of matchmaker and bringing about a "literary romance" between nations.

Since complete and thoroughgoing "transformation" is an all but unrealizable ideal, and some degree of "misrepresentation" in certain connections is all but unavoidable, the act of transmitting and enticing takes on a new significance. Translation is to save people the trouble of learning foreign languages and reading the original works, but now it entices the readers into doing that very thing. It arouses the readers' curiosity, causing them to yearn for the original: it lets them have a taste of the real thing, whetting their appetite without satisfying their hunger. The readers of a translation will always feel as if gazing at flowers through a fog. Thus, Goethe rather unceremoniously linked the translator to a professional go-between — because he half-reveals and half-conceals the features of the original, causing his readers to wonder how beautiful it must be. In order to

tear away the bridal veil and have a good look, the readers must try to read the original work. In this sense, a good translation is self-defeating; it leads us to the original, and as soon as we get to read the original, we will toss aside the translation. A very self-confident translator may feel that, reading his translated version, one will not need to read the original, but he will be disappointed. Anyone who is able to enjoy the real thing would heartlessly abandon the substitute that the translator has labored so long and hard to fashion. On the other hand, the inferior translation would have the effect of destroying the original. Clumsy and obscure translations inevitably turn the reader away; if he cannot stomach the translation, he will have no appetite for the original. This type of translation alienates the reader; it makes him lose what interest he has in the work and, in process, does harm to the reputation of the author. (Translated by George Kao)

In Qian's mind, "a good translation annihilates itself"; by enhancing readers' interest in the original, it encourages them to seek out the source text, leaving the translation behind. By contrast, a bad translation "annihilates the original"; the reader will not want to read either. In his role as mediator between the original and the translation, the translator uses all the energies and skills at his disposal to effect a successful transformation. By thus re-orienting the perspective of the translator, Qian opens the door to the possibility that the translated text can be an improvement of the original, and the translator can exercise judgements as to how his source text can be best translated.

With Qian Zhongshu's notion of total transformation and of the original text being "reborn" as a translation, we also come very close to a contemporary Western conception of the autonomy of the translated text which lives a life of its own, and which may even bring the original work to completion.

For Qian, the Chinese character for "translation" (译) has etymological and associative connections with the characters for "seduction" (诱), "error" (讹), "mediator" (媒), and "transformation" (化). In his view, these words express precisely the manifold aspects of translation: the translator seeks to seduce the reader, to lure him to the original; the translator is always liable to errors in crossing from one language to another, from one culture to another; and of course, the translator "transforms." Therefore, like his Western counterparts, Qian forges linkages between terms, which he then uses to build his theory.

According to Qian, "sublimity" (化) has at least the following connotations. First, as is argued above, it implies both changing (the form) and retaining (the content and style or spirit) at the same time. Second, a translation should be both smooth and idiomatic in the target language. While changing the form, translators should try their utmost to avoid any evidence of artificiality and thus avoid translationese in the translated work. As Fu Lei puts it, "the ideal translation is the Chinese writing of the writer." Third, a translation should be faithful to the original in content or spirit and style. While transforming the form, translators should neither "follow the dictates of their heart" nor "overstep the boundaries of right." That is, "the external shell is replaced" (i.e., the appearance is transmuted), yet "the inner spirit or style is remained without any deviation" (i.e., the essence is retained). Fourth, Qian is clear-minded enough to recognize that complete and thoroughgoing "sublimity" is an all but unrealizable ideal. "Sublimity" is a flexible concept that allows change in various aspects. In other words, when a translator makes some changes out of necessity, he can also be said to have attained the perfection of "sublimity," although the gap between languages (Chinese and Western languages, for instance) is so great that even a language virtuoso like Qian himself would give up his efforts to pursue the state of absolute, ideal sublimity.

③ Qian's Translation Practice

(1) O! One glimpse of the human face, and shake of the human hand, is better than whole reams of the cold, thin correspondence, etc.

> 得与其人一瞥面、一握手，胜于此等枯寒笔墨百函千牍也。噫！（钱锺书《谈艺录》）

(2) Why, at the height of desire and human pleasure-worldly, social, amorous, ambitious, or even avaricious-does there mingle a certain sense of doubt and sorrow?

> 入世务俗，交游酬应，男女爱悦，图营势位，乃至贪婪财货，人生百为，于兴最高，心最欢时，辄微觉乐趣中杂以疑虑与忧伤，其故何耶。(Ibid.)

(3) Just as we see the bee settling on all the flowers, and sipping the best from each, so also those who aspire to culture ought not to leave anything untasted, but should gather useful knowledge from every source.

> 独不见蜜蜂乎，无花不采，吮英咀华，博雅之士亦然，滋味遍尝，取精而用弘。(Ibid.)

(4) In summer I'm disposed to shirk, /as summer is no time for work. /In winter inspiration dies/For lack of outdoor exercise. /In spring, I'm seldom in the mood, /Because of vernal lassitude. /The fall remains. But such a fall! /We've really had no fall at all.

> 炎夏非勤劬之时；严冬不宜出户游散，无可即景生情，遂尔文思枯涸；春气困人，自振不得；秋高身爽，而吾国之秋有名乏实，奈何! (Ibid.)

(5) Virtues and vices have not in all their instances a great landmark set between them, like warlike nations separate by prodigious walls, vast seas, and portentous hills; but they are oftentimes like bounds of a parish.

> 善德与过恶之区别，非如敌国之此疆彼圉间以墉垣关塞、大海崇山，界画分明，而每似村落之比连邻接。(Ibid.)

4 Exercises

(1) Give examples of Qian Zhongshu's own translation to illustrate his translation ideas.

(2) Can "realm of transformation" be used as highest translation criterion of other genres of texts?

5 References and Further Readings

(1) CHAN T L. Twentieth-Century Chinese Translation Theory: Modes, Issues and Debates [M]. Amsterdam: John Benjamins, 2004.

(2) 钱锺书. 林纾的翻译 [M] // 七缀集. 上海: 上海古籍出版社, 1996.

Chapter Fourteen

Wang Zuoliang's Translation Theory and Practice

 1 **An Introduction to Wang Zuoliang**

Wang Zuoliang (1916–1995), born in 1916 in Shangyu District of Shaoxin City, Zhejiang Province, is a learned scholar of tremendous accomplishments enjoys high reputation in the academic circles both at home and abroad with many titles (an educator, a foreign literature critic, an expert of comparative literature, a translator, a translation theorist, a linguist, a writer, a poet, and the like) simultaneously conferred on him, and is thus dubbed as "a versatile man of the Renaissance".

Wang Zuoliang has made great contributions to translation in China. Of an abundance of his translated works, most are classical poems and essays, and some are short novels, drama etc., among which are not only the translations from English to Chinese but also the ones from Chinese to English. His translations are usually typical of clarity and novelty in terms of both language and meaning, and his art for translation is really perfect, especially his art for E-C translation of verse, because poems are his favorite. As a result, he translated a large number of them, which have been mainly collected in his three books —— *Selected Poems of Robert Burns* (《彭斯诗选》), *Selected Poems and Essays of England* (《英国诗文选译集》) and *Selected Poems of Scotland* (《苏格兰诗选》). The poems he translated almost involve a large number of influential poets like John Milton (1608–1674), Robert Burns (1759–1796), George Gordon Byron (1788–1824), Percy Bysshe Shelley (1792–1822), Alexander Pope (1688–1744), Sir Walter Scott (1771–1832), Hugh MacDiarmid (1892–1978) as well as the Irish poet William Butler Yeats (1865–1939), etc. *Selected Poems of Robert Burns*, a book of making a name for himself, is the only verse anthology of a single poet Wang Zuoliang has ever translated, which can be said to have reached the acme of Robert Burns' translated poems and their studies in China, primarily reflecting Wang's ideas for translation.

In addition, he plays an important role in translation studies and has never stopped learning from his own experience of translation practice so as to propose some translation theory of his own, which has already developed into a systematic one that is made up of five ideas — the idea of stylistic translation (文体翻译观), the idea of cultural translation (文化翻译观), the idea of verse translation (译诗观), the idea of unity of translation theory with practice (理论与实践统一观) as well as the idea of translation study in a new age (新时期翻译观).

Wang Zuoliang has left a valuable legacy to the translation studies in China. His translation theory, rich in connotation, systematic in content and strategic in significance, hits the nail on the head in terms of Chinese translation studies in a new age as well as provides a foresight and far-reaching perspective for Chinese translation studies.

2 Wang Zuoliang's Translation Ideas

I The Idea of Stylistic Translation

Wang Zuoliang points out in his book *Introduction to English Stylistics* (1987) that stylistics can be analyzed both broadly and narrowly. In narrow sense, it refers to the literary style and writing style. In broad sense, it refers to different forms in a language, such as colloquial style and written style, which is what we are going to study. "The task of stylistics is not to enumerate the names of different styles, but to observe and describe the linguistic features (including phonetic, syntactic, lexical and textual features) of commonly used styles in order to enable the scholars to better understand the text and apply the styles properly." Having applied stylistics in translation practice and study, Wang Zuoliang forms his own insightful view on stylistic translation that mainly includes four parts.

The Translator Shall Have a Thorough Understanding of the Original (强调对原文理解的透彻性)

Having a thorough understanding of the original requires the translator to grasp the content and ideas of the original and be clear about its quality and style, thus managing to achieve resemblance in spirit rather than in form. Some scholars summarized Wang Zuoliang's translation idea as "understanding the original thoroughly and expressing it flexibly". Wang Zuoliang offers an effective method of thoroughly understanding the original from the stylistic point of view: It is rather difficult to comprehend literary works since every reader may respond differently, yet it is not completely over our heads. Stylistic training enables the translator to grasp certain features of tone, rhythm, syntax, vocabulary, image or structure, including how they are used in the text, thus facilitating the understanding of the highlights as well as the main ideas of literary works.

Emphasis Must Be Placed on Appropriateness of Style (译文要讲究文体适合性)

Wang Zuoliang points out that the research of stylistics "includes not only written style, but also colloquial style, with each having a number of categories. For instance, written style covers legal instruments and epistles. As for colloquial style, the way of giving a speech or class is quite different from that of answering phone calls. Colloquial style also includes advertisements, product descriptions, scientific reports and news reports, etc." Therefore, he concludes that it is of vital importance to translation to have a command of stylistic knowledge and stylistic awareness of the original. Wang also lays stress upon an essential concept in stylistics: varieties, namely, different styles related to science, business, sports and religion. From his point of view, "translation is supposed to vary in accordance with styles." For example, bulletins, advertisements, notices and political articles should be translated respectively as their appropriate styles. As for translating novels, it is essential to make the storyline and dialogue clear through smooth expression. When translating verse, the translator should attach great importance to the tone of the verse apart from the rhythm, rhyme and image, which Wang Zuoliang deems significant in translating all types of texts. "If the original adopts the ironic tone, the tone of translation shall stay the same. It is far from success to reserve the funny part of sarcasm." In a word, Wang Zuoliang advocates that emphasis must be placed on appropriateness of style.

The Target Language Shall Fit into the Specific Social Occasions in Which It Is Spoken (译语要体现社会场合适合性)

Wang Zuoliang said, "The essence of stylistics lies in studying how language fits into specific social occasions." "Although all people share the same system of phonetics, vocabulary and syntax, it is the social and cultural environment that makes a difference in their usage, thus necessitating the process of selecting. The language that perfectly fits into the social and cultural occasions will guarantee smooth communication." For instance, scientists will not talk to their families in the same way as they discuss with their colleagues on scientific issues. Meanwhile, the conversation between adults differs from that between adults and children. It is the matter of "register," namely, the vocabulary and sentence used by a certain social group (e.g. colleagues of the same business) in a particular social situation (e.g. discussion of professional issues). The study of register, entailing the exploration of direct relation between language and context, is of vital importance in stylistics.

Wang Zuoliang believes that the translator must focus on the relation between language and social occasions and the translation shall fit into the specific social occasion by using the proper style and language, which is called adaptability. For example, "油漆未干" shall be translated into "Wet Paint" instead of "The paint is not dry". The translator should seek equivalent expressions or equivalent style under the same occasion of both countries rather than translate literally in that "adaptability is priority"(适合就是一切). He also draws the conclusion that "The translator's task is to reproduce the spirit and ideas of the original. Namely, the translation shall emphasize rigorous reasoning if the original is a logic one; and the translation shall highlight creativity to the utmost if the original is an imaginative one. The style of an article is the author's private way of expressing ideas and is tightly related to the content, which shall not be deemed as a potential source of additional embellishment." (译者的任务在于再现原作的面貌和精神：原作是细致说理的，译文也细致说理；原作是高举想象之翼的，译文也高举想象之翼。一篇文章的风格只是作者为表达特定的内容而运用语言的个人方式，它与内容是血肉一体，而不是外加的、美化的成分。)

The Translator Shall Improve his Sensitivity to Language Variation (译文要提高对语言变异的敏感性)

Wang Zuoliang thinks every language has some of its own conventional rules in use, yet its use usually varies somewhat from person to person with a view to attracting readers. That is to say, people will use language in their own ways by "making variations here and there" in order to achieve certain rhetoric effects. He deems the variations as "the creative use of language regarding intonation, vocabulary, syntax as well as the art of writing, such as metaphors, images and unexpected collocations of some rarely-seen words or scenes. The abnormal frequency and distribution of words could result in special variations even if the language phenomenon is totally normal." He also points out that variation is most prominent and frequently seen in the literary style (especially verse) where the writer's (especially poet's) imaginations are fully displayed. Wang Zuoliang quotes two examples as a way of proving his ideas: "two martinis ago", a straightforward and common expression, was used in one of the best sellers to indicate a certain period of time. However, Dylan Thomas (1914–1953), a British poet of the twentieth century, created the variant phrase "a grief ago", getting readers into confusion — "Does it refer to the specific time before a tragedy or an accident?" Wang Zuoliang suggests that the translator shall improve his sensitivity to the language variation, which may change in accordance with writers' styles, meaning that he should be good at recognizing it and reflecting it in his translation. Hence, he concludes that "the translator shall take on the dual task: (1) He shall be sensitive enough to recognize variations in the original, which requires proficiency in the source language; (2) he shall be capable of reproducing the variations in translation, which requires proficiency in the target language."

II The Idea of Cultural Translation

Translation Is to Culture What a Robe Is to Underwear (翻译之于文化，犹如棉袍之于内衣)

In terms of the relation between translation and culture, Wang Zuoliang believes that a great deal of practice in translation "enriches people's cultural life". Translation and culture are interdependent, and translation can promote cultural prosperity, which may in turn lead translation into its heyday. "It's the native culture of a country that plays a decisive role in the destiny of foreign cultures." He points out in his article *Understanding Yan Fu* (《严复的用心》), "A great cultural movement in history

has always been accompanied or preceded by a translation movement. A great culture movement was brewing in China at the beginning of the 20th century, giving rise to a huge translation movement as well." He believes that "translation, especially literary translation, is of great benefit to any national literature and culture. It not only helps to open the door to the outside world, but also gives new vitality to the national literature. Without translation, the culture of any nation would be greatly impoverished and the world would lose its vitality, which is like a man with only underwear after taking off his robe."(如果去掉翻译，每个民族的文化都将大为贫乏，整个世界也将失去光泽，宛如脱了锦袍，只剩下单调的内衣。) Besides, he adds that, with the development of culture, the translation practice is improving in its scale and quality. As for its scale, translation was gaining momentum in the second half of the 20th century with the wider spread of new communication tools, the increasing number of foreign language learners and unprecedentedly frequent cultural exchange, which is deemed as "translation explosion". As to its quality, the level of English and American literature translation in the world is "once again approaching that of Elizabethan Age" and the Chinese translators have clinched unparalleled achievements since Liberation.

The Translator Must Be Bicultural (翻译者必须是一个真正意义上的文化人)

Wang Zuoliang holds that one could not master a language without fully understanding its social culture. Here "understanding" is not a general concept, but refers to getting acquainted with the past and present of the people who speak the language, including their history, social trend, customs, economic base, emotional life, philosophy, scientific and technological achievements, and political and social organizations, etc. The deeper the understanding is, the better it will be for language learning. Therefore, many people could not speak English fluently despite their abundant English knowledge and skills. The crux does not lie in phonetics, grammar or vocabulary, but in their education and cultural awareness. When it comes to translation, he holds the view that the first difficulty encountered by the translator is the understanding of the original. Translation could be possibly done however complicated the original is in that people of different countries have much in common, but the original usually contains factors that are unfamiliar to foreigners, thus again making it necessary to have a deep understanding of the foreign culture. He also points out that it is far from enough for the translator to acquaint himself with the foreign culture only but need to gain an in-depth understanding of his own culture, for translation is at once a bilingual exchange and a cross-cultural communication. And translation is aimed to break the language barrier and promote cultural exchange, which is a two-way interaction in essence. In a nutshell, "the translator must be bicultural."

Translation Is a Process of Comparing Two Cultures and Adapting to Social Occasions (翻译是不断对两种文化进行比较并适合社会文化的过程)

Wang Zuoliang holds that the translator is not only supposed to be bicultural, but also constantly compares two cultures in that translation is a dynamic process in which the greatest and most direct difficulty for the translator arises from cultural differences. "He seems to be translating individual words, but is actually dealing with two cultures."(他处理的是个别的词，他面对的则是两大片文化。) In this case, the translator has to make a comparison between two cultures when looking for the "equivalents", the words with the same meaning, function, register, emotional color and effects in the target language. Otherwise, readers may fall into a trap by taking the words literally. For instance, if the Chinese sentence "一位学者帮助青年研究人员修改论文" is translated into "He often helps his younger colleagues to complete their research papers anonymously", readers will take it as "He often ghostwrites papers for his colleagues"! Besides, Wang Zuoliang also emphasizes that cultural comparisons made by the translator is usually more comprehensive and profound than others since the question of how to make translations fit into social occasions should be taken into consideration. In other words, the translator has to search for "equivalents" in the target text that adapt to social occasions in terms of genre and style according to his awareness of the relations between language and culture.

The Cultural Perspective in Translation Studies is Conducive to the Construction of Translation Theory (翻译研究的文化视野有利于翻译理论建设)

When it comes to the status quo of translation studies, Wang Zuoliang thinks that we have come a long way in the study of translation principles and skills. Besides, advances in modern linguistics, stylistics, literary theory and computer technology have witnessed new approaches for translation studies. In this case, if we can do translation studies from cultural perspective or by combining translation studies with "comparative culture", it will add a new dimension to translation studies. In this way, the research achievements scholars have made will not only promote cultural exchanges, but also provide a better perspective for translation studies, enable us to have a clearer picture of historical development of translation theory and thus better help to improve the construction of translation theory.

III The Idea of Verse Translation

As for translation, Wang Zuoliang is mainly interested in verse translation and is famous for his abundant verse translations. His understanding of verse translation is extremely deep and his theoretical thinking is particularly profound. His idea of verse translation is mainly included in such articles as *Some Observations on Verse Translation* (《论诗歌翻译》, 1991), *Between Verse Translation and Verse Writing* (《译诗和写诗之间》, 1989), *Another Mirror: How Do British and Americans Translate Foreign Poems* (《另一面镜子：英美人怎样译外国诗》, 1997) and his book *On Verse Translation* (《论诗的翻译》, 1992). His idea of verse translation fully reflects the highest goal he pursues in translation — "everything should be translated according to the original, i.e. the target text should be tantamount to the source text in elegance, depth, speaking tone and style." (一切照原作，雅俗如之，深浅如之，口气如之，文体如之。)

Verses are Translatable (诗歌是可译的)

Verses have long been deemed as untranslatable by quite a few people, among whom the American poet Robert Frost (1874–1963) is the most famous, saying, "Poetry is what gets lost in translation." In this regard, Wang Zuoliang, based on his own experience as a verse translator, eloquently argues in *Selected Poems and Essays of England· Preface*:

"People never stop translating verses although they deem verses untranslatable. Just as Goethe once mentioned that the contradiction consists in the fact that verse translation, on one hand, is almost impossible and, on the other hand, is absolutely necessary. Goethe, the great poet, has his own experience of verse translation, for instance, he translated some of the verses at the beginning of Byron's *Don Juan* after reading it. In China, verse translation has not only been practiced for quite a long time, but also played a significant role in promoting the rise and development of free verse."(谁都说诗不可能翻译，然而历来又总有人在译。诚如歌德所言，这里的矛盾在于译诗一方面几乎不可能，而另一方面又有绝对的必要。这位大诗人本人就译过诗，例如他在读了拜伦的《唐璜》之后，就动手译了那部史诗的头上几节。在我们中国，诗的翻译不但行之已久，而且对于新诗的兴起和发展起了重大的促进作用。)

Wang Zuoliang holds the view that "verses are translatable" "because people of different countries think in similar way, otherwise daily communications can't even be made. However, in verse translation, something is bound to be lost in distinguishing the nuances of phrases, or in dealing with the associations that a phrase evokes, or in conveying the general mood of a verse." "In fact, many people are trying to translate verses and I do find it a great joy." Wang Zuoliang is expecting more translators to engage in verse translation. He also points out that, as a creative activity, verse translation is a high demanding and challenging task, and that he once had a difficulty in dealing with the Scottish dialect in Burns' verses. He finds dialects more rarely seen in verses than in novels, thus bringing more challenges to verse translation. When translating the dialect, he "treats it as the Scottish national language and uses the standard Chinese in the translation, just as we translate the text of any national language. As for the specific rendering of the verses, we avoid doing it too modernly by making words easy to understand, rhyming like folk songs and using old-fashioned sentence patterns". In Wang Zuoliang's opinion, verse translation is really a project worth studying, and is of great help to any national literature and culture. It not only provides a vision towards the outside world, but also gives new life to the national literature by unearthing the essence of language and makes it vitalized and activated through refinement and refreshment.

Translating Verse as Verse (以诗译诗)

Verse is a literary genre "reflecting social life and people's spiritual world with condensed language, sincere emotion and vivid imagination in accordance with syllables, tones and rhythms" (*Ci Hai*). When doing verse translation, Wang Zuoliang points out that the translator should "remain faithful to the original in terms of content, tone and rhythm (rhymed or free) but need not make the words of each line equal to the original. In addition, the language should be as novel and sharp as the original and literal translation should be adopted for imagery description. More importantly, we should analyze the verse as a whole by figuring out the spirit, tone and style, and then deal with its details". In other words, we should "translate verse as verse." In verse translation, it is of vital importance for the translator, after having a thorough understanding of the original, to have the courage to innovate and explore the use of words, sentences, rhymes and poetic style. In response to Robert Frost, Wang Zuoliang said without losing interest, "Perhaps there is something lost in verse translation, but what we obtain is a new verse as well as a brighter new world." (诗歌也许在翻译中有所丢失，但是我们得到的却是一种新诗，而且我们还因此拥有了一个更灿烂的世界。)

Poet as Poetry Translator (诗人译诗)

As a translator and poet, Wang Zuoliang is interested in reading, translating and writing verses and is full of exuberant creativity throughout his life. He offers some creative and insightful observations in his article *Some Observations on Verse Translation* that there are at least three crucial elements in verse translation — verse's meaning, poetic art and the language used by the translator.

As for verse's meaning, he points out in *Another Mirror: How Do British and Americans Translate Foreign Poems* (1997: 522-523) that the translator should figure out the meaning of the original in verse translation, including its literal meaning, tone, sentence structure, rhythm, style (colloquial style or written style) and the implications of words or phrases specially intended by poets. He believes meaning is the sum of all these elements without which the translator could not comprehend the verse to the ground. As for poetic art, Wang Zuoliang is sure that "those who translate verses tend to translate like verse"(大凡译诗的人，总想所译像诗), and what on earth the verse is, however, changes with time and what people think about it. The innovation of verse will be beyond doubt lift the quality of verse translation. As for the use of language, he holds that verse translation requires the translator to "find a pure, transparent and living language at which only the poets are the most adept (需要译者有能力找到一种纯净的、透明的、然而又是活的本质语言——这又只有诗人最为擅长)." All things considered, only poets can do well in all the three aspects, so "only poets are the best poetry translators (只有诗人才能把诗译好)".

In addition, he believes that poets can benefit more from verse translation since "verse translation is the two-way communication in which the translator can not only apply his experience of writing verses to verse translation, but also draw inspiration from doing so." (译诗是一种双向交流，译者既把自己的写诗经验用于译诗，又从译诗中得到启发。) "For instance, poets may have a new understanding of the theme and poetic art in verse translation." "Verse translation could also be beneficial to their creation." He emphasizes that in order to achieve the expected effect in verse translation, "the translator should not only have gift and accomplishment, but also use the language that is flexible enough to adapt to any new usage and resilient enough to withstand any rough manipulation." (除了译者个人的天才和素养之外，他所使用的语言必须处于活跃状态，即一方面有足够的灵活性能够适应任何新的用法，另一方面又有足够的韧性能够受得住任何粗暴的揉弄。) In short, language used in verse translation should be alive, clear and novel, which can be achieved by the poct only.

The Translator Shall Translate Works Close to His Own Style (译者只应翻译与自己风格相近的作品)

Wang Zuoliang believes that the translation done by a translator should have something in common with his own works. A translator shall "select what is close to his own style to translate" instead of translating works of various styles, otherwise the translator will definitely be put at a disadvantage since no one could actually acquaint himself with all styles of works. Most people could only master a certain literary style even in their mother tongue. Therefore, the translator shall translate works close to his own style for the sake of achieving the best translation. Wang Zuoliang takes translation as a process in which the translator adapts himself to the style of others and imposes his own personality on the translation (翻译是一个让译者适应他人风格的过程，又是一个对译作施加自己个性的过程). "If readers can't tell the differences between the translated works of Shakespeare, Milton, Donne, Tarleton, Pope, Wordsworth, Byron, Shelley and Keats, it is the very negation of translation as well as literature itself." (如果莎士比亚、密尔顿、邓恩、特莱顿、蒲柏、华兹华斯、拜伦、雪莱、济慈等等读起来都差不多，那可真是翻译的否定了，也是文学本身的否定了。)

IV The Idea of Unity of Translation Theory with Practice

As a translation theorist as well as a translator, Wang Zuoliang embodies the high unity of translation theory and practice, which is also fully reflected in his book *Translation: Experiments and Reflections*(《翻译：思考与试笔》, 1989). He has sightful views on the unity of translation theory and practice by saying in his article *Meaning, Style and Translation* (《词义·文体·翻译》), "There are two achievements worth noticing in the translation field: (1) The scale and quality of translation is improving significantly both at home and abroad, forming the worldwide trend. (2) The research of modern linguistics has provided some new insights which may facilitate translation studies." It not only summarizes the current situation of translation practice, but more importantly provides theoretical thinking and prospects for translation problems arising from translation practice, including "the idea of stylistic translation," "the idea of cultural translation" and "the idea of verse translation," all of which reflect the high unity of translation theory and practice. Aiming at the cognitive deviations held by some translators in their understanding of translation theory, Wang Zuoliang points out:

"Above all, I want to make it clear that translators should not deem it boring or mysterious on hearing the word 'theory' because translation theory originates from translation practice and will in turn guide practice. We should summarize several points based on our translation experience that are concise and not mysterious and that are able to guide our translation practice. Yan Fu's 'faithfulness, expressiveness and elegance is the translation theory. It is awesome that Yan Fu, a great translator, could summarize his translation practice in such three words, showing what the theory should be like. Coming up with a concise theory of this kind is the most challenging task, which is the same case with science. Einstein had a famous formula: $E=mc^2$. How simple it is! Anyone can see it clearly and there is a special beauty. That is the very theory we need." (我首先要说明，大家不要听到"理论"这两个字就感到不妙，以为是很枯燥的，或者玄而又玄的。其实理论应是出自翻译实践又能指导翻译实践的。我们要能够通过丰富的翻译经验总结出几条来，这几条要很精练，不是很玄，能对以后的翻译工作起指导作用。严复的信、达、雅这三点就是理论。他是一个伟大的翻译家，能够把他的实践总结出这么三个字，了不得。我们要的理论是这样子的，但是不

要以为这个很容易，这个最难，而且据我所知，科学界也是这样。爱因斯坦有一个有名的公式，$E=mc^2$。你看多么简洁，任何人一看都很清楚的，而且有一种特殊的美。我们就要这样的一种理论。)

His words clarify the dialectical relationship between theory and practice and reveal the direction for translation studies: the concise and practical translation theory originates from practice and can in turn guide translation activities. As for how to better promote the unity of translation theory and practice, Wang Zuoliang believes that translation studies "is of direct help to material and spiritual construction because of its abundant translation subjects, practical activities and research materials. It also has the brightest future in theoretical development since it is a comparative, cross-language and interdisciplinary activity related to culture, society and history. Backed by experience from translators throughout the history and confronted with an ever-changing world, translation will keep going with new challenges and projects". He points out that the scope of theory has expanded to unnoticed linguistic factors with the wider use of language. Therefore, he deems it necessary to conduct translation studies for creating valuable theories instead of just analyzing words and phrases. Translation studies should be interdisciplinary and based on new findings on linguistics and literature. Besides, Wang Zuoliang believes that translation is the starting point as well as an open field with accumulated experience and bright future and is closely related to both practice and esoteric theory. Only if the translator keep learning, studying and practicing can the translation theory and practice achieve the unity (Wamg Zuotiang, 1989: 36). That is what Wang Zuoliang says and does in his life.

V The Idea of Translation Study in a New Age

Since China entered a new age, the majority of translators have been talking about "faithfulness, expressiveness, elegance," "resemblance in spirit," "sublimation" or foreign theory like "functional equivalence," which is deemed lacking in new idea. Wang Zuoliang, however, could provide new insights instead of making summary from pre-existing theories mentioned above. He stresses that "active language" should be adopted to show the "dynamic state" of the original, rendering the translation to perfection, which is the essence of his translation theory in a new age. To sum up, Wang Zuoliang's translation theory in a new age includes two parts: reviewing the tradition (感悟传统) and practicing new theories (践行新说).

Reviewing the Tradition （感悟传统）

Reviewing the translations of ancient Buddhist scriptures, modern social sciences and literary works, Wang Zuoliang (1989: 2) believes that the Chinese translators had at least three features. First, they had the strong sense of mission and deep concern for the country and the people. Second, they had the great courage to translate books and even a set of books with esoteric content and a large amount of words. Third, they employed a variety of translation methods like literal translation, free translation, transliteration, and translating based on other's interpretation. (至少具有三个特点：一是高度使命感，忧国忧民，不辞辛劳；二是不畏艰难，勇挑难书、大书甚至成套书翻译；三是翻译方法多种多样，如直译、意译、音译、听人口译而下笔直书，等等。) He points out that many great writers also acted as translators in modern China, such as Lu Xun, Guo Moruo, Mao Dun, Bing Xin, Cao Yu, Xu Zhimo, Dai Wangshu, Ai Qing and Bian Zhilin, whose translation facilitated their own literary creation which in turn boosted the translation cause in China.

In terms of "faithfulness, expressiveness and elegance" put forward by Yan Fu, Wang Zuoliang states that if we do not take Yan Fu's proposition of using the ancient Chinese before the Han Dynasty too seriously, his "elegance" is tightly related to "faithfulness", the foremost word of the three. Here "elegance" is not polishing the text into an elegant one, but it aims to express the author's intention and the spirit of the text more complicated and delicate than the literal meaning of words and sentences. (雅不是美化，不是把一篇原来不典雅的文章译得很典雅，而是指一种努力，要传达一种比词、句简单的含义更高、更精微的东西：原作者的心智特点，原作的精神光泽。)

With regard to "equivalence", he advocates "resemblance in spirit" instead of equivalence in words and sentences by saying, "People tend to attach importance to 'equivalents' without noticing that real equivalence is supposed to cover emotions, settings, novelty and popularity of language, rhythms and associations triggered by words. In the translation of literary works, especially verses, 'The resemblance in spirit' to the original as a whole is more significant than the equivalence regarding words and sentences."

As to "binary opposition", Wang Zuoliang suggests taking it in a dialectical way: the translator should try his best to translate freely and adopt the literal translation method when necessary. Any good version has always resulted from the combination of free translation and literal translation.

In translation, Wang Zuoliang advocates using lively and fresh language by saying, "Some people pursue beauty of words by reading ancient books to look for ornate phrases or reading foreign magazines to look for new expressions and buzzwords. The use of language as such is beneficial on certain occasions but they may lose their value when used for ornament only. The vernacular Chinese is the most useful and the most beautiful language for the translator to better express the ideas between lines. Sharp and fresh words can only come from sharp and fresh minds." (白话文往往是最顶用，也是最美的。美不在文词，而在文词后面的思想。要语言锐利、新鲜，首先要头脑锐利、新鲜。) Therefore, he finds it necessary for the translator to comprehend the author's thoughts and feelings, including the most delicate and complicated aspects.

Practicing New Theories （践行新说）

(1) Pragmatic perspectives of translation studies: the word meaning is determined according

to its context and the author's intention. Wang Zuoliang thinks that the translator should figure out the meaning of the original, which is quite challenging. He believes that "the word meaning should be determined according to its context instead of the dictionary" (Wang Zuoliang, 1989: 7). That is to say, besides the direct and superficial explanations in the dictionary, a word may also have connotative, emotional and other associated meanings, and its structure, pronunciation, intonation, rhythm and tempo all make sense, too. He adds that the context, which provides a social occasion determining the word meaning, is more related to the social activity than language itself. Therefore, "one can only get the meaning of a word or a sentence from the context where the same word or sentence is repeated several times." (一词一句的意义有时不是从本身看得清楚的, 而要通过整段整篇——亦即通过这个词或这句话在不同情境下的多次再现才能确定。) In addition, he believes that apart from linguistic factors, the word meaning has much to do with the author's intention, stressing the great importance of social occasions to the language use. Wang Zuoliang advises the translator to "convey the author's intention and the nuances of tone, attitude and the like" (Wang Zuoliang, 1989: 9), showing his contributions to the studies on modern pragmatics.

(2) New development of functional equivalence: the reader-oriented. Wang Zuoliang emphasizes that it is the readers who make a work because its author will always cater to the readers' taste and reflect on their response. As for translation, he believes that, instead of following the principles, the translator shall try to figure out what readers are really concerned about. Readers may at least expect the translation to be reliable (faithful to the original without missing or distorting its information) and readable (smooth and easy to understand even if it is done by way of literal translation). Hence, "translation should cater to the readers apart from the author, the translator and some critics." This is because, according to Wang Zuoliang, sometimes the translator is obsessed over some issues that the readers consider unimportant, but neglects what is really important to the readers. But he insists that "translations should not vary from reader to reader". For this purpose, he warns seriously, saying, "I am skeptical about an extreme theory of making different translations for different groups of readers. If so, there would be nothing left except for the outline of the story in the simplified version intended for the less educated readers, which would be like a simplified classic specially made for the foreign language learners. However, it is definitely recommendable to consider the readers' potential response and keep improving the translation." (现在甚至有一种极端说法, 即针对不同类型的读者, 出版不同的译文。我对此是怀疑的, 因为我怕出现一种针对教育程度不高的读者群而准备的简化的译文, 那就会像外语学生读的简化名著一样, 只剩下了故事大概, 而形象、气氛、文采等都不存在了。但是, 确要考虑读者, 考虑读者可能有的反应, 这一点是完全正确的。这就是说我们译本要不断地更新。) His "idea of readers' response" not only further the development of Nida's functional equivalence, but also seems to be a

pertinent criticism to some of the views on foreign functionalist approaches.

(3) Stylistic and sociolinguistic perspective of translation studies: adaptability is priority. First of all, Wang Zuoliang believes that translation should fit with the style of the original. For example, formal style should be applied in treaties, laws and academic works; colloquial style should be used in drama translation; and verse translation, however, should not only have literary talent, but also artistic conception. Besides, he holds that the target language shall fit into social occasions, saying, "The essence of stylistics lies in studying how language fits into specific social occasions." "Although all the people share the same system of phonetics, vocabulary and syntax, it is the social and cultural environment that makes a difference in their usage, thus necessitating the process of selection. The language that perfectly fits into the social and cultural occasions will guarantee the smooth communication." He also suggests that the translator must pay attention to the relationship between language and social occasions, and that the translation should fit into the specific social occasions by using the proper style and language. In a word, "adaptability is priority." "Everything should be translated according to the original, namely, the target text should be tantamount to the original in elegance, depth, speaking tone and style." However, Wang Zuoliang suggests that even a talented and skilled translator should "select what is close to his own style to translate" instead of translating works of various styles, which will definitely put the translator at a disadvantage. Wang Zuoliang takes translation as a process in which the translator adapts himself to the style of others and imposes his own personality on the translation since no one could acquaint himself with woks of all styles. Having applied stylistic and sociolinguistic knowledge into translation studies, Wang Zuoliang provides a new theoretical perspective for the development of translation studies in China.

(4) The cultural turn of translation studies: the translator must be bicultural. Since the second half of the 20th century, an important change has taken place in contemporary Western translation studies following the linguistic turn — the cultural turn, transforming translation studies from analyzing cross-language communication to studying cultural exchange. Hence, more and more scholars begin to conduct translation studies from the cultural perspective. Wang Zuoliang believes that one could not master a language without fully understanding its social culture, history, developing trends, customs, economic basis, emotional life, philosophy, scientific and technological achievements as well as political and social organizations, etc. When it comes to translation, he holds the view that the first difficulty encountered by the translator is the understanding of the original that usually contains factors that are unfamiliar to foreigners, thus making it necessary to have a deep understanding of the foreign culture. More than that, the translator shall get acquainted with their own culture, for translation is aimed to break the language barrier and promote the cultural exchange. The greatest and most direct difficulty for the translator arises from cultural differences. "He seems to

be translating individual words, but is actually dealing with two cultures." In this way, the translator has to make a comparison between two cultures when looking for the "equivalents", the words with the same meaning, function, register, emotional color and effects in the target language. Otherwise, readers may fall into a trap by taking the words literally. Wang Zuoliang's idea of cultural translation seems to be closely related to the cultural turn of contemporary Western translation studies.

③ Wang Zuoliang's Translation Practice

(1) Wang Zuoliang loves poems all his life. He wrote poems, studied poems, compiled books of poems, wrote papers on poems and translated poems. Verse translation is his favorite in the case of his translation work, which he did most and best as well. His verse translation theory of "translating verse as verse" and "poet as poetry translator" had been very well put into his practice. What he liked to do most with devoted efforts in terms of verse translations is of course the English poems of Great Britain. *Selected Poems of Robert Burns*, *Selected Poems and Essays of England* and *Selected Poems of Scotland* are the most famous, covering the poems of almost all the influential poets in Great Britain as well as the poems by Irish poet W. B. Yeats and the like. His verse translation *My Luve Is Like a Red, Red Rose* by Robert Burns is widely read as a good version in Chinese. Through a detailed contrastive analysis of the three versions by Wang Zuoliang, Guo Moruo and Yuan Kejia respectively, Wang Zuoliang's version is the closest to the original in poem's meaning, poetic art and language use.

我的爱人像朵红红的玫瑰

王佐良 译

呵，我的爱人像朵红红的玫瑰，

六月里迎风初开；

呵，我的爱人像支甜甜的曲子，

奏得合拍又和谐。

我的好姑娘，多么美丽的人儿！

请看我，多么深挚的爱情！

亲爱的，我永远爱你，

纵使大海干涸水流尽。

纵使大海干涸水流尽，

太阳将岩石烧作灰尘，

亲爱的，我永远爱你，

只要我一息犹存。

珍重吧，我唯一的爱人，

珍重吧，让我们暂时别离，

但我定要回来，

哪怕千里万里！

(2) Wang Zuoliang has translated some essays (though not so many in quantity as verse translations), most of which are from English to Chinese. The originals he selected (such as *Of Studies*) are so classical and his translations are so well-received and influential that he is recognized as one of the most outstanding translators in China. Compared with other translators in rendering *Of Studies*, Wang Zuoliang has extraordinary abilities and skills in understanding the original, weighing his word to express the feelings and ideas. Besides, his version is faithful and felicitous with an appropriate, terse and precise diction as well as a coherent and clear arrangement of discourse. Furthermore, he is sensitive to the style and is really an expert of language. His essay translation not only faithfully transfers the original content or ideas, but also felicitously reproduces the stylistic features and aesthetic value pertaining to the original. That is to say, his essay translation — the good version in both form and spirit — is the very unity with form, content and style of the source text.

> 读书足以怡情，足以博采，足以长才。其怡情也，最见于独处幽居之时；其博采也，最见于高谈阔论之中；其长才也，最见于处世判事之际。练达之士虽能分别处理细事或——判别枝节，然纵观统筹、全局策划，则舍好学深思者莫属。
>
> 读书费时过多易惰，文采藻饰太盛则矫，全凭条文断事乃学究故态。读书补天然之不足，经验又补读书之不足，盖天生才干犹如自然花草，读书然后知如何修剪移接；而书中所示，如不以经验范之，则又大而无当。有一技之长者鄙读书，无知者慕读书，唯明智之士用读书，然书并不以用处告人，用书之智不在书中，而在书外，全凭观察得之。读书时不可存心诘难作者，不可尽信书上所言，亦不可只为寻章摘句，而应推敲细思。（王佐良译，《论读书》）

(3) *Thunderstorm* (《雷雨》), the maiden works by the noted playwright Cao Yu written in 1933, is one of the best-known theatrical plays in modern China. Its extraordinary artistic accomplishment and the important role it plays in the history of modern Chinese drama gave rise to the appearance of its English version by Wang Zuoliang and A.C. Barnes in 1958. Through analyzing Wang Zuoliang's translation *Thunderstorm*, we find that the scenario of the English version is as twisty, vivid, intense and exciting as the original; that the language he used in the target text is plain and clear, felicitous and natural as well as terse and implicit, which effectively keeps such features of drama discourse as colloquialism, characterization and poetic dramatization; and that the target text successfully reduplicates the ideas and emotions as well as artistic taste of the source text by

firmly grasping the plurality and diversity of the inner world of the characters. In other words, Wang Zuoliang has faithfully and felicitously conveyed the stylistic markers inherent in the original into the English version.

CHUNG：Sometimes I forget the present — (with a rapt expression on his face) I forget my home, I forget you, I forget my mother — I even forget myself. It seems like a winter morning, with a brilliant sky overhead... on a boundless sea... there's a little sailing-boat, light as a gull. When the sea breeze gets stronger, and there's a salty tang in the air, the white sails billow out like the wings of a hawk and the boat skims over the sea, just kissing the waves, racing towards the horizon. The sky is empty except for a few patches of white cloud floating lazily on the horizon. We sit in the bows, gazing ahead, for ahead of us is our world.

— Act Three, *Thunderstorm* translated by Wang Zuoliang & A.C. Barnes

HAI (struggling): Let go of me, you hooligans!

PING (to the servants): Hustle him outside!

MA (breaking down): You are hooligans, too! (Going across to Chou Ping.) You're my — mighty free with your fists! What right have you to hit my son?

PING: Who are you?

MA: I'm your — your victim's mother.

— Act Two, *Thunderstorm* translated by Wang Zuoliang & A.C. Barnes

4 Exercises

(1) Try to summarize Wang Zuoliang's contribution to the verse translation.

(2) Try to summarize Wang Zuoliang's essay translation style.

(3) Translate the following paragraph into Chinese and then compare your translation with Wang Zuoliang's translation and summarize the differences.

Some books are to be tasted, others to be swallowed, and some few to be chewed and digested; that is, some books are to be read only in parts; others to be read, but not curiously; and some few to be read wholly, and with diligence and attention. Some books also may be read by deputy, and extracts made of them by others; but that would be only in the less important arguments, and the meaner sort of books; else distilled books are, like common distilled waters, flashy things.

Reading maketh a full man; conference a ready man; and writing an exact man. And therefore, if a man write little, he had need have a great memory; if he confer little, he had

> need have a present wit; and if he read little, he had need have much cunning, to seem to know that he doth not. (Francis Bacon: *Of Studies*)

🔍 ⑤ References and Further Readings

(1)WANG Z. Degrees of Affinity: Studies in Comparative Literature [M]. Beijing: Foreign Language Teaching and Research Press, 1985.

(2)WANG Z. A Sense of Beginning: Studies in Literature and Translation [M]. Beijing: Foreign Language Teaching and Research Press, 1991.

(3)北京外国语大学外国文学研究所. 王佐良先生纪念文集 [M]. 北京：外语教学与研究出版社，2001.

(4)黎昌抱. 王佐良翻译风格研究 [M]. 北京：光明日报出版社，2009.

(5)王佐良. 英语文体学论文集 [M]. 北京：外语教学与研究出版社，1980.

(6)王佐良. 英国诗文选译集 [M]. 北京：外语教学与研究出版社，1980.

(7)王佐良. 翻译：思考与试笔 [M]. 北京：外语教学与研究出版社，1989.

(8)王佐良. 论诗的翻译 [M]. 南昌：江西教育出版社，1992.

(9)王佐良. 王佐良文集 [M]. 北京：外语教学与研究出版社，1997.

(10)王佐良，丁往道. 英语文体学引论 [M]. 北京：外语教学与研究出版社，1987.

Chapter Fifteen

Yang Xianyi, Gladys Yang and Translation of Chinese Classics

1 An Introduction to Yang Xianyi and Gladys Yang

Yang Xianyi (1915–2009), born into a wealthy banker family in Tianjin, was sent to Merton College, Oxford, in 1934 to study classical languages and literature. As a major member of the Oxford China Society, he met Gladys Tayler. Tayler's father served as a British missionary in China. Tayler was born in Beijing and became Oxford's first graduate in Chinese literature in 1940. With the same interest in Chinese classical literature, they got married and returned to China in 1940. Tayler became Gladys Yang and Yang Xianyi's partner in both life and introducing Chinese classics to the English-speaking world.

The couple began working together as translators and, despite opposition from their families, married in China in 1940. After 1949, working for the Foreign Languages Press in Beijing, Yang translated scores of major Chinese works, written from the 10th century to the present, into English (most of them are included in Panda Books), usually in collaboration with his wife, Gladys. Their translations included *Selected Works of Lu Xun* and a complete English version of *A Dream of Red Mansions*, which began in the early sixties and finished in the following decade after a spell in prison during the Cultural Revolution. He also translated works by George Bernard Shaw and other English-language writers into Chinese. He is also the first one to render Homer's *Odysseia*(《奥德修斯》) into Chinese from the ancient Greek original. He has also translated Aristophanes's *Ornites*, Virgil's *The Georgics* (维吉尔的《农事诗》), *La chanson de Roland* （《罗兰之歌》）and Bernard Shaw's *Pygmalion*（萧伯纳的《卖花女》）into Chinese. In 1952, Yang Xianyi was appointed as chief editor of Chinese literature, a magazine founded in 1951. It served as a portal for introducing elite Chinese literature to the outside world, especially before China's reform and opening up policy.

Mr. Yang said he considered his most important accomplishment to be the translation of *A Dream of Red Mansions*, an 18th-century novel viewed by many scholars as the greatest Chinese literary work in history. He and his wife began working on that translation in the early 1960s and finished it in 1974. When asked to help translate *Selected Works of Mao Zedong*, he declined, citing work on *A Dream of Red Mansions* as his priority. Considered representative of the Yangs, *A Dream of Red Mansions* continues to be highly received worldwide for its exact rendering of the Chinese literary classic. The couple has been credited with making the work accessible to the outside world and it is regarded as the genuine version that has allowed Westerners to understand the traditional Chinese love story. Many colleges in the US and throughout the world use the Yang's version as textbooks to study Chinese literature.

From their published translations, we find that Yang Xianyi had produced about 10 Chinese translations from different foreign languages, including Greek, Latin, English and Medieval French. Yang Xianyi and Gladys had done more than 50 English translations of Chinese works, most of them literary in nature, and Gladys alone had done more than 20 English translations of modern

Chinese novels. The couple's translations have been internationally recognized for their accuracy, likeness and faithfulness to the original work, while at the same time catering to the taste of the target language. According to critics and experts alike, their translations are second to none among Chinese translators in terms of both quality and significance.

② The Translation of Li Sao

When he was 24, Yang translated the Chinese masterpiece *Li Sao* into English. In 1953, as a special CPPCC member, Yang Xianyi met Chairman Mao with a group of scientists and artists. Yang Xianyi recalled, "He (Chairman Mao) had already begun to put on weight, but he looked very healthy. He walked over and shook hands with each of us. Zhou Enlai was beside him and introduced each of us to him. Zhou said to Mao: 'This is a translator who has rendered *Li Sao* into English.'

Chairman Mao loved classical Chinese poetry, and *Li Sao* was one of his favorite works. As he extended a sweaty palm to shake my hand, he said, 'So you think that *Li Sao* can be translated, hmm?' 'Chairman, surely all works of literature can be translated.'"

Yang translated *Li Sao* with rhymed English verse. Yang believed the poem was a fake and approached it in that spirit. David Hawkes, a friend of Yang's who did his own translation of *Li Sao* (as well as another complete edition of 《红楼梦》 as *The Story of the Stone*, with John Minford), made the comment that the resulting translation "bears as much resemblance to the original as a chocolate Easter egg to an omelette," an observation that amused Yang.

As to the translatability, Yang replied in an interview, "There were those that could be solved, and counterparts could be found in English. Those that could be translated, we translated, and for the others, we added a footnote. Of course, the ones that were solvable were in the minority. Chairman Mao was of the opinion that *Li Sao* could not be translated. I think that everything can be translated."

③ Collaboration Translation

Yang acknowledged his wife's significance in their translations. "Our works could never have been that good without her. She was the real translator, not me," Yang said. And he said in an interview that their work procedure had always been that he translated the first draft and she polished it. "After all, she was the native speaker and had been immersed in English classical literature since a young age."

He continued, "Generally, people would prefer to work alone. But Gladys and I are a couple and we both know two different languages. We have cooperated quite well. If you want to work in a team, you must be team-spirited. Otherwise, there will be arguments. For example, Lin Shu didn't know foreign languages at all but managed to translate so many foreign novels. He was successful because he could cooperate with his good friends who knew these foreign languages."

④ Yang Xianyi and Glady Yang's Translation Ideas

I Faithfulness

Yang believed that we can not explain too much in translation. A translator should be faithful to the original images, without exaggeration or personal comments. If equivalents cannot be found, then surely some original meanings will be lost in the process. Overemphasis of creativity in translation is not recommended for if so, it is not translation at all; instead, it is rewriting. In this sense, a translation must be faithful to the original.

Faithfulness, Yang believed, meant that a translation should not be far from the original. For example, Western people think highly of rose, while Chinese prefer Mudan (a tree peony). So if we translate rose into Mudan in Chinese, then our translation obtain expressiveness at the sacrifice of faithfulness. The best translation, while preserving the original meaning, has as little footnotes as possible, so that readers can enjoy reading and appreciating it. But faithfulness doesn't mean word-for-word translation. When asked about the question of translation unit, Yang said, "We have seldom

translated word-for-word. We think it is good to translate according to the unit of meaning without feeling bound by the original syntax."

II Culture and Translation

Translation is more than language switching. What's more important is the culture behind the words. Yang said in an interview: "In *The Book of South*, we have '昔我往矣，杨柳依依。今我来思，雨雪霏霏。' You may translate these two sentences freely into English by replacing the '杨柳 (willows and poplars)' with 'roses'. But this cannot reflect the particular meaning associated with 'willows and poplars' in Chinese. Such meanings are culturally bound and specific. So we have to keep the original image and add a footnote or an endnote when necessary."

Arthur Waley's translation of *The Book of Songs* is of high quality, but his version is westernized. Full of *castles* and *knights*, the translated poems are more like a folk song in the mediaeval England rather than in ancient China.

III Poetry Translation with or without Rhyme

Keeping the rhyme is secondary to keeping the meaning. We are dealing with a different culture when translating from one language into another. There are some translators in China today, who think that Chinese poetry is very good and so everything, including the rhyme, should be kept when they translate these poems. It is impossible to do so. For example, when translating into Chinese "To be or not to be, that is the question" in Shakespeare's *Hamlet*, a translator once tried very hard to keep the original iambic in Chinese. Finally, he failed. The same is true when translating Tang poems and Song Ci-poems. Therefore, keeping the rhyme is not as important as keeping the meaning. If you are translating Chinese ballads that are strikingly rhymed, then you may try to

make your translation partly rhymed.

When asked why he did not try to make his translations of Tang and Song poetry rhymed, he said, "That is because of the differences in the two cultures. Not all English poems are rhymed. For example, poems of the Anglo-Saxon era do not rhyme, such as *Beowulf*. But Chaucer's *Canterbury Tales* are rhymed. Different genres may have different patterns of rhyme. For example, the patterns of rhyme in sonnets could be this way or that way. Each line in a Tang poem may be composed of five or seven characters.

But you cannot translate it into an English line of 5 or 7 words. The prosody of different languages is different. If you strive for rhyme for rhyme's sake, the English translation would sound very ridiculous. The original Chinese poem may be about something serious, but if your translation turns it into something like doggerel and loses some of the original flavor, then that translation is a failure."

⑤ Yang Xianyi and Gladys Yang's Translation Practice

(1) 因此步步留心,时时在意,不肯轻易多说一句话,多行一步路,惟恐被人耻笑了去。自上了轿,进入城中, 从纱窗向外瞧了一瞧, 其街市之繁华, 人烟之阜盛,自与别处不同。(曹雪芹《红楼梦》)

> She must watch her step in her new home, she decided, be on guard every moment and weigh every word, so as not to be laughed at for any foolish blunder. As she was carried into the city she peeped out through the gauze window of the chair at the bustle in the streets and the crowds of people, the like of which she had never seen before. (Yangs' version)

> When she arrived at their house, she would have to watch every step she took and weigh every word she said, for if she put a foot wrong they would surely laugh her to scorn. Dai-yu got into her chair and was soon carried through the city walls. Peeping through the gauze panel which served as a window, she could see streets and buildings more rich and elegant and throngs of people more lively and numerous than she had ever seen in her life before. (Hawkes' version)

(2) 满纸荒唐言，一把辛酸泪！

都云作者痴，谁解其中味？(曹雪芹《红楼梦》)

Pages full of fantastic talk

Penned with bitter tears;

All men call the author mad,

None his message hears. (Yangs' version)

Pages full of idle words

Penned with hot and bitter tears:

All men call the author fool;

None his secret message hears. (Hawkes' version)

(3) 一面说，一面递眼色与刘姥姥.刘姥姥会意，未语先飞红的脸，欲待不说，今日又所为何来？只得忍耻说道："论理今儿初次见姑奶奶，却不该说，只是大远的奔了你老这里来，也少不的说了。

She winked at Granny Liu, who took the hint. Although her face burned with shame, she forced herself to pocket her pride and explain her reason for coming.

"By rights, I shouldn't bring this up at our first meeting, madam. But as I've come all this way to ask your help, I'd better speak up. " (Yangs' version)

(4) 鲁镇的酒店的格局，是和别处不同的：都是当街一个曲尺形的大柜台，柜里面预备着热水，可以随时温酒。做工的人，傍午傍晚散了工，每每花四文铜钱，买一碗酒，——这是二十多年前的事，现在每碗要涨到十文，——靠柜外站着，热热的喝了休息；倘肯多花一文，便可以买一碟盐煮笋，或者茴香豆，做下酒物了，如果出到十几文，那就能买一样荤菜，但这些顾客，多是短衣帮，大抵没有这样阔绰。只有穿长衫的，才踱进店面隔壁的房子里，要酒要菜，慢慢地坐喝。（鲁迅《孔乙己》）

The layout of Luzhen's taverns is unique. In each, facing you as you enter is a bar in the shape of a carpenter's square where hot water is kept ready for warming rice wine. When men come off work at midday and in the evening they spend four coppers on a bowl of wine — or so they did twenty years ago; now it costs ten -- and drink this warm, standing by the bar, taking it easy. Another copper will buy a plate of salted bamboo shoots or peas flavored with aniseed to go with the wine, while a dozen will buy a meat dish; but most of the customers here belong to the short-coated class, few of whom can afford this. As for those in long gowns, they go into the inner room to order wine and dishes and sit drinking at their leisure. (Yangs' version)

6　Exercises

(1) Read Yangs' translation of chapter titles in *A Dream of Red Mansions.*

(2) Select a few paragraphs in *Hong Lou Meng* and compare Yangs' translation with David Hawkes'.

7　References and Further Readings

(1) 冯庆华. 红译艺坛——《红楼梦》翻译艺术研究 [M]. 上海: 上海外语教育出版社, 2006.

(2) 杨宪益. 我有两个祖国: 戴乃迭和她的世界 [M]. 桂林: 广西师范大学出版社, 2003.

(3) 邹霆. 永远的求索: 杨宪益传 [M]. 上海: 华东师范大学出版社, 2004.

Chapter Sixteen

Yu Guangzhong's Translation Theory and Practice

Yu Guangzhong (余光中, also written as Yu Kwang-Chung, 1928–2017) is a great Taiwanese writer, poet, educator, critic and translator.

① An Introduction to Yu Guangzhong

Yu was born in Nanjing, China but fled with his family during the Japanese Army's invasion in World War II. Yu entered the University of Nanking for English Major in 1947, and then transferred to Xiamen University. Later, Yu and his family went to Taiwan via Hong Kong in 1950. He was enrolled at Taiwan University and was one of the first students to graduate with a degree in foreign languages. He also held a master of fine arts degree from the University of Iowa.

After graduation, he began his career as a university teacher in 1956. He was Professor Emeritus at Sun Yat-sen University in Kaohsiung. He had taught in the United States, including Gettysburg College. As a prolific and versatile writer, Yu had published 40 books, of which 16 are in verse and the rest in prose, criticism, and translation. In recently years, seven books by or on him have been published in Chinese mainland. A dozen or so of his lyrics enjoy popularity as songs, notably *Nostalgia*, *Nostalgia in Four Rhymes*, and *A Folk Song*. Yu's poetry since the 1970s had focused on the theme of longing for Chinese mainland felt by many people who left for Taiwan after 1949.

Yu in his works often focused upon four fundamental aspects of literature, namely, poetry, prose, translation, and commentary. Amongst the writers using Chinese, Yu has made himself well-received to readers by showing innovative humor in his essays, exhibiting wit in his appreciations, and evincing his understanding of humanistic culture in his poetry. As a former professor at the Chinese Language and Literature Faculty at the Chinese University of Hong Kong, Yu is internationally acclaimed for his command in traditional Chinese as well as modern literature.

Among Yu's translation are *The Old Man and the Sea*, *Lust for Life*, *Bartleby the Scrivener*, and *Anthology of Modern English and American Poetry*. His Chinese version of Oscar Wilde's *The*

Importance of Being Earnest and *Lady Windermere's Fan* has been successfully staged in Hong Kong and Taiwan.

 ## 2 Yu Guangzhong's Translation Ideas

In 1969, Yu Guangzhong wrote a paper entitled *Translation and Creative Writing*. After the illustration of fundamental similarities and differences between translation and creative writing, he elaborated on the impact that one has on the other. The following is an excerpt from the paper.

Under normal circumstances, the impact is enormous as far as the style is concerned. If a writer also translates, his translation style will inevitably be affected by his own creative writing style. Conversely, if a writer does a special kind of translation for long, his own writing style will not remain unaffected.

In commenting on *Modern English and American Poetry*, Zhang Jian said, "In general, the poet who translates often renders others' poetry in a style resembling his own. That is of course a common occurrence. Because of my personal preference for classical Chinese syntax in writing poetry, it shows itself too in my poetry translations. For instance, translators of the 'National Language School' will definitely not translate the last few lines of Robinson Jeffer's *Divinely Superfluous Beauty* the way I did. At least Hu Shi would not have done so. Now this reminds me of how he rendered Tennyson's 'Ulysses' into fluent vernacular Chinese. He translated in a lucid, straightforward manner reminiscent of his writing style. But his extra effort was wasted when he attempted to render Tennyson's antiquated, rhymeless style in the vernacular of the May Fourth period. A comparable case is Su Manshu's experiment in translating Byron's excited, flamboyant style in *The Isles of Greece* using five-character regulated verse in Chinese.

In fact, similar situations have occurred frequently in the West. For example, Homer's rap-tapping dactylic hexasyllabic meter was turned, in the hands of the gentle and affable Alexander Pope of the 18th century, into the latter's heroic couplets. The heroes in fierce combat in ancient battlefields were tamed and transformed into gentlemen engaged in refined drawing-room conversations. Another lively example is that of Ezra Pound. T. S. Eliot was right when he said Pound 'discovered' Chinese poetry. His classical Chinese poetry, in itself delicate and poignant, exuded the uninhibited, sketchy style of Imagist poetry. The translator is somewhat like a character actor: his personal style surfaces in whatever role he plays. T. S. Eliot once emphasized the 'impersonality' of poetry. While I may not agree totally with this idea, I can borrow it and use it in relation to his predecessor Ezra Pound, for in the best translated poetry the translator does not show his own presence. In terms of acting, the ideal translator should be a many-faced Janus, and not a character actor.

On the other hand, creative writing is inevitably influenced by translations. The influence of *The Authorized Version of the English Bible* (1611) on subsequent English prose writing was immense. European literature of the Middle Ages consisted almost entirely of translations. As far as my personal experience is concerned, when I was invited by Lin Yiliang to translate Emily Dickinson's poetry for *Selected American Poetry* over ten years ago, I went so far as to use Dickinson's balladic style in my own poetry as well. Then, my translations of Yeats's poetry did affect the style of my own poems two years ago. We can even go so far as to assert that May Fourth 'New Literature' could not have come into being without translation; it would not have developed the way it did, to say the least. Generally speaking, translations of Western literature have fostered rather than hindered the growth of May Fourth 'New Literature', though their detrimental effect on creative writing in our country must not be underestimated.

As it is, translation is a 'necessary evil', a substitute we rely on for lack of something better. Not even a good translation can convey the true meaning of the original. In the case of bad translations, besides distorting the original meaning, they often have a pernicious impact on indigenous writing styles.

Inferior writers, as well as youths learning to write, find themselves totally incapable of resisting the kind of stilted, awkward writing style — or 'translationese' — perpetuated by translations. When the influence persists, their own creative writing will be affected. In fact, translationese has already spread far and wide within the literary circles in our country. Bombarded by the various mass media (newspapers, television and advertising), those sensitive to the beauty of the Chinese language are tortured by translationese — God knows how many times a day!" (Translated by Leo T. H. Chan)

3 Yu Guangzhong's Translation Practice

(1) In an interview, Yu described his way of translating play, "In the translation of poetry and novels, especially poetry, I cannot lightly make changes to the words on the page. Poetry is designed

to be read with care and patience. In a play, on the other hand, the words are spoken by actors, and pass rapidly through the ears' of the audience. For this reason, the way I deal with the translation of plays is very different from how I approach poetry. It needs to be much more accessible." Yu said that the linguistic subtleties of Wilde made him a great challenge to the translator, but added that on occasion, the nature of the Chinese language made his translations superior to the original. "Wilde loved using symmetrical phrases for effect, and no language on Earth is as good at this kind of symmetrical composition as Chinese," Yu said. Here is the example.

Jack: Well, that is no business of yours.

Algernon: If it was my business, I wouldn't talk about it. [Begins to eat muffins.] It is very vulgar to talk about one's business. Only people like stockbrokers do that, and then merely at dinner parties. (Oscar Wilde: *The Importance of Being Earnest*)

> 杰克：哼，这跟你毫无关系。亚吉能：要是跟我有关系，我才不讲呢。（吃起松饼来。）讲关系最俗气了。只有政客那种人才讲关系，而且只在饭桌上讲。(Yu's version)

(2) He lives, then, on ginger-nuts, thought I; never eats a dinner, properly speaking; he must be a vegetarian then; but no; he never eats even vegetables, he eats nothing but ginger-nuts. (Herman Melville: *Bartleby the Scrivener*)

> 那么他就靠姜饼为生了，我想；正确地说，从不用膳的；那他该是个吃素的了；又不是的，他从不吃蔬菜，只吃姜饼。(Yu's version)

(3) But it was the color of the countryside that made him run a hand over his bewildered eyes. The sky was so intensely blue, such a hard, relentless, profound blue that it was not blue at all; it was utterly colorless. The green of the fields that stretched below him was the essence of the color green, gone mad. The burning lemon-yellow of the sun, the blood-red of the soil, the crying whiteness of the lone cloud over Montmajour, the ever reborn rose of the orchards... such colorings were incredible. How could he paint them? How could he ever make anyone believe that they existed, even if he could transfer them to his palette? Lemon, blue, green, red, rose; nature run rampant in five torturing shades of expression. (Irving Stone: *Lust for Life*)

(4)

> 可是使他伸手翼蔽自己愕视的双眼的，却是四野的色彩。天空蓝得如此强烈；蓝得硬朗，苛刻，深湛，简直不是蓝色，完全没有色彩了。展开在他脚下的这一片绿田，可谓绿色之精，且中了魔。燃烧的柠檬黄的阳光，血红的土地，蒙马茹山头那朵白得夺目的孤云，永远是一片鲜玫瑰红的果园……这种种彩色都令人难以置

信。他怎么画得出来呢？就算他能把这些移置到调色板上 去，又怎能使人相信世上真有这些色彩呢？柠檬黄、蓝、绿、红、玫瑰红；大自然挟五种残酷的浓淡表现法暴动了起来。 (Yu's version)

Stopping by Woods on a Snowy Evening	**雪晚林边歇马**
Whose woods these are I think I know.	我想我认得这座森林
His house is in the village though;	林主的房子就在前村
He will not see me stopping here	却看不见我在此歇马
To watch his woods fill up with snow.	看他林中飘满的雪景
My little horse must think it queer	我的小马一定很惊讶
To stop without a farmhouse near	周围望不见什么人家
Between the woods and frozen lake	竟在一年最暗的黄昏
The darkest evening of the year.	寒林和冰湖之间停下
He gives his harness bells a shake	马儿摇响身上的串铃
To ask if there is some mistake.	问我这地方该不该停
The only other sound's the sweep	此外只有轻风拂雪片
Of easy wind and downy flake.	再也听不见其他声音
The woods are lovely, dark and deep.	森林又暗又深真可羡
But I have promises to keep,	但是我已经有约在先
And miles to go before I sleep,	还要赶多少路才安眠
And miles to go before I sleep.	还要赶多少路才安眠。
(Robert Frost)	(Yu's version)

(5)

With you a part of me hath passed away;

For in the peopled forest of my mind

A tree made leafless by this wintry wind

Shall never don again its green array.

Chapel and fireside, country road and bay,

Have something of their friendliness resigned;

Another, if I would, I could not find,

And I am grown much older in a day.

But yet I treasure in my memory

Your gift of charity, your mellow ease,

And the dear honor of your amity;

For these once mine, my life is rich with these.

And I scarce know which part may greater be, —

What I keep of you, or you rob of me. (George Santayana: *To. W. P.* Part Ⅱ)

我生命的一部分已随你消亡；

因为在我心里那人物的林中，

一棵树飘零于冬日的寒风，

再不能披上它嫩绿的春装。

教堂、炉边、郊路和港湾，

都丧失些许往日的温情；

另一个，就如我愿意，也无法追寻，

在一日之内我白发加长。

但是我仍然在记忆里珍藏

你仁慈的于性、你轻松的童心，

和你那可爱的、可敬的亲祥；

这一些曾属于我，但充实了我的生命。

我不能分辨哪一分较巨——

是我保留住你的，还是你带走我的。(Yu's version)

The following is Li'ao's (李敖) translation, so a comparison is possible to be made.

冬风扫叶时节，一树萧条如洗，

绿装已卸，卸在我心里。

我生命的一部分，已消亡

随着你。

教堂、炉边、郊路和港湾，

情味都今非昔比。

虽有余情，也难追寻；

一日之间，我不知老了几许？

你天性的善良、慈爱和轻快，

曾属于我，跟我一起。

我不知道哪一部分多——

是你带走的我，还是我留下的你。(Li'ao's version)

Exercises

(1) Compare the three translation versions of *The Old Man and the Sea* by Yu Guangzhong, Zhang Ailing and Wu Lao.

(2) Analyze the interaction between Yu Guangzhong's writing and translation.

5 **References and Further Readings**

(1) 林以亮. 美国诗选[M] // 张爱玲, 林以亮, 余光中, 邢光祖, 译. 北京: 生活·读书·新知三联书店, 1989.

(2) 余光中. 余光中谈翻译[M]. 北京: 中国对外翻译出版公司, 2002.

Chapter Seventeen

Hu Gengshen's Translation Theory and Practice

① An Introduction to Hu Gengshen

Hu Gengshen(1949–) is an eminent Chinese translation theorist, translator and professor. Born in Zhengzhou, Henan Province, he finished his undergraduate study in the Department of Foreign Languages in Zhengzhou University in 1976, and then worked as a translator for a Metallurgical Industry in Wuhan for six years after graduation. Later he entered the Wuhan Institute of Physics, Chinese Academy of Sciences as an associate professor of translation. In 1987, he came to Boston University for a master's degree in the School of Communication and then came back for further education in Hong Kong Baptist University. After receiving his Ph.D. in Translation in 2003, he came to Cambridge University for further study in the same year. It was during his study for a Ph.D. in translation that he began to explore translation theories from the perspective of ecological translation.

He now works as a professor of Tsinghua University, and he is also Chairman of the Asia-Pacific Institute of International Exchange English Studies, recipient of Special Government Grants of the State Council. And more importantly, he is the pioneer of Eco-translatology and the president of the International Association for Eco-translatology Research.

Mainly engaged in cross-cultural, international communication and translation studies, he has published a variety of works including *International Communication Pragmatics: From Practice to Theory* (2004), *Translation and Intercultural Communication: Progress and Interpretation* (2010), *International Conference Communication* (2013), and *Eco-translatology: Construction & Interpretation* (2013). At the same time, more than 180 of his papers have been published at home and abroad.

The concept of eco-translatology was first put forward in 2001, but Hu's research on this new perspective has long been underway. The origin ostensibly began with his doctoral studies in 2001, but the related issue (the application of the Darwinism of adaptation/selection) began in the early 1990s. At that time, he gave courses to graduate students on Linguistics at Tsinghau University,

introducing the Theory of Linguistic Adaptation by Jef Verschueren, who used Darwin's natural selection-adaptation theory to introduce the biological sciences into linguistics, creating a new theoretical framework for the study of language use: the theory of linguistic adaptation. During his teaching process, he was aware that this kind of adaptation and selection should be more prominent in the translation activity. Determined to find out how translators "adapt" and "select" in the translation process, he initially had a theoretical hypothesis. When he was offered a Ph.D. in 2001, he gave the first translation lecture entitled "From the Darwinian Principle of Adaptation and Selection to Translation Studies" at the Translation Research Centre of Hong Kong Baptist University, which described the philosophical rationale and feasibility of using Darwin's "natural selection" to explore translation activities. The preliminary idea of establishing "translation adaptation selectivity theory" was put forward. On December 6 of the same year, a paper entitled "An Initial Exploration into an Approach to Translation as Adaptation and Selection" was presented at the third Asian Translators Forum of the International Translation Federation. This preliminary exploration redefines the translation from the perspective of adaptation and selection, expounds the relationship between the translator's adaptation and selection, and makes a new description of the translation process, the principle of translation, the method of translation, initially forming the basic framework of translation adaptation and selection theory.

② An Introduction to Eco-translatology

According to Hu, eco-translatology is a paradigm of ecological translation studies rooted in eco-reason and synthesized from an ecological perspective. It originated in an upsurge of worldwide ecological theories to synthesize and describe the entire ecology of translating and translation theories proper (including the essence, processes, criteria, principles, methods, and factual cases of translation) from the ecological perspective, drawing support from the isomorphic metaphor

between the translation ecosystem and the natural ecosystem; conceived in ecological holism; subordinated to Eastern ecological wisdom; probing into textual ecology, translator-community ecology, translation environment ecology, and their interrelationship; and narrated in ecological terms and an ecological manner.

Currently, this theory involves nine major research focuses and theoretical perspectives: Ecological Paradigm, the Sequence Chain, Ecological Principles, "Translator-Centeredness", "Doing Things with Translation", Translational Eco-environment, "Translation as Adaptation and Selection", Three-Dimensional Transformation, and Mechanism of "Post-event Penalty".

I Ecological Paradigm

A "paradigm" is a complex of beliefs, values, techniques, etc., shared by members of a community. As the theoretical basis and operational norm on which the natural sciences rely, a "paradigm" sets the values and behavioral patterns followed by researchers of a given science. A paradigm is not only a prerequisite for scientific research but also a sign of a mature science. In his book *Eco-translatology: Construction & Interpretation*, Hu state that an "ecological paradigm," or an ecological approach to translation, is gradually taking shape and accumulating concern and approval with such concepts as the basic notions, value judgments, research methods, terminology, and findings of many translation investigations with a strong ecological tint. Hu hold that as an interdisciplinary approach to translation, eco-translatology is an ecological paradigm that regards Translation as Adaptation and Selection to delve synthetically into translation via ecological rationale

II The Sequence Chain

At the beginning of his research on the basic theory of eco-translatology, Hu explained the correlation and interaction between translation activities and nature, and illustrated a chain of cognitive vision expansion from "translation" to "nature" with internal logical connection, which is called the sequence chain (Figure 17.1). A detailed transcription of the diagram based on "the Sequence Chain" is as follows: translation studies are a part of language studies, which are a part of cultural studies; cultural studies are a part of sociological studies, which are a part of anthropological studies, while anthropological studies are a part of ecological studies.

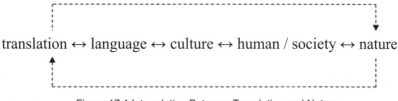

Figure 17.1 Interrelation Between Translation and Nature

Through this sequence chain, we can observe the interconnection between translation activities and biological nature, as well as the basic features of the co-interaction between natural and human ecosystems.

III Ecological Principles for Eco-Translatology

When approached from an ecological perspective and an ecosystem perspective, translation studies display an intense color of ecological rationality, regardless of whether a study is of a natural ecosystem or translation ecosystem and whether the system is large or small or at the superior or lower level. In his book *Eco-translatology: Construction & Interpretation*, Hu labeled rational features of these ecosystems as follows: 1) emphasizing holism and relevance, 2) seeking a dynamic balance, 3) reflecting ecological aesthetics, 4) identifying the "translation community", 5) adhering to Eco-translation ethics, and 6) highlighting unity in diversity. These features or principles of ecological rationality are illuminative of translation studies in terms of conceptualization, technical route, and methodology.

IV "Translator-Centeredness" in the Translation Process

The translator is highlighted in eco-translatology, not merely because eco-translatology has been developed from "An Approach to Translation as Adaptation and Selection" but also because the idea of the "translator as the center" of the translation process was initiated in the approach, which is related to the meso-level and micro-level research on eco-translatology. What is more important is that the exploration of the relationship between the translators of the translational eco-environment is one of the research objects of eco-translatology. The issue of the translator's survival and ability development is one of the "three eco-themes" of eco-translatology, namely, text ecology, translator-community ecology, and translation-environment ecology.

V Doing Things with Translation

In his paper entitled "On Initial Exploration of An Approach to Translation as Adaptation and Selection," presented at the "The Third FIT Asian Translators' Symposium" held in Hong Kong in 2001, the phrase "doing things with translations" was used for the first time. It is illustrated in two main aspects: first, the translator has a certain motivation (focus on subjective motivation) in undertaking translation activity; second, something can be done with the translated target text (focus on objective effect).

The translator undertakes translation activity for fame and reputation, for love of ethical virtue, for reasons rooted in religious faith, for a thirst for universal truth and meet his / her daily requirements. Therefore, from the perspective of the translators subjective motivation, the reason for "doing things with translation" can be 1) "survival," 2) the "realization" of ideals, 3) the "pursuit of the interesting," 4) the "transfer" of moods, and 5) "competition".

The translation that is discussed here includes various types of translation, such as oral translation (interpreting), written translation, and machine translation. Undoubtedly, the tremendous functions and great achievements of translation are undeniable. In Hu' s opinion, translation is "done" to promote communication and exchange, to stimulate lingual innovation, to stimulate cultural evolution, to stimulate social reform, to promote eco-civilization, to shape the reputation of the country, and to promote the development of translation studies.

VI Translational Eco-environment

According to Hu, the components of translational eco-environment include the source text, the source and the target language, which are the overall environment for the translator and translation. Therefore, the concept of translational eco-environment is a bit broader than the "context" in translation. With further researches, Hu found the "translational eco-environment" more clearly refers to the world constituted by the original text, the source language and the target language, including the language, communication, culture and society, as well as the interactions of the author, the reader and the client. In other words, the translational eco-environment consists of the source language, the original text and the translation system, and is the overall environment of the translator. It is not only a collection of factors restricting the translator's best adaptation and optimal choice, but also the premise and basis for the translator's multi-dimensional adaptation and adaptive choice.

In recent years, the definition of translational eco-environment has become broader, referring to the collection of the text in question, the cultural context and the "translation community," as well as the spiritual and material components. The eco-environment of translation is hierarchical and is split into macroscopic, mesoscopic, and microscopic environments. It can be said that for translation, everything exterior to the translator is accumulated into the eco-environment of translation and that each translator is a component of the other's translational eco-environment.

VII Translation as Adaptation and Selection (TAS)

Translation as Adaptation and Selection is proposed by assimilating the metaphorically Darwinian theory of "adaptation / selection" to probe into material translation issues. Based on the theory of "adaptation / selection," Hu defines translation as "a selection activity of the translator's adaptation to fit the translational eco-environment via textual transplants, dominated by the translator to targeting of cross-cultural transmission of messages".

Selective adaptation and adaptive selection in the translation process feature (1) "adaptation" — the adaptations of a translator to the translational eco-environment and (2) "selection" — the selections of the TT by a translator who stands for the translational eco-environment. Translation in this translation process is depicted as a cycling process of adaptations and selections on the part of the translator.

VIII Three-Dimensional Transformation

The translation method of eco-translatology can be called "multidimensional" transformation, with a focus on "three-dimensional" transformation. In other words, in the principle of "multidimensional adaptation and multidimensional selection," the transformation of adaptive selection relatively focuses on the lingual dimension, cultural dimension and communicative dimension. In terms of translation as "textual transformation", what is concerned in textual transformation is the textual transformation in the "three-dimensional" (the linguistic dimension, cultural dimension, and communicative dimension) eco-environment in the system of the source-text language and the target-text language.

Adaptive selection transformation from the linguistic dimension means the translator adapts and selects linguistic forms from different layers and different perspectives. Linguistic form can be analyzed at lexical level, syntactical level and textual level, including and adaptation to language forms like words, rhetoric, tone, manner, writing style and so forth. The most important aspect of this part is whether the author's stylistic features are appropriately transformed in the translation.

Adaptive transformation from the cultural dimension means the translator notices the transmission and interpretation of bilingual cultural connotations in the translation process. It takes the differences in nature and content between the original culture and the translated culture into consideration, to avoid misinterpreting the original culture from the translator's point of view. Translators should pay attention to the whole cultural system to which the language belongs while carrying out the original language conversion.

Adaptive transformation from the communicative dimension means the translator should notice the adaptive selection of bilingual communicative intentions in the translation process. It requires the translator to focus on the communicative level in addition to the conversion of linguistic information and the transfer of cultural connotation, concerning whether the communicative intention in the original language is reflected in the target language.

IX Mechanism of "Post-event Penalty"

The history of translation studies shows that in translation theory, there are two kinds of situations of translator confinement: the "pre-event precaution" and "postevent penalty," both of which can be regarded as metaphors used to distinguish two situations for the sake of convenience. The so-called "pre-event precaution" refers to the "regulations," "restrictions," and "criteria" that serve as precautions for translation in translation theory. The so-called "post-event penalty" is also a metaphor, referring to the judgment and disposition of the target text after the translation activity. It refers not to the beforehand "direction," "warning," or "confinement" of the translation activity but to the translator's active "dominance/management/handling/rewriting" of each stage of the translation activity; that is, all is left to the translator for his/her adaptive selection. After the translator's selection at each stage, the final selection and adaptation will be made by the translator according to the principles of "survival of the fittest" and "elimination of the weak" applied in the translational eco-environment, and the translator as "the center," "the dominator," or "the ruler" will fully embody the translation activity.

To conclude, eco-translatology emphasizes the organic entirety of translational environments, source and target texts, and translator actions; advocates the interaction, balance, and harmony of the translational ecosystem; and pursues ecological aesthetics and diverse unity. Therefore, the development of eco-translatology will contribute to promoting and guiding the evolution of many aspects of translatological studies.

First, it can broaden academic vision. Ecology, the metascience based on holism, is inclusive of and takes the lead in other disciplines. Meanwhile, ecological orientation is an interdisciplinary orientation with a research method that emphasizes the integrity of interaction. Consequently, from the perspective of academic vision, translation theory maintains consistency on the whole with the path of the expansion of human cognitive vision. Moreover, the vision of eco-translatology has surpassed the single dimension and instrumental rationality and has extended from a single discipline to interdisciplinary integrity.

Second, eco-translatology is taking the lead in constructing the ecological paradigm. It is a research paradigm that makes an integrated study of translation from ecological perspectives. It is a kind of multiple integration. Some scholars have proposed an idea of related study of eco-translatology from the perspective of different disciplines, such as translatology, linguistics, cultural studies, anthropology, and ecology. From

the perspective of different disciplines, they have also pointed out "interdisciplinary integration" that is eventually incorporated into their mutually reliant ecosystem and thus constitutes the organic whole of the translational ecosystem.

Third, it stimulates cross-disciplinary research because the concept of Translation as Adaptation and Selection was proposed by borrowing the idea from the theory of biological evolution and the eco-translatology is explored from the modern ecological perspective of holism. Translation activity is an interdisciplinary integration of various social and natural factors. And the development of eco-translatology indicates that translation studies are moving towards the combination of social science and natural science.

Fourth, it is nourishing new translation schools of thought. It points out that the formation and development of the ecological paradigm in translation studies, as an enrichment, innovation and leap forward, have given domestic and overseas researchers new insights into theoretical research. The explorative and pioneering spirit that it demonstrates plays an important role in orienting and stimulating the further scientific development of translatology.

Eco-translatology has made considerable progress in the past decades, but it has some limitations for it still needs continuous improvement. The translational eco-environment is defined as the overall environment for the translator and translation, thus the linguistic and cultural ecological constructs of the source language and target language is neglected, which leads to a superficial understanding of the translational eco-environment. In addition, it overemphasizes the "translator-centeredness" in the translation process, which highlights the central position and leading role of the translator in the translation process. It reflects the innate and natural needs of translators. In the translation process, out of the instinct of survival, the translator will make choices with the aim of maximizing personal interests, which may betray the source text or violate the basic morality of the translator.

All in all, as an emerging eco-translation paradigm of translation studies from ecological perspectives, eco-translatology provides a unique perspective to describe and interpret translation phenomena. Further research and discussion are needed to improve the development of eco-translatology to address relevant limitations.

③ Applicatiion of Hu Gengshen's Translation Theory

The source of theory is practice, and the value of theory is also reflected by practice. In the practice and development of eco-translatology in recent years, researchers in different fields have developed colorful applied studies and theoretical applications to fill various "vacancies" of translation studies on the basis of understanding ecology, mastering translatology, and grasping eco-translatology in combination with their personal research interests and the existing results. For instance, scholars apply the eco-translatological ideas to the translation studies on such fields as literary works, philosophical and sociological literature, sci-tech materials, commercial materials, legal documents, public signs as well as the Internet translation, interpretation, dubbing translation, subtitling translation, translator studies, translation teaching, translation history, translation theory, translation methodology, translation ethics, translation criticism, translation terminology, etc.

According to Hu Genshen, who tries to interpret and analyze with examples the functions of basic concepts of eco-translatology in translation, "mutidimentional transplantation", one of the significant ecological translation concepts and methods of eco-translatology, usually manifests itself as the translator changing a single-dimensional translation treatment in the wake of an overall consideration of a whole sentence, paragraph, passage and text. That is, the translator should not only execute language transformation but also take care of such multiple dimensions as cultural connotations, communicative intentions, psychological hints, and aesthetic pursuits, especially the balance between the source language ecology and the target-language ecology, and the holistic and interrelated factors of the micro-, meso-, and macro-translational eco-environments.

For example, the precise translations of a public sign concerning a crocodile.

ST: The last one was delicious; bring me another one!

TT1: 上一个好吃，再带来一个。

TT2: 鳄鱼伤人，禁止入水！

TT3: 人肉真香，再来一口！ (At the top of the Chinese signboard is painted a crocodile opening a big mouth stained with blood.)

TT1 is a word-for-word translation from the linguistic perspective. The first and second parts each consist of five Chinese characters, which appear to be symmetric. However, it is evident that the communicative intention of the original is not achieved, nor are the "Western" cultural expression and sense of humor adequately reflected on the Chinese sign. From the perspectives of adaptation to the translational eco-environment and "multidimensional transplantation," the translator has neither carried out multidimensional adaptation to the translational eco-environment nor performed selective transformation to adapt to the translational eco-environment.

TT2 is neat in its use of words with antithesis, and, more importantly, the translation, from the communicative perspective, better realizes the "sign" function of the original. In this sense, version 2 is indeed a good translation. However, in TT2 the "identity" of the "speaker" in the original has been changed, and the Western cultural expression and sense of humor are gone. In addition, this translated version, in terms of the "sign" function fulfillment, appears to "warn" rather than "attract."

In other words, TT2 retains "communicative ecology" of the source language, but damage the original "cultural ecology" and "linguistic ecology"

TT3 better keeps the Western cultural expression and sense of humor. Considering that the original speaks in the voice of the crocodile, the translator has painted a crocodile opening a big mouth stained with blood above the Chinese version on the signboard, which is similar to the crocodile speaking, matching the original tone; thus, the "narrator" identity of the source language ecology is explicitly and vividly "reproduced." With the help of the adaptive translation selection of symbolic language, the translator succeeds in rendering the translation accurate, expressive, vivid, and intuitive, thus better fulfilling the original communicative and "warning" functions.

Through the comparative analysis of the three translation examples mentioned above, we can see that in TT3, the original content and its communicative significance are transplanted together with a graphic from multiple dimensions (including linguistic, cultural, communicative, and aesthetic dimensions), the client's intention, the pragmatic scenario and the readers' needs. And all this better reflects the translation principles of "selective adaptation" and "adaptive selection" of Translation as Adaptation and Selection, resulting from the translator's multidimensional adaptation and adaptive selection of the specific translational eco-environment. That is, in version 3, the translator better maintains the balance between the original ecology and the ecology of the translation and constructs an eco-environment closer to the source-text ecology, enabling the "survival" of the translation in the target text ecology.

The above analysis not only illustrates the translation principles of "multidimensional selective adaptation and adaptive selection" of eco-translatology but also demonstrates that in accordance with the "multidimensional transplantation" concept and method, a translation with a higher "degree of holistic adaptation and selection" can be produced. At the same time, the above illustrations and interpretations show how to reduce the "damage" to the original text ecology and the target-text ecology in the process of translation as much as possible and how to maintain the coordination and balance of the original text ecology and the target- text ecology in the process of translation as much as possible. In other words, how to create and reconstruct the target eco-environment for the "survival" of the translated version. For more examples, see Hu (2020: 185-210).

4 Exercises

(1) Where does eco-translatology differ from the prevailing paradigms to translation? What is the addition of knowledge that eco-translatology can offer to the scholarship of Translation Studies in the world today?

(2) Compare the two translated versions and interpret Yan Fu's translation in terms of its specific translational eco-environment in the light of eco-translatology.

ST: No less certain is it that, between the time during which the chalk was formed and that at which the original turf came into existence, thousands of centuries elapsed, in the course of which, the state of nature of the ages during which the chalk was deposited, passed into that which now is, by changes so slow that, in the coming and going of the generations of men, had such witnessed them, the contemporary conditions would have seemed to be unchanging and unchangeable. (Huxley: *Evolution and Ethics*)

TT1：沧海扬尘，非诞说矣！且地学之家，历验各种殭 (僵) 石，知动植庶品，率皆递有变迁，特为变至微，其迁极渐。即假吾人彭聃之寿，而亦由暂观久，潜移弗知。是犹蟪蛄不识春秋，朝菌不知晦朔，遽以不变名之，真瞽说也。（严复译文）

TT2：还可以同样地肯定，在白垩形成和原始草皮出现之间，经历了几千个世纪，在这个过程中，从白垩沉积时代的自然状态变化到现在，由于变化如此缓慢，以致使亲眼见到这些变化的世世代代的人们，觉得他们那一代的情况好象是不曾变化过，也不会变化似的。（科学出版社译文）

(3) Compare the following translated versions and interpret the translators' translation in the light of eco-translatology.

ST: "道可道，非常道。"（《道德经》）

TT1: The Way that can be told of is not an Unvarying Way. (Waley's version)

TT2: The Tao that be told of,

　　　Is not the Absolute Tao. (Lin Yutang's version)

TT3: The way can be spoken of.

　　　But it will not be the constant way. (Lau's version)

TT4: As fot the Way, the Way that can be spoken of is not the constant Way. (Henricks' s version)

TT5: The ways that can be walked are not the eternal Way. (Mair's version)

TT6: The Tao that is utterable,

　　　Is not the eternal Tao. (Gu Zhengkun's version)

5 References and Further Readings

(1) HU G. Eco-Translatology: Towards an Eco-Paradigm of Translation Studies [M]. Singapore: Springer, 2020.

(2) 胡庚申. 翻译适应选择论[M]. 武汉：湖北教育出版社，2004.

(3) 胡庚申. 翻译生态 VS 自然生态：关联性、类似性、同构性[J]. 上海翻译，2010(4)：1-5.

(4) 胡庚申. 生态翻译学的研究焦点与理论视角[J]. 中国翻译，2011(2)：5-9.

(5) 胡庚申. 生态翻译学：建构与诠释[M]. 北京：商务印书馆，2013.

Part II

Western Translation Theory

Chapter One

The Romans: Cicero, Horace and Quintilian

Just as Alexander Gross observes, truly major periods in the history of translation tend to coincide with eras when a major differential or inequality exists between two cultures or two peoples employing different languages. One of these peoples perceives the need to absorb greater or higher or more detailed knowledge from another, whether this knowledge is conceived in political, religious, or scientific terms. In the translation history of the world, eleven periods exist. Let's first have a look at those golden times of translation.

(1) Prehistory: predominance of interpreting and "mediating" (by "marriage-brokers," "go-betweens," "deal-makers," "peace-seekers," all of these subsidiary meanings of the earliest words for "interpreters").

(2) Sumerians, Akadians, Assyrians: the need to make laws, creation tales and other scriptures, and economic norms known among peoples using different languages.

(3) Egyptians: the need to communicate with peoples in Southern Egypt and with the Hittites. The Rosetta stone is evidence of Egypt's assiduous concern with translation through the ages. If it were not for the deciphering of the Rosetta inscriptions (written in Hieroglyphic), the glory of Egyptian civilization could not have been revealed quite so soon. Translation was the key that granted the world entry into a world otherwise unknown.

(4) Greeks: the need to understand Egyptian civilization.

(5) Romans: the need to understand Greek civilization.

(6) Chinese (7th Century): the need to understand Indian civilization, especially Sanskrit and Pali scriptures.

(7) Arab and Persian World (Jundishapur and Baghdad, 8th to 10th Centuries): the need to absorb and integrate Sanskrit, Hebrew, Syriac, and Greek knowledge into Persian and Arabic cultures.

(8) Japanese (Heian Period, 9th to 10th Centuries): the need to understand and absorb

Chinese culture, with Korea as an important intermediary.

(9) Western Middle Ages: the need to reabsorb and integrate Arabic, Hebrew, and Greek knowledge in medieval Europe.

(10) Renaissance: reintegration of Ancient Greek culture in the West.

(11) Conquest and colonization: the need to understand American, African, and Asian languages and dialects.

(12) Enlightenment and 19th Centuries: decline of Latin, emergence of modern national languages as the measure of human knowledge.

(13) Modern Times: many competing major and minor national languages.

In the empires of Antiquity, interpreters were essential intermediaries in trade and the various matters of state. With the onset of printing, some of this work was transferred to translators, who also came to play a key role in disseminating, and passing on to later generations the documents that were to form the canons of literature, learning, and religion, and works such as the Homeric epics, the Bible, and Greek drama, philosophy, and history, to mention obvious examples in the Western tradition.

George Steiner, in *After Babel*, divided the literature on the theory, practice and Western history of translation into four periods. The first extends from the statements of Cicero and Horace on translation up to the publication of Alexander Fraser Tytler's "Essay on the Principles of Translation" in 1791. The central characteristic of this period is that of "immediate empirical focus," i.e. the statements and theories about translation stem directly from the practical work of translating. Steiner's second period, which runs up to the publication of Larbaud's *Sous I'invocation de Saint Jérome* in 1946 is characterized as a period of theory and hermeneutic enquiry with the development of a vocabulary and methodology of approaching translation. The third period begins

with the publication of the first papers on machine translation in the 1940s, and is characterized by the introduction of structural linguistics and communication theory into the study of translation. Steiner's fourth period, coexisting with the third has its origins in the early 1960s and is characterized by "a reversion to hermeneutic, almost metaphysical inquiries into translation and interpretation"; in short by a vision of translation that sets the discipline in a wide frame that includes a number of other disciplines: classical philology and comparative literature, lexical statistics and ethnography, the sociology of class-speech, formal rhetoric, poetics, and the study of grammar are combined in an attempt to clarify the act of translation and the process of "life between languages." In trying to establish certain lines of approach to translation, across a time period that extends from Cicero to the present, it seems best to proceed by following a loosely chronological structure, but without making any attempt to set up clear-cut divisions.

Up until the second half of the twentieth century, Western translation theory seemed locked in a sterile debate over the triad of literal, free and faithful translation. The distinction between word-for-word (i.e. literal) and sense-for-sense (i.e. free) translation goes back to Cicero (1st century BC) and St Jerome (late 4th century AD) and forms the basis of key writings on translation in centuries nearer to our own. Now let's start with Cicero, Horace and Quintilian.

 1　Cicero

> Marcus Tullius Cicero (106 BC–43 BC), a Roman philosopher, statesman, lawyer, political theorist, and constitutionalist, is widely considered one of Rome's greatest orators and prose stylists. What's more, he is credited with the formation of a Latin philosophical vocabulary.

Cicero is generally perceived to be one of the most versatile minds of ancient Rome. He introduced the Romans to the chief schools of Greek philosophy and created a Latin philosophical vocabulary, distinguishing himself as a linguist, translator, and philosopher. As an impressive orator and successful lawyer, Cicero probably thought his political career to be his most important achievement. Today, he is appreciated primarily for his humanism and philosophical and political writings. His voluminous correspondence, much of it addressed to his friend Atticus, has been especially influential, introducing the art of refined letter writing to European culture.

Cicero is considered to be one of the earliest translation theorists in the West; however, ironically, his translation ideas are reflected in his three works not intended for translation, *De Oratore* (*On the Orator*), *De Optimo Genere Oratorum* (*The Best Kind of Orator*) and *De Finibus Bonorum et Malorum* (*On the Limits of Good and Evil*). The following is an excerpt from *De Oratore* (*On the Orator*) in which he discusses his translation of Greek orations into Latin:

"Afterwards I resolved, and this practice I followed when somewhat older, to translate freely Greek speeches of the most eminent orators. The result of reading these was that, in rendering into Latin what I had read in Greek, I not only found myself using the best words, and yet quite familiar

157

ones, but also coining by analogy certain words such as would be new to our people, provided only they were appropriate."

Cicero outlines his approach to translation in *De Optimo Genere Oratorum* (*The Best Kind of Orator*), introducing his own translation of the speeches of the Attic orators Aeschines and Demosthenes:

"And this is our conclusion: that, since the most outstanding Greek orators were those from Athens, and that their chief was easily Demosthenes, anybody who imitates him will speak in the Attic style, and excellently to boot. Consequently, since Athenian orators are proposed for our imitation, to speak in the Attic style is to speak well. But, because there are many misconceptions over what constitutes this style of composition, I propose to undertake a task useful for students, but not completely necessary for myself. For I have translated into Latin two of the most eloquent and most noble speeches in Athenian literature, those two speeches in which Aeschines and Demosthenes oppose each other. And I have not translated like a mere hack, but in the manner of an orator, translating the same themes and their expression and sentence shapes in words consonant with our conventions. In so doing I did not think it necessary to translate word for word, but I have kept the force and flavor of the passage. For I saw my duty not as counting out words for the reader, but as weighing them out. And this is the goal of my project: to give my countrymen an understanding of what they are to seek from those models who aim to Attic in style, and of the formulas of speech they are to have recourse to."

And in the *De Finibus Bonorum et Malorum* (*On the Limits of Good and Evil*), Cicero stated:

"Yet it will not be necessary to render the Greek term by means of a Latin word that is a calque

of it, as is the custom of translators who do not know how to express themselves, when we already have a more common word that says the same thing. You could even do what I usually do: where the Greeks have one word I use more than one if I can't translate otherwise, but that does not mean that I should not have the right to use a Greek word whenever Latin is unable to offer an equivalent."

The "interpreter" in Cicero's mind is the literal ("word-for-word") translator, while the "orator" tries to produce a speech that moved the listeners. In Roman times, word-for-word translation was exactly what it said: the replacement of each individual word of the ST (invariably Greek) with its closest grammatical equivalent in Latin. This was because the Romans would read the TTs side by side with the Greek STs.

Cicero points out that mind dominates the body as a king rules over his subjects or a father controls his children, but warned that where Reason dominates as a master rules his slaves, 'it keeps them down and crushes them." With translation, the ideal SL text is there to be imitated and not to be crushed by the too rigid application of Reason. Cicero, in his remarks on translation, makes an important distinction between word-for-word translation and sense-for-sense translation. The underlying principle of enriching their native language and literature through translation leads to a stress on the aesthetic criteria of the TL product rather than on more rigid notions of "fidelity".

In *De Optimo Genere Oratum*, Cicero makes two major points: Firstly, word-for-word translation is not suitable Secondly, translators should seek in their own language expressions that reproduce as much as possible the cogency of the original. His sensitivity to words made him an excellent terminologist, and his work prepared the ground for most modern philosophical terminology. Cicero is important for a verse translation of Aratus, Phaenomena, for much rhetorical translation which has not survived, and for his translations of Greek philosophy into Latin. There are discussions of the problems created by Greek terms in Cicero's philosophical writings, the most important being the discussions of Epicureanism in the *De Finibus Bonorum ET Malorum* (The Ends of Good and Evil). Of equal importance to the development of translation is Horace, whose discussion of literary imitation in the *Ars Poetica* (The Art of Poetry) has had an influence on translation out of all proportion to his intent.

2 Horace

Quintus Horatius Flaccus, (65 BC–8 BC), known in the English-speaking world as Horace, was the leading Roman lyric poet during the time of Augustus. Horace was an outstanding lyric poet and satirist, friend of the Emperor Augustus and the great epic poet Virgil. His four books of Carmina or Odes are perhaps his most admired and translated works.

Horace is generally considered by classicists to be one of the greatest Latin poets. He coined many Latin phrases that still remain in use (in Latin or in translation) including "carpe diem" "("pluck the day" literally, more commonly used in English as "seize the day"); "Dulce et decorum est pro patria mori" ("It is sweet and fitting to die for one's country"); "Nunc est bibendum" ("Now we must drink") and "aurea mediocritas" ("golden mean").

Horace's *Ars Poetica* (also known as "*The Art of Poetry*"), published in 18 BC, is a treatise on poetics. It was first translated into English by Ben Jonson. Horace, in his *Art of Poetry*, warned against overcautious imitation of the source model:

"A theme that is familiar can be made your own property so long as you do not waste your time on a hackneyed treatment; nor should you try to render your original word for word like a slavish translator, or in imitating another writer plunge yourself into difficulties from which shame, or the rules you have laid down for yourself, preventing you from extricating yourself."

Since the process of the enrichment of the literary system is an integral part of the Roman concept of translation, it is not surprising to find a concern with the question of language enrichment also. So prevalent was the habit of borrowing or coining words, that Horace, whilst advising the would-be writer to avoid the pitfalls that beset 'the slavish translator', also advised the sparing use of new words. He compared the process of the addition of new words and the decline of other words to the changing of the leaves in spring and autumn, seeing this process of enrichment through translation as both natural and desirable, provided the writer exercised moderation. The art of the translator, for Horace and Cicero, then, consisted in judicious interpretation of the SL text so as to produce a TL version based on the principle non verbum de verbo, sed sensum exprimere de sensu (of expressing not word for word, but sense for sense), and his responsibility was to the TL readers.

The disparagement of word-for-word translation by Cicero, and indeed by Horace, who underlines the goal of producing an aesthetically pleasing and creative text in the TL, had great influence on the succeeding centuries. Drawing on the talent at his disposal, the Emperor Augustus (63 BC–14 AD) set up a translation office as part of the imperial household to assist in administering the Empire. As long as the Roman Empire existed, translation remained important, although after the third century knowledge of Greek became less common in the West. There is no record of translation from languages other than Greek. As the teaching of medicine developed at Rome, an increasing amount of medical and pharmacological translation began to appear, particularly after the fourth century. The Emperor Augustus's translation office in the imperial household seems to have had offshoots in the Eastern provinces. Most of this translation was done by Greeks who had come to Rome as slaves.

3 Quintilian

Marcus Fabius Quintilianus (35–100), a Roman rhetorician from Hispania, is widely referred to in medieval schools of rhetoric and in Renaissance writing. In English translation, he is usually referred to as Quintilian.

Quintilian, like Cicero, was trained as an orator and practised at the bar. Tutor to the family of the Emperor Domitian, he was primarily celebrated as a teacher. Quintilian retired in order to write, his principal work being *The Institutio Oratoria* (*Education of an Orator*), possibly intended as a primer for the young princes; it is regarded as a basic text in rhetoric, pedagogy and literary criticism. Translation becomes a way of improving or asserting the value of the vernacular through emulation of Classical models. Quintilian's remarks are in the Ciceronian tradition, whereby translation was seen not only as a tool in the acquisition of a foreign language, but as a means of enriching the target language. He systematizes much of what

earlier writers had to say, making clear, for instance, the distinction between metaphrasis or word-for-word translation and paraphrasis or phrase-by-phrase translation. He is concerned not so much with the painstaking reproduction of earlier texts, as with the preservation of a living tradition. His approach to education is of course highly influential.

In the first passage below, Quintilian makes it clear that it is permissible and indeed obligatory not only to emulate the Greek models but even to try to excel them.

"From these Greek authors, and others worthy to be read, a stock of words, a variety of figures, and the art of composition must be acquired; and our minds must be directed to the imitation of all their excellences; for it cannot be doubted that a great portion of art consists in *imitation*, since, though to invent is first in order of time, and holds the first place in merit, yet it is of advantage to copy what has been invented with success... We must, indeed, be either like or unlike those who excel and nature rarely forms one like, though imitation does so frequently. But the very circumstance that renders the study of all subjects so much easier to us, than it was to those who had nothing to imitate, will prove a disadvantage to us unless it be turned to account with caution and judgement.

Undoubtedly, then, imitation is not sufficient of itself, if for no other reason than that it is the mark of an indolent nature to rest satisfied with what has been invented by others. For what would have been the case, if, in those times which were without any models, mankind had thought that they were not to execute or imagine anything but what they already knew? Assuredly nothing would have

been invented…

It is dishonourable even to rest satisfied with simply equalling what we imitate. For what would have been the case, again, if no one had accomplished more than he whom he copied?… But if it is not allowable to add to what has preceded us, how can we ever hope to see a complete orator, when among those, whom we have hitherto recognized as the greatest, no one has been found in whom there is not something defective or censurable? Even those who do not aim at the highest excellence should rather try to excel, than merely follow, their predecessors; for he who makes it his object to get before another, will possibly, if he does not go by him, get abreast of him. But assuredly no one will come up with him in whose steps he thinks that he must tread, for he who follows another must of necessity always be behind him."

In the following passage, Quintilian advocates that translation is a struggle and rivalry.

"Our ancient orators believed that the most efficacious means of acquiring a command of their language was to translate Greek works into Latin. Crassus, quoted in Cicero, *De Oratore* l. 155, says he made a practice of it; and Cicero, speaking in his own name, recommended it very often. And indeed, he published books by Xenophon and Plato he had translated…The reason for this exercise is extremely obvious. For Greek authors abound in richness of expression and bring the greatest finesse into their oratory. And therefore those who would translate these authors must use the best of language while relying on their native resources. Because our Roman language is immensely different from Greek, we are bound by a certain need to rethink the many and varied figures with which a work is adorned.

For I do not want translation to be a mere paraphrase, but a struggle and rivalry over the same meanings."

4 Exercises

(1) Please summarize Cicero's translation ideas. Why did he translate the orations of Aeschines and Demonsthenes as an orator instead of an interpreter?

(2) Do you agree with Quintilian's idea that translation is not a mere paraphrase, but a struggle and rivalry over the same meanings? Why or why not?

5 References and Further Readings

(1) LEFEVERE A. Translation — History, Culture: A Sourcebook [M]. London & New York: Routledge, 1992.

(2) WEISSBORT D. & Eysteinsson, A. Translation — Theory and Practice [M]. London: Oxford University Press, 2006.

(3) ROBINSON D. Western Translation Theory: from Herodotus to Nietzsche [M]. Beijing: Foreign Language Teaching and Research Press, 2007.

Chapter Two

Bible Translation in the West

The Bible is the central religious text of Christianity. It consists of *The Old Testament* writtten primarily in Hebrew and *The New Testament* originally written in Greek. The history of Bible translation is a history of Western culture in microcosm. It is common knowledge that the Bible has been translated into more languages than any other piece of literature. But by the year 600 A.D., the four Gospels had been translated into only a very few languages. When the art of printing with movable type was invented by Johannes Gutenberg in 1456, only thirty-three languages had any part of the Bible. Even when the Bible society movement began some two centuries ago, only sixty-seven languages had any portions. During the 19th century, however, more than four hundred languages received some part of the Scriptures, and within the first half of the 20h century, this figure increased

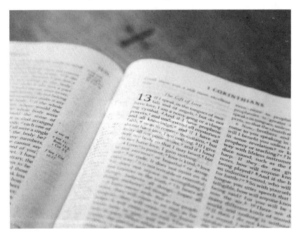

by more than five hundred. This rapid increase in the preparation of versions of the Bible is due to the role played by Bible societies, *Wycliffe Bible* Translators, and similar organizations.

The history of the translation of the Bible can be divided into four major periods. The first period includes the efforts to translate the Scriptures into several of the dominant languages of the ancient world. The second important period of Bible translating is related to the Reformation, when renderings are no longer made from the Latin Vulgate translation but from the original Hebrew and Greek text into the vernaculars of Europe. The third period may be called the great missionary endeavor, when pioneer translators undertook the preparation of renderings into hundreds of languages and dialects, in many of which there was previously often not even an alphabet. Such work is still going on, while a fourth period has already begun. This is characterized primarily by translations being produced in newly developing nations, where native speakers often assume primary responsibility, with missionaries sometimes serving as consultants. This has many advantages, since it is invariably easier for properly trained people to translate into their own mother tongue than into a foreign language, and the end product is likely to be more effective. By the opening of the year 2000, the entire Bible had been made available in 371 languages and dialects, and portions of the Bible in 1,862 other languages and dialects.

1 The Septuagint

The Septuagint is the traditional terms for the Old Greek translation of the Hebrew Scriptures. This is not only the earliest but also one of the most valuable of ancient biblical versions.

The word "Septuagint" means "seventy" and is often abbreviated by using the Roman numeral LXX, referring to the seventy-two translators reputed to have produced the version in the time

of Ptolemy II Philadelphus (285–246 BC) for Greek-speaking Jews living in the Graeco-Roman diaspora. The Greek language was the lingua franca of the eastern Mediterranean Basin from the time of Alexander the Great (356 BC–323 BC). According to a document called *Letter of Aristeas*, Ptolemy II, being of a literary disposition, wished to make a collection of the world's best literature. His librarian, Demetrius of Phalerum, called his attention to the Hebrew Scriptures as being worthy of a place "in your library since the law which they contain…is full of wisdom and free from all blemish." At once the king sent ambassadors to Eleazar, the Jewish high priest at Jerusalem, and requested him to send a copy of the Hebrew Scriptures, with learned men who could translate the text into Greek.

Upon their arrival in Alexandria, the seventy-two translators were conducted to a quiet house in the harbor of Alexandria, where every provision was made for their needs. So they set to work; as they completed their several tasks, they would reach an agreement on each by comparing versions. By happy coincidence, the task of translation was completed in seventy-two days. It was at once approved as an accurate rendering, and a curse was invoked on any who would alter the text by any addition, transposition, or deletion.

The importance of the Septuagint as a translation is obvious. Besides being the first translation ever made of the Hebrew Scriptures, it was the medium through which the religious ideas of the Hebrews were brought to the attention of the world. It was the Bible of the early Christian church, and when the Bible was quoted in *The New Testament*, it was almost always from the Septuagint version. Furthermore, even when not directly quoted in *The New Testament*, many of the terms used and partly created by the Septuagint translators became part and parcel of the language of *The New Testament*. At an early stage, the belief developed that this translation had been divinely inspired, and hence the way was open for several church fathers to claim that the Septuagint presented the words of God more accurately than the Hebrew Bible. The fact that after the 1st century very, very few Christians had any knowledge of the Hebrew language meant that the Septuagint was not only the church's main source of *The Old Testament* but was, in fact, its only source.

Although this translation and its interpretations of the Hebrew text have been criticized since its inception, the Septuagint has nevertheless served as a standard reference ever since its completion. It became the basis for daughter versions of the Old Testament in many languages, including Old Latin, Coptic, Gothic, Armenian, Georgian, Ethiopic, Christian Palestinian Aramaic, Arabic, and Slavonic. To this day, the Septuagint still retains considerable influence on questions of interpretation and textual matters, and its study continues to shed light on the principles of translation used in the ancient world.

2 Jerome's Latin Vulgate

It would be difficult to overestimate the importance of the influence exerted by the Latin versions of the Bible and particularly by Jerome's Latin Vulgate. Whether one considers the Vulgate from a purely secular point of view, with its pervasive influence on the development of Latin into Romance languages, or whether one has in view only the specifically religious influence, the extent of its penetration into all areas of Western culture is almost beyond calculation. The theology and the devotional language typical of the Roman Catholic Church were either created or transmitted by the Vulgate. Both Protestants and Roman Catholics are heirs of terminology that Jerome either coined or baptized with fresh significance — words such as salvation, regeneration, justification, sanctification, propitiation, reconciliation, inspiration, Scripture, sacrament, and many others.

Probably by the end of the second century A.D., Old Latin versions of the Scripture were in circulation in North Africa, but the pre-Jerome translations in general lack polish and are often painfully literal. By the close of the 4th century, there was such a confusing diversity among Latin manuscripts of *The New Testament* that Augustine lamented, "Those who translated the Scriptures from Hebrew into Greek can be counted, but the Latin translators are out of all number. For in the early days of the faith, everyone who happened to gain possession of a Greek manuscript (of *The New Testament*) and thought he had any facility in both languages, however slight that might have been, attempted to make a translation." In these circumstances, the stage was set for the most decisive series of events in the whole history of the Latin Bible. In the year 383, Pope Damasus commissioned Jerome, the most learned Christian scholar of his day, to produce a uniform and dependable text of the Latin Scriptures. He was not to make a totally new translation but to revise a text of the Bible in use at Rome. Jerome's first inclination was to say "No, thank you" to the Pope's invitation. He wrote:

"You urge me to revise the Old Latin version, and, as it were, to sit in judgment on the copies of the Scriptures that are now scattered throughout the world; and, inasmuch as they differ from one another, you would have me decide which of them agree with the original. The labor is one of love, but at the same time it is both perilous and presumptuous — for in judging others I must be content to be judged by all....Is there anyone learned or unlearned, who, when he takes the volume in his hands and perceives that what he reads does not suit his settles tastes, will not break out immediately into violent language and call me a forger and profane person for having the audacity to add anything to the ancient works, or to make any changes or corrections in them?"

Two factors, however, prompted Jerome to undertake this difficult task. One was the command laid upon him by the supreme pontiff. The other was the shocking diversity among the Old Latin manuscripts, there being, as he wrote, "Almost as many forms of text as there are manuscripts."

Jerome (Eusebius Hieronymus, 347–420) was born at Stridon on the borders of Dalmatia and Pannonia of a well-to-do Christian family. His early training was such as to fit him admirably for work as translator, for he received a first-class education in grammar and rhetoric at Rome under the illustrious teacher Aelius Donatus. He became familiar with the Latin classics and studied Plautus and Terence, Sallust, Lucretius, Horace, Virgil, Persius, and Lucan. These developed his feeling for literary style, and he became a follower of Ciceronian traditions. He also learned Greek and studied the Greek classics written by Hesiod, Sophocles, Herodotus, Demosthenes, Aristotle and others. His scholarly tools also came to include the Hebrew language which he learned with great labor in his mature years. Such was the philological training of the man who was destined to fix the literary form of the Bible of the entire Western Church.

Jerome started with the Gospels, using a Greek manuscript as his principal source. For the rest of the New Testament he stuck to the existing texts for the most part. Jerome then produced three revisions of the Psalms, all extant. In the meantime, Jerome realized the futility of revising the Old Latin solely on the basis of the Greek, and by the end of 405 he had executed his own Latin translation of the entire Old Testament based on the "Hebrew truth" (Hebraica veritas).

Because of the canonical status of the Greek version within the church, Jerome's version was received at first with much suspicion, for it seemed to cast doubt on the authenticity of the Septuagint and exhibited divergences from the Old Latin. The innate superiority of Jerome's version assured its ultimate victory, and by the 8th century it had become the Latin Vulgate ("the common version") throughout the churches of Western Christendom, where it remained the chief Bible until the Reformation. For nearly a thousand years, the Vulgate was used as the recognized text of the Scripture throughout Western Europe. It also became the basis of pre-Reformation vernacular Scriptures, such as Wycliffe's English translation in the fourteenth century, as well as the first printed Bibles in German (1466), Italian (1471), Czech (1488), and French (1530).

Jerome's translation idea is reflected in the following extract from his *Letter to Pammachius*:

"I admit and confess most freely that I have not translated word for word in my translations of Greek texts, but sense for sense, except in the case of the scriptures in which even the order of the words is a mystery. Cicero has been my teacher in this.

Do Plautus and Terence, for example, stick to the word, or do they try to preserve the beauty and the elegance of the original in translation? Educated people have coined the phrase *kako zelia*, misplaced zeal for what you call a faithful translation. I have derived my principles from the writers I mentioned when I translated the chronicles of Eusebius into Latin twenty years ago. In your opinion I committed the same mistakes as they did but I never suspected that you would go on to blame me for them. In those days I wrote in my introduction, among other things:

It is hard not to slip when you are translating a foreign text word for word. It is difficult to preserve the elegance of felicitous expression as you find it in a foreign language when you translate. Something may find its most poignant expression through the proper nature of *one* word. I cannot find the one that achieves the same effect. If I want to do justice to the sense I have to make a long detour to get just a little bit ahead. Add to this the irritating anacolutha, or sentences that do not make sense, the difference in cases, the multiplicity of images and, finally, the spirit that dwells in every language, your own and that of others. If I translate word for word I produce nonsense, but if I have to change something in the order of the words or their sound I could be accused of failing in my duties as a translator.

After a few more sentences that are of no interest to us here, I added: 'If people maintain that the beauty of a language does not suffer from translation let them simply translate Homer into Latin, word for word, or even better, let them simply render him in prose in his own language. The whole thing will turn into a ridiculous comedy and the greatest poet will be reduced to a mere stammerer'.

I only wanted to prove that I have always been opposed to sticking to words, from the days when I was young, and that I have always translated the sense. But my judgment is probably not of great importance in this matter. I advise people to read the short preface to the book that describes the life of Saint Antony. It says there:

A literal translation from one language into another obscures the sense in the same way as the thriving weeds smother the seeds. Since language depends on cases and images you sometimes have to waste time and make a detour to express what could be said with few words, and often to express it with great imprecision at that. I have skirted this danger and at your request I have translated the life of Saint Antony in such a way that the whole sense is there, even if I have not always kept to the sound of the words. Let others stick to syllables, or even to letters, you should try to grasp the sense!

It would lead us too far to point out how much the translators of the Septuagint have added and how much they have left out. In the manuscripts we use in our churches these passages are marked with small obelisk and small asterisks. Yet the Septuagint has become the accepted translation in churches, and rightly so, not only because it was the first translation and because it was already in use before the coming of Christ, but also because it was used by the apostles, though only in as far as it did not deviate from Hebrew."

3 Wycliffe Bible

So far as we know, the first complete English Bible was due to the influence and activity of John Wycliffe (1330–1384), an eminent Oxford theologian, called the "Morning Star of the Reformation" because of the religious convictions that he developed and propagated.

A strong believer in the Bible as the Word of God addressed to every person, John Wycliff felt the need to provide the Scripture in a form that the ordinary reader could use. He put forward the theory of "dominion by grace", according to which man was immediately responsible to God and God's law. Since Wycliffe's theory means that the Bible is applicable to all human life it follows that each man should be granted access to that crucial text in a language that he could understand, i.e. in the vernacular. At that time, only the educated (and those wealthy enough to become educated) could read and understand Latin. People mainly heard the Bible read to them by the clergy at church since they did not know how to read and the Bible was costly (before the printing press). Wycliffe's idea was to translate the Bible into the language of the common people, giving them the chance to read the Bible and develop their own interpretation of it.

When Wycliffe took on the challenge of translating the Bible he was breaking a long held belief that no person should translate the Bible on their own initiative, without church approval. When met with opposition to the translation he replied "Christ and his apostles taught the people in that tongue that was best known to them. Why should men not do so now?" Wycliffe also believed that it was necessary to return to the primitive state of *The New Testament* in order to truly reform the church. His attacks both on the privileges of the church and on such Catholic doctrines as transubstantiation earned him the Pope's condemnation for heresy.

The Wycliffe translation is probably mostly not by Wycliffe himself, but the project was at the heart of his aim to restore the Bible's authority in the life of church and nation. It was based not on the original languages (which were not available then in England) but on the Latin Vulgate text. The first version produced about 1382, was extremely literal, corresponding word for word to the Latin, even at the expense of natural English word order. The revised version, produced after Wycliffe's death in about 1388, probably by his secretary John Purvey and others, shows more respect for English idiom; the reviser's prologue describes the four stages of the translation process:

(1) a collaborative effort of collecting old Bibles and glosses and establishing an authentic Latin source text;

(2) a comparison of the versions;

(3) counselling "with old grammarians and old divines" about hard words and complex meanings; and

(4) translating as clearly as possible the "sentence" (i.e. meaning), with the translation corrected by a group of collaborators.

Since the political function of the translation was to make the complete text of the Bible accessible, this led to a definite stance on priorities by the translator: Purvey's Preface states clearly that the translator shall translate "after the sentence" (meaning) and not only after the words, "so that the sentence be as open (plain) or opener, in English as in Latin and go not far from the letter." What is aimed at is an intelligible, idiomatic version: a text that could be utilized by the layman. The extent of its importance may be measured by the fact that the bulk of the 150 copies of Purvey's revised Bible were written even after the prohibition, on pain of excommunication, of translations circulated without the approval of diocesan or provincial councils in July 1408.

In spite of the zeal with which the hierarchy sought to destroy it due to what they saw as mistranslations and erroneous commentary, there still exist about 150 manuscripts, complete or partial, containing the translation in its revised form. For this reason the Wycliffites in England were often designated by their opponents as "Bible men." Just as Luther's version had great influence upon the German language, so Wycliffe's, by reason of its clarity, beauty, and strength, influenced the English language as the King James version was later to do. It was, in effect, *the* English Bible throughout the fifteenth and early sixteenth centuries.

4 Martin Luther's Bible

Martin Luther (1483–1546), Augustinian monk and theologian, was the German leader of the Reformation. With his ninety-five theses, nailed to the door of Wittenberg University in 1517, he expressed his dissatisfaction with the penitential system of the Roman Catholic Church. By 1521, the breach with the Church had become irreparable. An effective publicist and great writer of treatises, with a rugged popular style, Luther came to emphasize original writing in the vernacular, but it was through his translation of the Bible *(The New Testament*, published in 1522, and *The Old Testament*, in 1534) that he was to establish a norm for written German, and to have a radical and lasting influence on German language and literature. Luther translated the Bible from Greek into German to make it more accessible to ordinary people, a task he began alone in 1521 during his stay in the Wartburg castle. He was not the first translator of it into German, but he was by far the greatest. A comment goes like this: Had Luther done nothing but this, he would remain one of the greatest benefactors of the German-speaking race.

As a translator, Luther was distinctly reader-oriented; his aim was to put together a Bible text for the general public. His translation, characterized by a combination of popular speech and poetic dignity, became for many Northern Europeans a new "original," and served as such as the basis of some Bible translations into the Nordic languages. Luther's *Open Letter on Translation* (1530) is an important text in the history of translation theory, not only because it is intimately connected to a groundbreaking translation, but further because it manifests vividly how the choice of words and expressions in a translation is sometimes intimately linked to a whole ideological and institutional matrix. Here is an excerpt from *Open Letter on Translation*.

"…Only an idiot would go ask the letters of the Latin alphabet how to speak German, the way these dumbasses do. You've got to go out and ask the mother in her house, the children in the street, the ordinary man at the market. Watch their mouths move when talk, and translate that way. Then they'll understand you and realize that you're speaking *German* to them.

Jesus says, for example, in Matthew 12:34, *Ex abundantia cordis as loquitur*. If I followed those jackasses, they would probably set the letters before me and have me translate it, 'Out of the abundance of the heart the mouth speaketh.' Tell me, is that how any real person would say it? Who would understand such a thing? What on earth is the 'abundance of the heart'?' Anybody who said that would probably mean he has too large a heart, or too much heart — and even that doesn't sound right. For 'abundance of the heart' sounds about as good in ordinary speech as 'abundance of the house,' or 'abundance of the stove', or 'abundance of the bench'. What the mother in her house and the common man would say is something like: 'Speak straight from the heart'. This is the kind of ordinary phrasing that I've always striven for, but alas, haven't always managed to find. The letters of the Latin alphabet make it pretty hard to speak good German.

…If I let the letters go their merry way and try to determine what the Hebrew speaker meant by '*isch hamudoth*', I find that the true meaning is something like 'Dan my man,' 'sweet Mary,' 'June honey,' 'you great gorgeous hunk of a man,' and the like. You see, the translator has to store up lots of words, so he'll have plenty to choose from if one doesn't always sound right.

And why should I go on and on about translation? If I wanted to trace every one of my words back to its original germ or idea, it would take me a year to write it. Whatever it takes to translate, I've done it, and I'm not going to let any wet-behind-the-ears papist jackasses and dumbasses line up and take potshots at me. Anybody who doesn't like my translation, let me give you a little helpful hint: *don't read it*! And I say, may the devil take anybody who doesn't like it or correct it without my knowledge or against my will. If anybody's going to correct it, I'll do it myself. And if I don't do it, everybody else should leave my translation alone. You got something to do with your life? Then go do it and have a nice day…"

⑤ The King James Bible (1611)

In 1603 when King James VI of Scotland became King James I of England, the text of the Bible, current in a variety of English translations, was a source of division among religious parties in England rather than a bond of unity. In order to reconcile differences among the various parties, the king called for a conference to be held in January 1604 at Hampton Court. Both bishops and Puritan clergy alike were invited to consult together on the subject of religious toleration.

Although the conference itself arrived at no conclusion on this or any other subject, King James, who had a personal interest in biblical study and translation, endorsed the idea of a new translation, stating that none of the existing English versions was translated well. Whatever his motives, James supported the project so vigorously that by July 1604 a translation committee of some fifty learned men and a list of rules of procedure had been provided, the first of which specified that the Bishops' Bible was to be followed and "as little altered as the truth of the original will admit".

James himself appears to have taken a leading role in organizing the work of the translation. Six panels of translators had the work divided among them; the Old Testament was allotted to three panels, the New Testament to two, and the Apocrypha to one. When any panel had finished the revision of a book, it was to be sent to all the rest for their criticism and suggestions, ultimate differences of opinion to be settled at a general meeting of the chief members of each panel.

The work, begun in 1607, had taken the incredibly short time of two years and nine months of strenuous toil to prepare for the press. The influence of this text on English literature has been enormous, indeed overwhelming at times. Barnstone writes: "It shaped the poetry of Milton as earlier versions had entered into the grandeur of Shakespeare's speech. No poet of stature after the seventeenth century has not been profoundly affected by its diction, syntax, and musical cadences, not to mention its content. Wordsworth and even free-speaking Shelley, pious though tormented Hopkins, profanely reverent Dylan Thomas, and T. S. Eliot after his conversion are more recent children of the King James Bible."

The following are excerpts from "The Translators to the Reader," preface to the King James Version of the Bible.

"Happy is the man that delighteth in the Scripture, and thrice happy that meditateth in it day and night.

But how shall men meditate in that which they cannot understand? How shall they understand that which is kept close in an unknown tongue? As it is written, '*Except I know the power of the voice, I shall be to him that speaketh a Barbarian, and he that speaketh shall be a Barbarian to me*'...Therefore as one complaineth that always in the Senate of Rome there was one or other that called for an interpreter; so lest the Church be driven to the like exigent, it is necessary to have translations in a readiness. Translation it is that openeth the window, to let in the light; that breaketh the shell, that we may eat the kernel; that putteth aside the curtain, that we may look into the most Holy place; that removeth the cover of the well, that we may come by the water, even as Jacob rolled away the stone from the mouth of the well, by which means the flocks of Laban were watered. Indeed without translation into the vulgar tongue, the unlearned are but like children at Jacob's well (which is deep) without a bucket or something to draw with; or that person mentioned by Isaiah, to whom when a sealed book was delivered, with the motion, '*Read this, I pray thee*', he was fain to make this answer, '*I cannot, for it is sealed*'.

...It is high time to leave them [earlier translators], and to show in brief what we proposed to ourselves, and what course we held in this our perusal and survey of the Bible. Truly (good Christian

Reader) we never thought from the beginning, that we should need to make a new Translation, nor yet to make of a bad one a good one...,but to make a good one better, or out of many good ones, one principal good one, not justly to be excepted against; that hath been our endeavor, that our mark.

...Another thing we think good to admonish thee of (gentle Reader) that we have not tied ourselves to an uniformity of phrasing, or to an identity of words, as some peradventure would wish that we had done, because they observe that some learned men somewhere have been as exact as they could that way. Truly, that we might not vary from the sense of that which we had translated before, if the word signified the same thing in both places (for there be some words that be not the same sense everywhere) we were especially careful, and made a conscience, according to our duty. But, that we should express the same notion in the same particular word; as for example, if we translate the Hebrew or Greek word once by *purpose*, never to call it *intent*; if one where *journeying*, never *traveling*; if one where *think*, never *suppose*; if one where *pain*, never *ache*; if one where *joy*, never *gladness*, etc. Thus to mince the matter, we thought to savour more of curiosity than wisdom, and that rather it would breed scorn in the Atheist, than bring profit to the godly Reader. For is the kingdom of God to become words or syllables? Why should we be in bondage to them if we may be free, use one precisely when we may use another no less fit, as commodiously?"

6 Exercises

(1) Compare the Bible translation with the Buddhist translation in China. What are the similarities and differences?

(2) Summarize Jerome's translation ideas.

(3) summarize Martin Luther's translation ideas.

7 References and Further Readings

(1) METZGER B M. The Bible in Translation [M]. Grand Rapids: Baker Academic, 2001.

(2) SCORGIE G G. et al. The Challenge of Bible Translation: Communicating God's Word to the World [M]. Grand Rapids: Zondervan, 2003.

Chapter Three

Translation Theory in Medieval and Renaissance Times

Anglo-Saxon England (450–1100) was the home to a vibrant literary culture which developed in the vernacular earlier than in most of medieval Europe. Writing came to Anglo-Saxon England with the conversion to Christianity, a culture of the book, initiated by Augustine's mission of 597. Early literary activity was mostly in Latin until King Alfred initiated a policy of translation, as he explains in the preface to his translation of Gregory's *Pastoral Care* below. Translation blossomed in late Anglo-Saxon England and reached a height in the works of Aelfric. Within such a culture of translation, there were multiple renditions of the Bible. A distinctive tradition of vernacular verse also developed in Anglo-Saxon England. While the most famous vernacular poem, *Beowulf*, is an original story rather than a translation, a similar style of verse was also used to retell incidents from the Bible, including the tower of Babel incident in Genesis.

1   King Alfred

In addition to being the most famous king of Wessex (871–899) and, arguably, the first king of a united England (that part, at least, which was not under Viking rule), King Alfred was also a significant translator in his own right and the initiator of a policy of translation. At a military level, Alfred's achievement involved fighting against the Vikings who had overrun most of the country until he finally reigned over a prosperous and expanding nation. At an educational level, his policy was spelled out in the preface to his translation of Gregory's *Pastoral Care*. Here the king initiated a programme both of translation and of vernacular education, recognizing that Latin learning had declined, aggravated by Viking assaults, to such an extent that it was now necessary to provide learning in the native tongue of his people.

Alfred began his project of translation with Gregory's *Pastoral Care*, presumably to educate and guide his bishops so that they could, in turn, educate the people. Gregory the Great (540–604) had a special resonance for the English as the pope who initiated Augustine's original mission to convert the country. Alfred's further contributions to those books most needful for all people to know comprise translations of Boethius' *Consolation of Philosophy*, Augustine's *Soliloquies*, and the first fifty Psalms, while his lawcode begins with a translation of Mosaic law. The king undertook such translations with the aid of a seminar of advisers gathered from outside his kingdom, as he outlined in the preface to Gregory's *Pastoral Care*. These advisers also produced other translations associated with Alfred's court, and probably the Old English translations of Bede's Ecclesiastical History and of the Martyrology. It is within this milieu, too, that the great work of original historical prose, *The Anglo-Saxon Chronicle*, was produced.

The text of the preface to Gregory's *Pastoral Care* below was translated from the edition by Dorothy Whitelock. The briefer preface to Boethius' *Consolation of Philosophy* shows more of the king's working method and outlines, in particular, his interesting treatment of the verse elements of the original prosimetrum. These he translated first into prose and subsequently versified from his own prose translation. The text is taken once again from the edition by Dorothy Whitelock in Sweet's *Anglo-Saxon Reader*.

The following is a paragraph taken from King Alfred's "Prose Preface" to his translation of *Gregory the Great's Cura Pastoralis*.

"When I recalled how the knowledge of Latin had declined before this throughout England, and yet many could read English writings, then I began among various and manifold cares of this kingdom to turn into English that book which is called in Latin *Pastoralis*, and in English *Shepherd-Book*, sometimes word for word, sometimes sense for sense."

The following is another paragraph taken from King Alfred's "Preface" to his Translation of Boethius' *Consolation of Philosophy*.

"King Alfred was the translator of this book and turned it from Latin into English, as it is now done. Sometimes he set it down word for word, sometimes sense for sense, just as he could relate it most clearly and most meaningfully in light of the various and manifold worldly cares which occupied him both in mind and body. Those cares are very difficult for us to count which occurred in his days in the kingdom which he had received, and yet, when he had understood this book and turned the substance from Latin into English, then he worked it over again into verse, as has now been done; and now he asks and in God's name beseeches each of those who desires to read this book to pray for him and not to blame him if they can understand it more rightly than he could, because every man must say what he says and do what he does in accordance with the measure of his understanding and in accordance to the time available to him."

② Aelfric

Aelfric (990–1010) was a monk of Cerne Abbas, Dorset, and (from 1005) abbot of Eynsham, a newly founded monastery in Oxfordshire. Aelfric was very concerned with the issue of translation: his most characteristic writings were homilies, which begin with a translation of a gospel pericope and continue with his own conspectus of commentary tradition, translated, combined, and augmented with original moral and topical exhortation. Aelfric showed a strong sensitivity to language, discussing in his homilies, for example, the special processes of signification of the real presence in the Eucharist. Such linguistic sensitivity along with his copious composition in the vernacular make Aelfric particularly qualified to pronounce upon the process of translation.

Aelfric's general practice is like that of Alfred. He declared repeatedly that he translated sense for sense, not always word for word. Furthermore, he desired rather to be clear and simple than to adorn his style with rhetorical ornament. Instead of unfamiliar terms, he used "the pure and open words of the language of this people." In connection with the translation of the Bible he laid down the principle that Latin must give way to English idiom. For all these things Aelfric had definite reasons. Keeping always in mind a clear conception of the nature of his audience, he did whatever seemed to him necessary to make his work attractive and, consequently, profitable. Preparing his Grammar for "tender youths," though he knew that words may be interpreted in many ways, he followed a simple method of interpretation in order that the book may not become tiresome. The Homilies, intended for simple people, are put into simple English, that they may more easily reach the hearts of those who read or hear.

The following excerpt is taken from Preface to Book I of *Catholic Homilies*.

"…However rashly or presumptuously undertaken, I have nevertheless formed this book out of Latin writers and from Holy Scripture, translating into our ordinary speech, for the edification of the simple, who know only this language both for reading and for hearing; and for that reason I have used no difficult words, but only plain English; so that our message might the more readily reach the hearts of those who read or hear, to the profit of the souls of those who cannot be taught in any other tongue than that to which they were born."

The following paragraph is taken from the preface to his *Excerptiones de Arte Grammatica Anglice* (conveniently known as Aelfric's Grammar):

"I, Aelfric, as one knowing little, have applied myself to translating into your language these excerpts from the lesser and greater Priscian for you tender little boys so that, having read through Donatus's eight parts of speech, you may in this book apply to your tenderness both languages, namely Latin and English, in the time until you reach more perfect studies. Now I know that many will blame me because I have desired to occupy my mind in such studies, namely turning the art of grammar into the English language, but I intend this text to be fitting for ignorant boys, not for their elders. I know it is possible to translate words in many ways but I follow a simple translation for the sake of avoiding putting off the reader. If, nevertheless, our translation displeases anyone, let him express it however he wants: we are content to express it just as we mastered it in the school of the venerable prelate, Aethelwold, who inspired many to good. It must be known, nevertheless, that the Ars Grammatica in many places does not easily receive translation into the English language as, for example, the parts about feet or metres, about which we here keep silent; but we have reckoned, nevertheless, this translation to be useful as a beginning for children, as we have said before."

③ Etienne Dolet

> Estienne Dolet (1509–1546) was a French humanist printer, translator, and scholar. He encouraged people to read the Bible in the vernacular and published many Calvinist works. Dolet's fame rests on his commentary on the Latin language (1536–1538). As a printer he published his own translations and editions of Classical authors, *The New Testament* and Psalms, as well as works by Francois Rabelais.

Etienne Dolet was one of the first writers to formulate a theory of translation. In 1540 Dolet published a short outline of translation principles, entitled *La Manière de Bien Traduire D'une Langue En Aultre* (The Way to Translate Well from One Language into Another) and established five principles for the translator.

Dolet's principles, ranked as they are in a precise order, stress the importance of *understanding* the SL text as a primary requisite. The translator is far more than a competent linguist, and translation involves both a scholarly and sensitive appraisal of the SL text and an awareness of the place the translation is intended to occupy in the TL system. The following is the main part of his essay on translation — *The Way to Translate Well from One Language into Another*.

"To translate well from one language into another requires in the main five things.

In the first place, the translator must understand perfectly the sense and matter of the author he is translating, for having this understanding he will never be obscure in his translations, and if the author he is translating is difficult in any way he will be able to render him easy and entirely understandable... It is important and necessary for every translator to fathom perfectly the sense of the author he is turning from one language into another. And without that he cannot translate reliably and faithfully.

The second thing that is required in translating is that the translator have perfect knowledge of the language of the author he is translating, and be likewise excellent in the language into which he is going to translate. In this way he will not violate or diminish the majesty of the one language or the other. Do you believe that a man can translate any of Cicero's orations well into French if he be not perfect in the Latin and French tongues? Bethink you that every language has its own properties, turns of phrase, expressions, subtleties, and vehemence that are peculiar to it. If the translator ignores the which, he does injustice to the author he is translating, and also to the language he is turning him into, for he does not represent or express the dignity and richness of the two tongues which he has taken in hand.

The third point is that in translating one must not be servile to the point of rendering word for word. And if someone does that, he is proceeding from poverty and lack of wisdom. For if he has the qualities aforesaid (which he needs in order to be a good translator), he will give thought to meanings without regarding the order of words, and set to work in such a way that the author's intention will be expressed while preserving precisely the property of the one and the other language. And it is too great a precision (or should I say stupidity, or ignorance?) to begin one's translation at the beginning of the sentence: if by changing the order of the words you can express the intention of him you are translating, no one can reprove you for it. Here I do not want to overlook the folly of some translators who submit to servitude in lieu of liberty. That is to say, they are so foolish as to make an effort to render line for line or verse for verse. By which mistake they often corrupt the sense of the author they are translating and do not express the grace and perfection of the one and the other language. You should diligently avoid this vice, which demonstrates nothing but the translator's ignorance.

The fourth rule, which I shall give at this place, is more to be observed in languages not reduced to an art than in others. Not yet reduced to a fixed and accepted art I call such languages as French,

Italian, Spanish, that of Germany, of England, and other vulgar tongues. Should it therefore happen that you translate a Latin book into one or another of these (even into French), you should avoid adopting words too close to Latin and little used in the past, but be content with the common tongue without introducing any new terms foolishly or out of reprehensible curiosity. If some do so, do not follow them in this, for their arrogance is of no worth, and is not tolerable among the learned. From this do not understand me to say that the translator should entirely abstain from words that are not in common use, for it is well known that the Greek and Latin languages are much richer in terms than is French. This often forces us to use rare words. But it should be done only out of sheer necessity. I am further well aware that some might say that most terms in the French language have been derived from the Latin, and that if our predecessors had the authority to introduce them, we moderns and our descendants may do the same. Let all that be debated by babblers, but the best thing is to follow the common tongue.

Let us now move on to the fifth rule that should be observed by a good translator, which is of such great import that lacking it any composition is ponderous and displeasing. But what does it consist of? Nothing other than the observation of rhetorical numbers: that is to say, a joining and arranging of terms with such sweetness that not alone the soul is pleased, but also the ear is delighted and never hurt by such harmony of language. I speak of these rhetorical numbers more copiously

in my *Orateur*; hence I shall not discourse of them further here. But here I do advise the translator to have a care for them, for without observing numbers one cannot be admirable in any composition whatsoever, and without them thoughts cannot be serious and have their required and legitimate weight. For do you think that it is enough to have correct and elegant terms without a good joining of them? I say to you that it is just as in a confused heap of various kinds of precious stones, which cannot display their luster because they are not properly arranged. Or just as when various musical instruments are badly played by performers who are ignorant of the art of music and know little of its tones and measures. In fine, there is little splendor in words if their order and pattern be not as it should be. And for that in times past the Greek orator Isocrates was esteemed above all, and likewise Demosthenes. Among the Latins Mark Tully Cicero was a great observer of numbers. But do not think that orators should observe them more than historiographers.

And that being true you will find that Caesar and Sallust kept their numbers no less than Cicero. The conclusion in this regard is that without closely observing numbers an author is nothing, and if he does observe them he cannot fail to become renowned for eloquence, providing he also is precise in his choice of words, serious in his thoughts, and ingenious in his arguments. These are the points of a perfect orator, one truly arrayed in all glory of eloquence."

4 George Chapman

Chapman (1559-1634) wrote much poetry and drama, but is best known for his translations of Homer, which remained the standard version at least until Pope's translation a century later--and a century after that, in 1815, it still inspired John Keats to write his famous sonnet, "On First Looking into Chapman's Homer". He published the first seven books of *The Iliad* in 1598, followed by the whole work (1611), the *Odyssey* (1614–1615) and *Homeric "Hymns"* (1616), as well as translations from Petrarch (1612), Musaeus (1616), Hesiod (1618), and Juvenal (1629).

Keats's resonant sonnet is of interest, taking Chapman at his word, and testifying to the translation's enduring freshness and originality.

> Oft of one wide expanse had I been told
>
> That deep-brow'd Homer ruled as his demesne;
>
> Yet did I never breathe its pure serene
>
> Till I heard Chapman speak out loud and bold:
>
> Then felt I like some watcher of the skies
>
> When a new planet swims into his ken…

Chapman's observations on translation in the verse preface to the 1611 Iliad, "To the Reader," hardly describe his method, but embody a passionate defense of Homer and a defiant attack on the translator's detractors. Chapman's insistence on non-literalism makes it clear that accusations of inaccuracy were a staple of criticism. As regards his tendency to elaborate, Chapman pointed to his predecessors. Only poetic license or inspiration can help in the translation of poetry. He did not argue but simply affirmed the appropriateness of the fourteener (fourteen-syllable line). Regarding the use of fourteeners in the Iliad as against pentametric couplets in the *Odyssey*, the longer line works well enough if the enjambments, varying the otherwise jog-trot alternation of 4-stress 3-stress hemistiches, are carefully observed.

Chapman translated directly from the original, with errors due to ignorance or haste. He vindicated his "varietie of new words." If "my country language were a usurer, he would thank me for enriching him." He dismisses Scaliger, the greatest Classical scholar of the time, as "soul-blind Scaliger," and compares Virgil and Homer to the disadvantage of the former, Homer's poem being "writ from a free fury," whereas Virgil's comes out of a "courtly, laborious, and altogether imitatory spirit."

In his dedication of the *Seven Books* (1598) Chapman declared:

"The work of a skillful and worthy translator is to observe the sentences, figures and formes of speech proposed in his author, his true sence and height, and to adorn them with figures and formes of oration fitted to the original in the same tongue to which they are translated: and these things I would gladlie have made the questions of whatsoever my labours have deserved."

Chapman repeated his theory more fully in the *Epistle to the Reader* of his translation of *The Iliad*. He stated that a translator must:

(1) avoid word for word renderings; (2) attempt to reach the "spirit" of the original; (3) avoid overloose translations, by basing the translation on a sound scholarly investigation of other versions and glosses.

The Platonic doctrine of the divine inspiration of poetry clearly had repercussions for the translator, in that it was deemed possible for the "spirit" or "tone" of the original to be recreated in another cultural context. The translator, therefore, is seeking to bring about a "transmigration" of the original text, which he approaches on both a technical and metaphysical level, as a skilled equal with duties and responsibilities both to the original author and the audience.

5 Exercises

(1) Compare Dolet's translation principles with Yan Fu's translation criteria. What are the similarities and differences?

(2) Why do King Alfred's translation ideas vary in different translations?

6 References and Further Readings

(1) METZGER B M. The Oxford History of Literary Translation in English [M]. London: Oxford University Press, 2008.

(2) WEISSBORT D, EYSTEINSSON A. Translation — Theory and Practice [M]. London: Oxford University Press, 2006.

Chapter Four

John Dryden's Translation Theory

① An Introduction to Dryden

John Dryden (1631–1700) was an influential English poet, literary critic, translator, and playwright who dominated the literary life of Restoration England (1660–1688) to such a point that the period came to be known in literary circles as the Age of Dryden.

Dryden was the dominant literary figure and influence of his age. He established the heroic couplet as the standard meter of English poetry, by writing successful satires, religious pieces, fables, epigrams, compliments, prologues, and plays in it; he also introduced the Alexandrine (a line of English verse composed in iambic hexameter) and triplet into the form. In his poems, translations, and criticism, he established a poetic diction appropriate to the heroic couplet that was a model for his contemporaries and for much of the 18th century. Dryden's heroic couplet became the dominant poetic form of the 18th century.

Dryden was born at the vicarage of Aldwinkle, Northamptonshire, on August 9, 1631. He attended Westminster School, and was an avid student of the classics. He entered Trinity College, Cambridge, in 1650, and took a BA in 1654.

Dryden moved to London around 1657, and first gained notice with his *Heroic Stanzas* (1659) on the death of Lord Protector Cromwell. In 1662, Dryden wrote verses *To My Lord Chancellor Clarendon*, and was elected to the Royal Society. The theatres had been reopened, demand for entertainments was high, and Dryden set to writing plays. His first play was the prose comedy of humors *A Wild Gallant* (1663), a wholly unremarkable piece, followed by the tragicomedy *The Rival Ladies* (1664) and *The Indian Queen* (1664).

In 1668, Dryden began a fruitful period of both critical and dramatic writing. His first major critical work was the *Essay of Dramatic Poesy* (1668), followed by *A Defence of an Essay* (1668), and *Essay of Heroic Plays* (1672). His plays from this period include the

comedy *Secret Love* (1667); the heroic drama *Tyrannic Love* (1669).

Dryden's writings on translation are best considered not as a fixed body of theory or doctrine, but as the working notes of a practitioner, based on broad principles established early in his translating career, but continually modified, enriched, and transformed by subsequent discoveries and challenges in the field. Dryden's translations, from the classical poets Homer, Horace, Juvenal, Lucretius, Ovid, Persius, Virgil, and Theocritus, and from the medieval writers Chaucer and Boccaccio, constitute about two-thirds of his non-dramatic verse. They are the poet's main source of income in the last decade of his life, and are widely regarded, for well over a hundred years after his death, as the crown of his creative achievement. Dryden was, by inclination, an "occasional" translator, who preferred to select poems and passages which had "affected" him with a particular vividness and urgency "in the reading," or to whose authors he felt he had a "soul congenial." (His version of the works of Virgil — his only attempt at rendering another author's oeuvre in its entirety, and the only one of his translations about which he expresses any weariness or misgivings — is the exception which proves the rule). Dryden's translations reveal him constantly (in T. S. Eliot's words) "giving the original through himself and finding himself through the original." A study of Dryden's translating practice is thus, necessarily and simultaneously, a study of the poet's imaginative communings with a number of his favorite fellow-writers.

② Dryden's Translation Ideas

Dryden's main reflections on translation are to be found in the prefaces and dedicatory epistles prefixed to the various miscellanies and collections in which his versions appeared between 1680 and 1700. These discussions focus on a number of recurring questions and preoccupations: the kinds of knowledge that any successful translator needs to possess; the kind of fidelity to his original which he should seek; the ways in which he might best preserve the distinctive "character" of each of their originals; the degree to which he might properly add to, subtract from, or "update" material in his original; the larger contribution which translation might make to the culture and language of the nation. In the "Preface to *Ovid's Epistles*" (1680), Dryden proposed his celebrated tripartite division of translation into 'metaphrase,' 'paraphrase,' and "imitation." He said it like this:

"All translation, I suppose, may be reduced to these three heads.

First, that of metaphrase or turning an author word by word and line by line, from one language into another. Thus, or near this manner, was Horace his *Art of Poetry* translated by Ben Johnson. The second way is that of paraphrase, or translation with latitude, where the author is kept in view by the translator so as never to be lost, but his words are not so strictly followed as his sense, and that too is admitted to be amplified, but not altered. Such is Mr. Waller's translation of Virgil's Fourth *Aeneid*. The third way is that of imitation, where the translator (if now he has not lost that name) assumes the liberty not only to vary from the words and sense, but to forsake them both as he sees occasion, and taking only some general hints from the original, to run division on the groundwork as he pleases. Such is Mr. Cowley's practice in turning two Odes of Pindar, and one of Horace, into English."

"Metaphrase" is rejected on the grounds that it produces versions of such crabbed awkwardness that they can give little idea of the artistic quality of their originals. He pointed out the hazards of metaphrase as follows:

"'Tis almost impossible to translate verbally and well at the same time; for the Latin (a most severe and compendious language) often expresses that in one word which either the barbarity or the narrowness of modern tongues cannot supply in more… The verbal copier is encumbered with so many difficulties at once that he can never disentangle himself from all. He is to consider at the same time the thought of his author and his words, and to find out the counterpart to each in another language; and besides this, he is to confine himself to the compass of numbers, and the slavery of rhyme. 'Tis much like dancing on ropes with fettered legs: a man may shun a fall by using caution; but the gracefulness of motion is not to be expected: and when we have said the best of it, 'tis but a foolish task; for no sober man would put himself into a danger for the applause of 'scaping without breaking his neck."

Imitation is criticized because of an excessive freedom which makes it more properly regarded as original poetry than translation. The following is his concept about imitation:

"I take imitation of an author to be an endeavor of a later poet to write like one who has written before him, on the same subject; that is, not to translate his words, or to be confined to his sense, but only to set him as a pattern, and to write, as he supposes that author would have done, had he lived in our age, and in our country…'Tis no longer to be called their work, when neither the thoughts nor words are drawn from the original; but instead of them there is something new produced, which is almost the creation of another hand…Yet he who is inquisitive to know an author's thoughts will be disappointed in his expectation. And 'tis not always that a man will be content to have a present made him, when he expects the payment of a debt. To state it fairly: imitation of an author is the most advantageous way for a translator to show himself, but the greatest wrong which can be done to the memory and reputation of the dead…Imitation and verbal version are, in my opinion, the two extremes which ought to be avoided."

Of these types Dryden chose the second as the more balanced path. "Paraphrase" — translation in which the contours of the original are attentively observed, but with a freedom which allows the translator to convey the "spirit" and "sense" rather than merely the "letter" of the original -- is offered as the ideal via media between the two extremes. To translate poetry, Dryden argued, the translator must be a poet, must be a master of both languages, and must understand both the characteristics and "spirit" of the original author, besides conforming to the aesthetic canons of his own age. He used the metaphor of the translator/portrait painter, which was to reappear so frequently in the 18th century, maintaining that the painter has the duty of making his portrait resemble the original.

"No man is capable of translating poetry who, besides a genius to that art, is not a master both of his author's language and of his own. Nor must we understand the language only of the poet, but his particular turn of thoughts and of expression, which are the characters that distinguish, and, as it were, individuate him from all other writers. When we are come thus far, 'tis time to look into ourselves, to conform our genius to his, to give his thought either the same turn, if our tongue will bear it, or, if not, to vary but the dress, not to alter or destroy the substance. The like care must be taken of the more outward ornaments, the words. When they appear (which is but seldom) literally graceful, it were an injury to the author that they should be changed. But since every language is so full of its own proprieties, that what is beautiful in one is often barbarous, nay sometimes nonsense, in another, it would be unreasonable to limit a translator to the narrow compass of his author's words: 'tis enough if he choose out some expression which does not vitiate the sense. I suppose he may stretch his chain to such a latitude; but by innovation of thoughts, methinks he breaks it. By this means the spirit of an author may be transfused, and yet not lost: and thus 'tis plain that the reason alleged by Sir John Denham has no farther force than to expression; for thought, if it be translated truly, cannot be lost in another language; but the words that convey it to our apprehension (which are the image and ornament of that thought) may be so ill chosen as to make it appear in an unhandsome dress, and rob it of its native lustre. There is therefore a liberty to be allowed for the expression, neither is it necessary that words and lines should be confined to the measure of their original. The sense of an author, generally speaking, is to be sacred and inviolable."

Dryden broadly adhered to "paraphrase" throughout his translating career, but his later prefaces and practice reveal him constantly modifying his theory both in details (elements of "metaphrase" and "imitation" are frequently incorporated piecemeal at the local level) and in larger responses to specific challenges posed by particular writers. In "The Preface to *Sylvae*" (1685), Dryden, buoyed up with confidence by the "hot fit" of activity which had recently produced his masterly renderings of Lucretius, Horace, and Virgil, claimed the right to exercise a greater degree of freedom than he had exercised hitherto, in order to produce translations which, if his original "were living, and Englishman... are such as he would probably have written." And when preparing his versions of the

highly allusive and topical Roman satirists Juvenal and Persius, Dryden clearly became convinced that further liberties were necessary if his versions were to convey to cultivated English readers a comprehensible and vivid impression of the pointed and acerbic wit which characterized his originals. The following is an excerpt from his "The Preface to *Sylvae*" (1685).

"I have both added and omitted, and even sometimes very boldly made such expositions of my authors, as no Dutch commentator will forgive me. Perhaps, in such particular passages, I have thought that I discovered some beauty yet undiscovered by those pedants, which none but a poet could have found. Where I have taken away some of their expressions, and cut them shorter, it may possibly be on this consideration, that what was beautiful in the Greek or Latin would not appear so shining in the English: and where I have enlarged them, I desire the false critics would not always think that those thoughts are wholly mine, but that either they are secretly in the poet, or may be fairly deduced from him: or at least, if both those considerations should fail, that my own is of a piece with his, and that if he were living, and an Englishman, they are such as he would probably have written.

For, after all, a translator is to make his author appear as charming as possibly he can, provided he maintains his character, and makes him not unlike himself. Translation is a kind of drawing after the life; where everyone will acknowledge there is a double sort of likeness, a good one and a bad. 'Tis one thing to draw the outlines true, the features like, the proportions exact, the coloring itself perhaps tolerable; and another thing to make all these graceful by the posture, the shadowing, and chiefly by the spirit which animates the whole. I cannot without some indignation look on an ill copy of an excellent original; much less can I behold with patience Virgil, Homer, and some others, whose beauties I have been endeavoring all my life to imitate, so abused, as I may say to their faces, by a botching interpreter. What English readers, unacquainted with Greek or Latin, will believe me, or any other man, when we commend those authors, and confess we derive all that is pardonable in us from their fountains, if they take those to be the same poets whom our Ogilbys have translated? But I dare assure them that a good poet is no more like himself in a dull translation, than his carcass would be to his living body. There are many who understand Greek and Latin, and yet are ignorant of their mother tongue. The proprieties and delicacies of the English are known to few; 'tis impossible even for a good wit to understand and practise them, without the help of a liberal education, long reading, and digesting of those few good authors we have amongst us, the knowledge of men and manners, the freedom of habitudes and conversation with the best company of both sexes; and, in short, without wearing off the rust which he contracted while he was laying in a stock of learning."

In the same Preface, Dryden also stressed the importance of maintaining the character and style of the original in translations:

"Thus it appears necessary that a man should be a nice critic in his mother tongue before attempts to translate a foreign language. Neither is it sufficient that he be able to judge of words and style; but he must be a master of them too. He must perfectly understand his author's tongue, and absolutely command his own; so that to be a thorough translator, he must be a thorough poet. Neither is it enough to give his author's sense in good English, in poetical expressions, and in musical numbers. For, although all these are exceeding difficult to perform, there yet remains a harder task; and 'tis a secret of which few translators have sufficiently thought. I have already hinted a word or two concerning it; that is, the maintaining the character of an author, which distinguishes him from all others, and makes him appear that individual poet whom you would interpret. For example, not only the thoughts, but the style and versification of Virgil and Ovid are very different. Yet I see, even in our best poets who have translated some parts of them, that they have confounded their several talents; and by endeavoring only at the sweetness and harmony of numbers, have made them both so much alike that, if I did not know the originals, I should never be able to judge by the copies which was Virgil and which was Ovid. It was objected to a late noble painter, that he drew many graceful pictures, but few of them were like. And this happened to him because he always studied himself more than those who sat to him. In such translators I can easily distinguish the hand which performed the work, but I cannot distinguish their poet from another."

In the Preface to his translation of *Aeneid*, Dryden compared the translator to a slave, who could only labor on others' plantation and had to accept the fact that the wine brewed belonged to his master. "But slaves we are, and labor on another man's plantation; we dress the vineyard, but the wine is the owner's; if the soil be sometimes barren, then we are sure of being scourged: if it be fruitful, and our care succeeds, we are not thanked; for the proud reader will only say, the poor drudge has done his duty. But this is nothing to what follows; for being obliged to make his sense intelligible, we are forced to untune our own verses, that we may give his meaning to the reader. He who invents is master of his thoughts and words; he can turn and vary them as he pleases, till he renders them harmonious; but the wretched translator has no such privilege; for being tied to the thoughts, he must make what music he can in the expression; and, for this reason, it cannot always be so sweet as the original."

③ Exercises

(1) Summarize Dryden's tripartite division of translation. What are the major features of each type?

(2) Compare the following translation versions of Li Qingzhao's ci-poem "声声慢" and classify them into the three categorie — metaphrase, paraphrase and imitation.

The original text: 寻寻觅觅，冷冷清清，凄凄惨惨戚戚。

Translation versions:

1) Seek-seek, search-search, cold-cold, quiet-quiet, sad-sad, sorrowful-sorrowful, grieved-grieved. (刘若愚)

2) Search. Search. Seek. Seek. Cold. Cold. Clear. Clear. Sorrow. Sorrow. Pain. Pain. (王红公)

3) Seek, seek. Search, search. Cold, cold. Empty, empty. Misery, misery. Sorrow, sorrow. Sadness, sadness. (茅于美)

4) Seeking, seeking, Chilly and quiet, Desolate, painful and miserable. (戴乃迭)

5) I look for what I miss; / I know not what it is.

I feel so sad, so drear, / so lonely, without cheer. (许渊冲)

6) So dim, so dark, so dense, so dull, so damp, so dank, so dead! (林语堂)

(3) To translate verbally is "much like dancing on ropes with fettered legs: a man may shun a fall by using caution; but the gracefulness of motion is not to be expected: and when we have said the best of it, 'tis but a foolish task; for no sober man would put himself into a danger for the applause of 'scaping without breaking his neck." How do you understand this remark?

(4) Do you agree with Dryden's argument that the translator is but a slave who could only labor on others' plantation? Why or why not?

④ References and Further Readings

(1) SCHULTE R. Theories of Translation: An Anthology of Essays from Dryden to Derrida [M]. Chicago: The University of Chicago Press, 1992

(2) FROST W. Dryden and the Art of Translation [M]. New Haven: Yale University Press, 1955.

(3) WINN J A. John Dryden and His World [M]. New Haven: Yale University Press, 1987.

Chapter Five

Alexander Fraser Tytler and *Essay on the Principles of Translation*

① An Introduction to Tytler

Alexander Fraser Tytler (1747–1813) was a Scottish-born British lawyer and writer. Tytler was also a historian, and for some years was Professor of Universal History, and Greek and Roman Antiquities, in the University of Edinburgh.

Tytler was born in Edinburgh on October 15, 1747, went to the High School there, and after two years at Kensington entered Edinburgh University.

It was in 1790 that Tytler read in the Royal Society his papers on Translation, which were published soon afterwards, without his name. Hardly had the work seen the light, when it led to a critical correspondence with Dr. Campbell, then Principal of Marischal College, Aberdeen. Dr. Campbell had at some time previous to this published his translations of the Gospels, to which he had prefixed some observations upon the principles of translation. When Tytler's anonymous work appeared he was led to express some suspicion that the author might have borrowed from his dissertation, without acknowledging the obligation. Thereupon Tytler instantly wrote to Dr. Campbell, acknowledging himself to be the author, and assuring him that the coincidence, such as it was, "was purely accidental, and that the name of Dr. Campbell's work had never reached him until his own had been composed... There seems to me no wonder," he continued, "that two persons, moderately conversant in critical occupations, sitting down professedly to investigate the principles of this art, should hit upon the same principles, when in fact there are none other to hit upon, and the truth of these is acknowledged at their first enunciation. But in truth, the merit of this little essay (if it has any) does not, in my opinion, lie in these particulars. It lies in the establishment of those various subordinate rules and precepts which apply to the nicer parts and difficulties of the art of translation; in deducing those rules and precepts which carry not their own authority *in gremto*, from the general principles which are of acknowledged truth, and in proving and illustrating them by examples."

Mr. Tytler's essay attained a rapid and extraordinary celebrity. Complimentary letters flowed in upon its author from many of the most eminent men in England; and the book speedily came to be considered a standard work in English criticism. Mr. Tytler had now attained nearly the highest pinnacle of literary repute. His name was widely known, and was in every case associated with esteem for his worth, and admiration of his talents.

Tytler died on the January 5, 1813, in the 66th year of his age; leaving a name which will not soon be forgotten, and a reputation for taste, talent, and personal worth, which will not often be surpassed.

② Tytler's *Essay on the Principles of Translation*

In English, perhaps the first systematic study of translation is Alexander Fraser Tytler's *Essay on the Principles of Translation* (1790), which was "throughout the nineteenth century, and far into the twentieth, the best known and most read of books in English on the nature of translation," as James S. Holmes observed in the introduction to his shortened version of Tytler's *Essay on the Principles of Translation, Modern Poetry in Translation.*

Tytler's book is divided into 15 chapters. In Chapter 1, Tytler gives his definition of "a good translation" as follows:

"If it were possible accurately to define, or, perhaps more properly, to describe what is meant by *a good translation*, it is evident that a considerable progress would be made towards establishing the rules of the *art*; for these rules would flow naturally from that definition or description. But there is no subject of criticism on which there has been so much difference of opinion. If the genius and character of all languages were the same, it would be an easy task to translate from one into another; nor would anything more be requisite on the part of the translator than fidelity and attention. But as the genius and character of languages are confessedly very different, two opinions have thence arisen regarding the proper task of a translator. On the one hand, it has been affirmed that it is the duty of a translator to attend only to the sense and spirit of his original, to make himself perfectly master of his author's ideas, and to communicate them in those expressions which he judges to be best suited to convey them. It has, on the other hand, been maintained that, in order to constitute a perfect translation, it is not only requisite that the ideas and sentiments of the original author should be conveyed, but likewise his style and manner of writing, which, it is supposed, cannot be done without a strict attention to the arrangement of his sentences, and even to their order and construction. According to the former idea of translation, it is allowable to improve and to embellish; according to the latter, it is necessary to preserve even blemishes and defects; and to these must be likewise be superadded the harshness that must attend every copy in which the artist scrupulously studies to imitate the minutest lines or traces of his original.

As these two opinions form two opposite extremes, it is not improbable that the point of perfection should be found between the two. I would therefore describe a good translation to be, *That in which the merit of the original work is so completely transfused into another language as to be as distinctly apprehended, and as strongly felt, by a native of the country to which that language belongs as it is by those who speak the language of the original work.*"

He then presents the laws of translation which may be deduced from it:

(1) That the Translation should give a complete transcript of the ideas of the original work.

(2) That the style and manner of writing should be of the same character with that of the original.

(3) That the translation should have all the ease of original composition.

Chapters 2 to 4 are devoted to the discussion of the first rule, while Chapters 5 to 8 the second rule, and Chapters 9 to 15 the third rule.

I The First Principle

"In order that a translator may be enabled to give a transcript of the ideas of the original work, it is indispensably necessary that he should have a perfect knowledge of the language of the original, and a competent acquaintance with the subject of which it treats. If he is deficient in either of these requisites, he can never be certain of thoroughly comprehending the sense of his author...

Where the sense of an author is doubtful, and where more than one meaning can be given to the same passage or expression, (which, by the way, is always a defect in composition), the translator is called upon to exercise his judgement, and to select that meaning which is most consonant to the train of thought in the whole passage, or to the author's usual mode of thinking, and of expressing himself. To imitate the obscurity or ambiguity of the original is a fault; and it is till a greater, tp give more than one meaning...

If it is necessary that the translator should give a complete transcript of the ideas of the original work, it becomes a question, whether it is allowable in any case to add to the ideas of the original what may appear to give greater force or illustration; or to take from them what may seem to weaken them from redundancy.

To give a general answer to this question, I would say, that this liberty may be used, but with the greatest caution. It must be further observed, that the superadded idea shall have the most necessary connection with the original thought, and actually increase its force. And, on the other hand, that whenever an idea is cut off by the translator, it must only be such as is an accessory, and not a principal in the clause or sentence. It must likewise be confessedly redundant, so that its retrenchment shall not impair or weaken the original thought.

Analogous to this liberty of adding to or retrenching from the ideas of the original, is the liberty which a translator may take of correcting what appears to him a careless or inaccurate expression of the original, where that inaccuracy seems materially to affect the sense.

I conceive it to be the duty of a poetical translator, never to suffer his original to fall. He must maintain with him a perpetual contest of genius; he must attend him in his highest flights, and soar, if he can, beyond him; and when he perceives, at any time, a diminution of his powers, when he sees a drooping wing, he must raise him on his own pinions. Homer has been judged by the best critics to fall at times beneath himself, and to offend, by introducing low images and puerile allusions. Yet how admirably is this defect veiled over, or altogether removed, by his translator Pope.

It is always a fault when the translator adds to the sentiment of the original author, what does not strictly accord with his characteristic mode of thinking, or expressing himself."

II The Second Principle

"Next in importance to a faithful transfusion of the sense and meaning of an author, is an assimilation of the style and manner of writing in the translation to that of the original. This requisite of a good translation, though but secondary in importance, is more difficult to be attained than the former; for the qualities requisite for justly discerning and happily imitating the various characters of style and manner, are much rarer than the ability of simply understanding an author's sense. A good translator must be able to discover at once the true character of his author's style. He must ascertain with precision to what class it belongs; whether to that of the grave, the elevated, the easy, the lively, the florid and ornamented, or the simple and unaffected; and these characteristic qualities he must have the capacity of rendering equally conspicuous in the translation as in the original. If a translator fails in this discernment, and wants this capacity, let him be ever so thoroughly master of the sense of his author, he will present him through a distorting medium, or exhibit him often in a garb that is unsuitable to his character.

But a translator may discern the general character of his author's style, and yet fail remarkably in the imitation of it. Unless he is possessed of the most correct taste, he will be in continual danger of presenting an exaggerated picture or a caricature of his original. The distinction between good and bad writing is often of so very slender a nature, and the shadowing of difference so extremely delicate, that a very nice perception alone can at all times define its limit. Thus, in the hands of some translators, who have the discernment to perceive the general character of their author's style, but want this correctness of taste, the grave style of the original becomes heavy and formal in the translation; the elevated swells into bombast, the lively froths up into the petulant, and the simple and naif degenerates into the childish and insipid.

From all the preceding observations respecting the imitation of style, we may derive this precept that a translator ought always to figure to himself, in what manner the original author would have expressed himself, if he had written in the language of the translation."

III The Third Principle

"It remains now that we consider the third general law of translation. In order that the merit of the original work may be so completely transfused as to produce its full effect, it is necessary, not only that the translation should contain a perfect transcript of the sentiments of the original, and present likewise a resemblance of its style and manner; but, that the translation should have all the ease of original composition.

When we consider those restraints within which a translator finds himself necessarily confined, with regard to the sentiments and manner of his original, it will soon appear that this last requisite includes the most difficult part of his task. To one who walks in trammels, it is not easy to exhibit an air of grace and freedom. It is difficult, even for a capital painter, to preserve in a copy of a picture all the ease and spirit of the original; yet the painter employs precisely the same colors, and has no other care than faithfully to imitate the touch and manner of the picture that is before him. If the original is easy and graceful, the copy will have the same qualities, in proportion as the imitation is just and perfect. The translator's task is very different: he uses not the same colors with the original, but is required to give his picture the same force and effect. He is not allowed to copy the touches of the original, yet is required, by touches of his own, to produce a perfect resemblance. The more he studies a scrupulous imitation, the less his copy will reflect the ease and spirit of the original. How then shall a translator accomplish this difficult union of ease with fidelity? To use a bold expression, he must adopt the very soul of his author, which must speak through his own organs.

If the order in which I have classed the three general laws of translation is their just and natural arrangement, which I think will hardly be denied, it will follow, that in all cases where a sacrifice is necessary to be made of one of those laws to another, a due regard ought to be paid to their rank and comparative importance. The different genius of the languages of the original and translation will often make it necessary to depart from the manner of the original, in order to convey a faithful picture of the sense; but it would be highly preposterous to depart, in any case, from the sense, for the sake of imitating the manner. Equally improper would it be, to sacrifice either the sense or manner of the original, if these can be preserved consistently with purity of expression, to a fancied ease or superior gracefulness of composition.

If a translator is bound, in general, to adhere with fidelity to the manners of the age and country to which his original belongs, there are some instances in which he will find it necessary to make a slight sacrifice to the manners of his modern readers. The ancients, in the expression of resentment or contempt, made use of many epithets and appellations which sound extremely shocking to our more polished ears, because we never hear them employed but by the meanest and most degraded of the populace. By similar reasoning we must conclude that those expressions conveyed no such mean or shocking ideas to the ancients, since we find them used by the most dignified and exalted characters."

In *Essay on the Principles of Translation*, Tytler also discusses the translation of poetry, arguing that "none but a poet can translate a poet."

"Whether a poem can be well translated into prose?

There are certain species of poetry, of which the chief merit consists in the sweetness and melody of the versification. Of these it is evident, that the very essence must perish in translating them into prose.

But a great deal of the beauty of every regular poem consists in the melody of its numbers. Sensible of this truth, many of the prose translators of poetry have attempted to give a sort of measure to their prose, which removes it from the nature of ordinary language.

If this measure is uniform and its return regular, the composition is no longer prose, but blank verse. If it is not uniform, and does not regularly return upon the ear, the composition will be more unharmonious, than if the measure had been entirely neglected. Of this, Mr. Macpherson's translation of *The Iliad* is a strong example.

But it is not only by the measure that poetry is distinguishable from prose. It is by the character of its thoughts and sentiments, and by the nature of that language in which they are clothed. A boldness of figures, a luxuriancy of imagery, a frequent use of metaphors, a quickness of transition, a liberty of digressing; all these are not only *allowable* in poetry, but to many species of it, *essential*. But they are quite unsuitable to the character of prose. When seen in a *prose translation*, they appear preposterous and out of place, because they are never found in an *original prose composition*.

The difficulty of translating poetry into prose is different in its degree, according to the nature or species of the poem. Didactic poetry, of which the principal merit consists in the detail of a regular system, or in rational precepts which flow from each other in a connected train of thought, will evidently suffer least by being transfused into prose. But every didactic poet judiciously enriches his work with such ornaments as are not strictly attached to his subject. In a prose translation of such a poem, all that is strictly systematic or receptive may be transfused with propriety; all the rest, which belongs to embellishment, will be found impertinent and out of place.

But there are certain species of poetry, of the merits of which it will be found impossible to convey the smallest idea in a prose translation. Such is Lyric poetry, where a greater degree of irregularity of thought, and a more unrestrained exuberance of fancy, is allowable than in any other species of composition. To attempt, therefore, a translation of a lyric poem into prose, is the most absurd of all undertakings; for those very characters of the original which are essential to it, and which constitute its highest beauties, if transferred to a prose translation, become unpardonable blemishes. The excursive range of the sentiments, and the play of fancy, which we admire in the original, degenerate in the translation into mere raving and impertinence.

We may certainly, from the foregoing observations, conclude that it is impossible to do complete justice to any species of poetical composition in a prose translation; in other words, that none but a poet can translate a poet."

Moreover, Tytler expounds the difficulty in the translation of idioms:

"While a translator endeavors to give to his work all the ease of original composition, the chief difficulty he has to encounter will be found in the translation of idioms, or those turns of expression which do not belong to universal grammar, but of which every language has its own, that are exclusively proper to it...

The translation is perfect, when the translator finds in his own language an idiomatic phrase corresponding to that of the original.

As there is nothing which so much conduces both to the ease and spirit of composition, as a happy use of idiomatic phrases, there is nothing which a translator, who has a moderate command of his own language, is so apt to carry to a licentious extreme.

In the use of idiomatic phrases, a translator frequently forgets both the country of his original author, and the age in which he wrote; and while he makes a Greek or a Roman speak French or English, he unwittingly puts into his mouth allusions to the manners of modern France or England...

A translator will often meet with idiomatic phrases in the original author, to which no corresponding idiom can be found in the language of the translation. As a literal translation of such phrases cannot be tolerated, the only source is, to express the sense in plain and easy language.

But this resource, of translating the idiomatic phrase into easy language must fail, where the merit of the passage to be translated actually lies in that expression which is idiomatical. This will often occur in epigrams, many of which are therefore incapable of translation..."

③ Exercises

(1) Please summarize Tytler's three principles of translation and make a brief comment on them.

(2) Why does Tytler argue that "none but a poet can translate a poet"? Do you agree with him? Why or why not?

(3) Compare Tytler's translation principles with Yan Fu's and find their similarities and differences.

④ References and Further Readings

(1) TYTLER A F. Essay on the Principles of Translation [M]. Amsterdam: John Benjamins Publishing Co., 1813.

(2) WEISSBORT D. Translation—Theory and Practice [M]. London: Oxford University Press, 2006.

(3) 罗书肆. 介绍泰特勒的翻译理论 [M] // 外国翻译理论评介文集. 北京: 中国对外翻译出版公司, 1983.

Chapter Six

Translation Theory in Germany: Goethe and Schleiermacher

Several of the key statements of the 19th-century philosophy and policy of translation were made by German scholars and writers who were, in one way or another, active in the period. Their texts were clearly linked to recent and contemporary practice of translation into German (especially translations of the Homeric epics, the Greek tragedies, and Shakespeare's plays), but they also made their mark as theoretical pronouncements both in and beyond the German sphere, especially some of Goethe's statements and Schleiermacher's *Different Methods of Translating*.

① Johann Wolfgang von Goethe

Johann Wolfgang von Goethe (1749–1832), pre-eminent German poet and writer, was also a lawyer, politician, civil servant, botanist, zoologist, physicist, painter, theatre manager, and literary critic. Author of *Faust, Die Leiden des jungen Werthers* (*The Sufferings of Young Werther*), *Iphigenie auf Tauris, Wilhelm Meisters Lehrjahre* (*Wilhelm Meister's Apprenticeship*), and several celebrated poems, Goethe is one of the most important European writers of his time, both as a master of many genres, and as someone who is instrumental in the whole crucible of movements and counter-movements: from *Sturm und Drang* (storm and stress) and early Romantic revolt against the rationalism of the Enlightenment, toward a reevaluation of Classicism and Humanism, along with the development of Romanticism. Goethe towers over German culture and literature like Dante over the Italian, Shakespeare over the English, Pushkin over the Russian -- and the fact that he paused her and there in his 133 volumes of collected works to remark upon translation hes helped make the German theoretical tradition one of the world's richest bodies of work in the field.

The following are three comments of Goethe on translation.

From *Dichtung und Wahrheit* (1811–1814):

"Wieland's translation [of Shakespeare] appeared. It was devoured, shared with and recommended to friends and acquaintances. We Germans had the advantage that many important works of foreign nations were first translated in a light and bantering vein. The translations of Shakespeare in prose, first Wieland's, then [Johann Joachim] Eschenburg's, could quickly spread as reading matter. They were generally intelligible and suited to the common reader. I honor both rhythm and rhyme, through which poetry become poetry indeed, but what is really deeply and thought operative, what really shapes and improves, is what is left of a poet when he has been translated into prose. What remains then is the pure, perfect essence which a blinding exterior often succeeds in deluding us with when it is not there, and in hiding when it is. That is why I think translations into prose are more advantageous than translations into verse in the first stages of education; one can see that boys, who turn everything into a joke, make fun of the sound of words, the fall of syllables, and destroy the deep essence of the noblest work out of a certain sense of parodistic devilry. I should therefore like you to consider whether we are not in need of a prose translation of Homer; it should, of course, be worthy of the level that German literature has reached by now. I leave this and what I said before to the consideration of our worthy pedagogues who can rely on extensive experience in this matter. I simply want to remind you of Luther's Bible translation as an argument in favor of my proposal. That this excellent man offered us in our mother tongue, and as it were in one piece, a work written in the most different styles, as well as its poetic, historical, imperative, didactic tone, has helped religion more than if he had aspired to recreate the idiosyncrasies of that original down to the smallest detail. Later translators have tried in vain to make us enjoy the book of Job, the Psalms, and other canticles in their poetic form. If you want to influence the masses, a simple translation is always best. Critical translations vying with the original are really of use only for conversations conducted by the learned among themselves."

From "*Zum bru¨derlichen Andenken Wielands*" (1813)

"There are two maxims in translation: one requires that the author of a foreign nation be brought across to us in such a way that we can look on him as ours; the other requires that we should go across to what is foreign and adapt ourselves to its conditions, its use of language, its peculiarities. The advantages of both are sufficiently known to educated people through perfect examples. Our friend [Wieland], who looked for the middle way in this, too, tried to reconcile both, but as a man of feeling and taste he preferred the first maxim when in doubt."

From *West-Ostlicher Divan* (1819):

"There are three kinds of translation. The first acquaints us with foreign countries on our own terms; a simple prosaic translation is best in this respect. For since prose totally cancels all peculiarities of any kind of poetic art, and since prose itself pulls poetic enthusiasm down to a common water-level, it does the greatest service in the beginning, by surprising us with foreign excellence in the midst of our national homeliness, our everyday existence; it offers us a higher mood and real edification while we do not realize what is happening to us. Luther's Bible translation will produce this kind of effect at any time.

A second epoch follows in which [the translator] really only tries to appropriate foreign content and to reproduce it in his own sense, even though he tries to transport himself into foreign situations. I would like to call this kind of epoch the parodistic one, in the fullest sense of that word. In most cases men of wit feel called to this kind of trade.

The French use this method in their translations of all poetic works. Just as the French adapt foreign words to their pronunciations, just so do they treat feelings, thoughts, even objects; for every foreign fruit they demand a counterfeit grown in their own soil.

Wieland's translations are of this kind; he too had a singular sense of understanding and taste which brought him close to antiquity and to foreign countries only to the extent to which he could still feel comfortable. This excellent man may be considered the representative of his time; he has had an extraordinary impact, precisely because what he found pleasing, how he appropriated it, and how he communicated it in his turn seemed pleasing and enjoyable also to his contemporaries.

Since it is impossible to linger too long either in the perfect or in the imperfect and one change must of necessity follow another, we experienced the third epoch, which is to be called the highest and the final one, namely the one in which the aim is to make the translation identical with the original, so that one would not be valued instead of the other, but in the other's stead.

This kind had to overcome the greatest resistance originally; for the translator who attaches himself closely to his original more or less abandons the originality of his nation, and so a third comes into existence, and the taste of the multitude must first be shaped towards it.

Voss [Johann Heinrich Voss, the translator of Homer into hexameters], who will never be praised enough, could not satisfy the public initially; yet slowly, bit by bit, it listened itself into his new manner and made itself comfortable in it. But whoever can now see what has happened, what versatility has come to the Germans, what rhetorical, rhythmical, metrical advantages are at the disposal of the talented and knowledgeable youngster, how Ariosto and Tasso, Shakespeare and Caldero'n are now presented to us twice and three times over as germanized foreigners, may hope that literary history will plainly state who was the first to take this road in spite of so many obstacles.

...

It remains to explain in a few words why we called the third epoch the final one. A translation which attempts to identify itself with the original in the end comes close to an interlinear version and greatly enhances our understanding of the original; this in turn leads us, compels us as it were, towards the source text, and so the circle is closed at last. Inside it the coming together of the foreign and the native, the unknown approximation and the known, keep moving towards each other."

2   Riedrich Schleiermacher

Riedrich Schleiermacher (1768–1834) was an influential German theologian and one of the key scholarly figures of German Romanticism; professor of theology, first at Halle, later in Berlin; often regarded as the founder of secular hermeneutics, since his theories of interpretation form a bridge from religion to the humanities in general. His important lecture "*On the Different Methods of Translating*," delivered to the Royal Academy of Sciences in Berlin in 1813, contains a systematic analysis of the Romantic concept of translation, urging that the reader be brought to the author, that the reader learn to accept "alienation," or what would now be called foreignization of translations. Schleiermacher's importance for the romantic theory of translation cannot be overestimated. His "*On the Different Methods of Translating*" is the major document of romantic translation theory, and one of the major documents of western translation theory in general.

Schleiermacher opens his lecture by discussing translation as a general feature of understanding and language, then narrows the focus to two kinds of transference: interpreting ("Dolmetchen"), whereby he refers not only to oral interpreting, but to this linguistic act in the general "field of commerce," whereas the "translator proper operates mainly in the fields of art and scholarship," especially as he tackles creative texts that constitute "a new element in the life of a language." It is the latter which is Schleiermacher's concern, but he goes on to exclude also looser versions of translation, namely "paraphrase" and "imitation." What we are left with then are the two basic methods of translation proper: moving the author to the reader or the reader to the author. Translators pursuing the first method often claim that they want to make their author speak the way he would have spoken had he written the work in the translator's language. This has long been a popular expression (Dryden is often quoted to this effect) among translators who wish to argue that the liberties they have taken are based on some more integral aspects of the work, aspects which are thus being rendered in spite of the changes made. In his lecture, Schleiermacher went after this formula with a vengeance, and argued in detail why the method behind it does not hold water. In fact, he more than once implied that this method often turns out to be imitation in disguise. Hence, there seems to be only one option left for the translator who wants to transmit "the living power" which "creates new forms by means of the plastic material of language"; the reader has to be brought to the author, and Schleiermacher came up with his own metaphoric formula to describe this translation: it will be "perfect in its kind when one can say that if the author had learnt German as well as the translator has learnt Latin he would not have translated the work he originally wrote in Latin any differently than the translator has done." This clever move of casting the author as a potential translator of his work (rather than a writer of it in another language) dramatizes the relationship between the author, translator and reader in a thought-provoking way. And while at one point he talked about moving the reader to the author, Schleiermacher also described them as meeting "at a certain point in the middle," i.e. they meet through and "in" a translator who opens up the gateway of the foreign.

However, this foreignizing method clearly challenges the reader and it places a strain on the language of the translation. Schleiermacher noted that not every language is ready for this, but he clearly had great faith in the German language and its ability not only to incorporate the foreign, but to house the extensive number of translated works which he found necessary for the method to make sense in the long run. Schleiermacher not only saw translation as a crucial national enterprise, but he also dreamed of the German language as a linguistic empire where the various works of world literary history are all gathered together.

The following are excerpts from "*On the Different Methods of Translating*":

"If his readers are to understand, they must perceive the spirit of the language which was the author's own and be able to see his peculiar way of thinking and feeling, and to realize these two aims the translator can offer them nothing but his own language, which at no point fully corresponds to the other, and his own person, whose understanding of his author is now more, now less clear, and whose admiration and approval of him is now greater, now less. Does not translation, considered in this way, seem a foolish enterprise? That is why people, in despair at not reaching this goal, or, if you prefer, before they had reached the stage at which all this could be clearly thought out, discovered two other methods of becoming acquainted with works in foreign languages, not with a view to gathering their real artistic or linguistic sense, but rather to fill a need and to contemplate spiritual art; in the methods some of these difficulties are forcibly removed, others slyly circumvented, but the concept of translation adduced here is completely abandoned. These two methods are paraphrase and imitation. Paraphrase strives to conquer the irrationality of languages, but only in a mechanical way. It says; even if I do not find a word in my language which corresponds to a work in the original language, I still want to try to penetrate its value by adding both restrictive expansive definitions... Imitation, on the other hand, submits to the irrationality of languages, it grants that one cannot render a copy — which would correspond precisely to the original in all its parts — of a verbal artefact in another language, and that, given the difference between languages, with which so many other differences are connected, there is no option but to produce an imitation, a whole which is composed of parts obviously different from the parts of the original, but which would yet in its effects come as close to that whole as the difference in material allows... The imitator, therefore, does not attempt to bring the two parties — the writer and the reader of the imitation—together, because he does not think a direct relationship between them is possible; he merely wants to produce on the reader an impression similar to that received from the original by its contemporaries who spoke the same language.

But what of the genuine translator, who wants to bring those two completely separated persons, his author and his reader, truly together, and who would like to bring the latter to an understanding and enjoyment of the former as correct and complete as possible without inviting him to leave the sphere of his mother tongue — what roads are open to him? In my opinion there are only two. Either the translator leaves the author in peace, as much as possible, and moves the reader towards him; or he leaves the reader in peace, as much as possible, and moves the author towards him. The two roads are so completely separate from each other that one or the other must be followed as closely as possible, and that a highly unreliable result would proceed from any mixture, so that it is to be feared that author and reader would not meet at all. The difference between the two methods, and the fact that they stand in this relationship, must be immediately obvious. For in the first case the translator tries, by means of his work, to replace for the reader the understanding of the original language that the reader does not have. He tries to communicate to the readers the same image, the same impression he himself has gained — through his knowledge of the original language — of the work as it stands, and in doing so he tries to move the readers towards his point of view, which is essentially foreign to them. But if the translation wants to let its Roman author, for instance, speak the way he would have spoken to Germans, but Latin; rather it drags him directly into the world of the German readers and transforms him into their equal — and that, precisely, is the other case. The first translation will be perfect in its kind when one can say that if the author had learnt German as well as the translator has learnt Latin he would not have translated the work he originally wrote in Latin any differently than the translator has done. But the second, which does not show the author as he himself would have translated but as he, as a German,

would have originally written German, can have no other measure of perfection than if it could be certified that, could all German readers be changed into experts and contemporaries of the author, the original would have meant exactly the same to them as what the translation means to them now -- that the author has changed himself into a German. This method is obviously meant by all those who use the formula that one should translate an author in such a way as he himself would have written German. From this opposition it is immediately obvious how different the procedure must be in every detail, and how, if one tried to switch methods in the course of one and the same project, everything would become unintelligible as well as unpalatable. I merely would like to add that there cannot be a third method, with a precisely delimited goal over and above these two. The two separated parties must either meet at a certain point in the middle, and that will always be the translator, or one must completely join up with the other, and of these two possibilities only the first belongs to the field of translation; the other would be realized if, in our case, the German readers totally mastered Latin, or rather if that language totally mastered them.

...

    Just as our soil itself has no doubt become richer and more fertile and our climate milder and more pleasant only after much transplantation of foreign flora, just so we sense that our language, because we exercise it less owing to our Nordic sluggishness, can thrive in all its freshness and completely develop its own power only through the most many-sided contacts with what is foreign. And coincidentally our nation may be destined, because of its respect for what is foreign and its nature which is one of mediation, to carry all the treasures of foreign art and scholarship, together with its own, in its language, to unite them into a great historical whole, so to speak, which would be preserved in the center and heart of Europe, so that, with the help of our language, whatever beauty the most different times have brought forth can be enjoyed by all people, as purely and perfectly as is possible for a foreigner. This appears indeed to be the real historical aim of translation in general, as we are used to it now."

3 Exercises

(1) Please summarize Goethe's and Schleiermacher's translation ideas.

(2) What are the differences between the translation methods put forward by Goethe and Schleiermacher?

4 References and Further Readings

(1) ELLIS R. Theories of Translation: An Anthology of Essays from Dryden to Derrida [M]. Chicago: The University of Chicago Press, 1992.

(2) WEISSBORT D, EYSTEINSSON A. Translation — Theory and Practice [M]. London: Oxford University Press, 2006.

Chapter Seven

Victorian Translation and Criticism: On Translating Homer

① The Newman-Arnold Debate

Britain was the scene of much translation activity during the nineteenth century and translation was taken very seriously in the critical forum. Publications such as The *Athenaeum*, *Classical Museum*, and *Edinburgh Review* regularly featured articles on translation as well as reviews of newly published translations. Some of these reviews are lengthy and include a good deal of general discussion about translation methods, most frequently in relation to the translation of poetry (lyrical, epic, dramatic). The discussion is clearly fuelled by a strong conviction that translation is crucial for literary life in Britain. The Homeric epics seem to become even

more important than before; how Homer is rendered in English is for many one of the key issues of contemporary literary activity. This is the source of the well-known controversy between Matthew Arnold (1822–1888), poet and professor of poetry at Oxford, and Francis W. Newman (1805–1897), professor of Latin at University College London. It started with Arnold's critique (in his lectures *On Translating Homer*, 1861) of Newman's translation of *The Iliad*. Newman wrote a detailed reply and Arnold responded in his *Last Words on Translating Homer*. It has often been assumed that Arnold had the last word in more than one sense; most readers have in fact approached the debate through editions of Arnold's criticism, where Newman's reply is printed in between Arnold's pieces, and it often feels as if Newman has been simply absorbed in, and "contained" by, the most powerful critical voice of Victorian England.

Newman's aim was an ambitious one, since he wanted to allude to a broad readership while at the same time staying true to the various "peculiarities" of Homer's epic, and the broad spectrum of expressions he found in it. He felt that Arnold was attacking the scholarly mainstay of his translation and answered accordingly; Arnold then turned the tables on him by claiming that it was not so much in the realm of scholarship as in poetic delivery that Newman had failed. From a contemporary point of view, the relationship between theory and practice becomes very complicated here. Several modern translation scholars seem to work on premises that are quite close to those of Newman; that does not mean they necessarily approve of his actual translation.

Translation scholars frequently refer to the Newman-Arnold controversy, but rarely discuss it in the context of Victorian translation criticism, but this is the context in which it appears here. Amidst the widespread interest in translation, there was an anxiety about the receptiveness of the literary public to older and more recent canonical works in English translation. This anxiety is echoed in an anonymous review of John Stewart Blackie's translation of Aeschylus' lyrical dramas. "There are few literary callings which have been more affected by the changes of public taste than that of the translator. From the time of the Restoration, if not earlier, to the beginning of the present century, the achievement of a decently successful version of a classic author conferred on a man a species of immortality. Those who stood highest as original poets felt that their assurance of posthumous fame was doubly sure when they had associated their names with Homer or Virgil." But why has this changed? The reviewer goes on, "After the public had once become accustomed to Byron and Scott, they began to care little for translations; And the more recent influences of Shelley and Wordsworth have not been more favourable to these unfortunate attempts to entwine the old with the new." It is probably true that in Britain, in some contrast to what happened in Germany, contemporary Romantic literature did not develop at close quarters with the translation of the canonical literature, and that many readers leaned more to the former than the latter. But the diminished status of the translator is also a result of the very criteria of some of the prominent views of translation. When the novelist George Eliot, herself a translator and an active spokeswoman of German culture in Britain, notes that "a good translator is infinitely below the man who produces good original works," she is not holding up any objective measuring stick, but rather following a dominant notion of the translator's task. To some extent it is summed up in a review of the translations of James Clarence Mangan, an important literary figure in 19th-century Ireland. The reviewer is full of praise, "Mr. Mangan's mind is precisely of that plastic character which is indispensable for spirited and truthful translations. He possesses, in a high degree, the art of thoroughly divesting himself, in his capacity of translator, of every individuality, of thought and of manner, and becoming, so to speak, the mere instrument of the author whom he translates." This is of course a well-known trope, the invisible translator, who does not remind readers that they are reading a translation.

Many critics (and translators) are skeptical of the overly visible or creative translator, and of what they perceive of as highly liberal translation methods in the past, even in the celebrated translations of Dryden and Pope, and they attempt to set up new parameters of accuracy. This debate, which can get quite heated, also sometimes becomes rather confusing, especially when it gets entangled with the question whether to translate classical epic or dramatic poetry into the same or somehow equivalent English metres, or whether to opt for prose. Some critics see prose translation as a means of guaranteeing a close rendering of the meaning of the original or even a "literal" transposition; yet at the same time prose clearly allows the translator more room to move in and such freedom also risks distancing the text from the original, the verse form of which has already been discarded.

The followings are paragraphs taken from F.W. Newman's preface to *The Iliad of Homer: Faithfully Translated into Unrhymed English Metre* (1856).

"In discerning the mind of Homer — as to its intellectual and moral tone — we get discernment not into one Greek only, but into all the Greeks, of whom he is emphatically a noble type. In this respect, the substance of what he tells is often of less importance to us than the manner in which he tells it, and it becomes a first-rate duty of a translator to adhere closely to his manner and habit of thought, as also to his moral sentiments.

[Homer] is alternately poet, orator, historian, theologian, geographer, traveller, jocose as well as serious, dramatic as well as descriptive... It suffices to warn the reader not to expect, or to wish, Homer to be always at the same high pitch of poetry. He rises and sinks with his subject, is prosaic when it is tame, is low when it is mean. To express this suitably, we need a diction sufficiently antiquated to obtain pardon of the reader for its frequent homeliness.

The style of Homer himself is direct, popular, forcible, quaint, flowing, garrulous, abounding with formulas, redundant in particles and affirmatory interjections, as also in grammatical connectives of time, place, and argument. In all those respects it is similar to the old English ballad, and is in sharp contrast to the polished style of Pope, Sotheby, and Cowper, the best known English translators of Homer.

...The first matter of all is to select the metre, with which the style is intimately connected. The moral qualities of Homer's style being like those of the English ballad, we need a metre of the same genius. It must be fundamentally musical and popular.

These considerations convinced me à *priori* that the English metre fitted to translate Homer's hexameter must be a long line composed of two short ones, having each either three beats or four beats... But beside this I held it as an axiom that rhyme must be abandoned... Yet on abandoning rhyme, to which our ears are accustomed in the popular ballad, I found an unpleasant void, until I gave a double ending to the verse, i.e., one (unaccented) syllable more than our Common Metre allows.

A few remarks here on the problem presented to a translator seem to me the more needful, because some reviewers of my translation of Horace's Odes lay down as axioms (to which they assumed my agreement), principles which I regard to be utterly false and ruinous to translation. One of these is, that the reader ought, if possible, to forget that it is a translation at all, and be lulled into the illusion that he is reading an original work. Of course, a necessary inference from such a dogma is that whatever has a foreign color is undesirable and is even a grave defect. The translator, it seems, must carefully obliterate all that is characteristic of the original, unless it happen to be identical in spirit to something already familiar in English. From such a notion I cannot too strongly express my intense dissent. I aim at precisely the opposite — to retain every peculiarity of the original, so far as I am able, *with the greater care the more foreign it may be* — whether it be a matter of taste, of intellect, or of morals."

The following is taken from Matthew Arnold's *On Translating Homer* (1861).

"It is disputed what aim a translator should propose to himself in dealing with his original. Even this preliminary is not yet settled. On one side it is said that the translation ought to be such 'that the reader should, if possible, forget that it is a translation at all, and be lulled into the illusion that he is reading an original work — something original (if the translation be in English) from an English hand." The real original is in this case, it is said, 'taken as basis on which to rear a poem that shall affect its natural hearers.' On the other hand, Mr. Newman, who states the foregoing doctrine only to condemn it, declares that he 'aims at precisely the opposite: to retain every peculiarity of the original, so far as he is able, *with the greater care the more foreign it may happen to be;* so that it may never be forgotten that he is imitating, and imitating in a different material.' The translator's 'first duty', says Mr. Newman, is a historical one: 'to be *faithful*'. Probably both sides would agree that the translator's 'first duty is to be faithful'; but the question at issue between them is, in what faithfulness consists.

My one object is to give practical advice to a translator; and I shall not the least concern myself with theories of translation as such. But I advise the translator not to try to 'rear on the basis of the *Iliad*, a poem that shall affect our countrymen as the original may be conceived to have affected its natural hearers;' and for this simple reason, that we cannot possibly tell how the *Iliad* 'affected its natural hearers.' It is probably meant merely that he should try to affect Englishmen powerfully, as Homer affected Greeks powerfully; but this direction is not enough, and can give no real guidance. For all great poets affect their hearers powerfully, but the effect of one poet is one thing, that of another poet another thing: it is our translator's business to reproduce the effect of Homer, and the most powerful emotion of the unlearned English reader can never assure him whether he has reproduced this, or whether he has produced something else. So, again, he may follow Mr. Newman's directions, he may "retain every peculiarity of his original," but who is to assure him, who is to assure Mr. Newman himself, that, when he has done this, he has done that for which Mr. Newman enjoins this to be done, "adhered closely to Homer's manner and habit of thought?" Evidently the translator needs some more practical directions than these. No one can tell him how Homer affected the Greeks; but there are those who can tell him how Homer affects them. These are scholars; who possess, at the same time with knowledge of Greek, adequate poetical taste and feeling. No translation will seem to them of much worth compared with the original; but they alone can say whether the translation produces more or less the same effect upon them as the original. They are the only competent tribunal in this matter: the Greeks are dead; the unlearned Englishman has not the data for judging; and no man can safely confide in his own single judgment of his own work. Let not the translator, then, trust to his notions of what the ancient Greeks would have thought of him; he will lose himself in the vague. Let him not trust to what the ordinary English reader thinks of him; he will be taking the blind for his guidance. Let him not trust to his own judgment of his own work; he may be misled by individual caprices. Let him ask how his work affects those who both know Greek and can appreciate poetry.

Mr. Newman says that 'the entire dialect of Homer being essentially archaic, that of a translator ought to be as much Saxo-Norman as possible, and owe as little as possible to the elements thrown into our language by classical learning'. Mr. Newman is unfortunate in the observance of his own theory, for I continually find in his translation words of Latin origin, which seem to me quite alien to the simplicity of Homer.

But, apart from the question of Mr. Newman's fidelity to his own theory, such a theory seems to me both dangerous for a translator and false in itself. Dangerous for a translator; because, wherever one finds such a theory announced (and one finds it pretty often), it is generally followed by an explosion of pedantry; and pedantry is of all things in the world the most un-Homeric. False in itself; because, in fact, we owe to the Latin element in our language most of that very rapidity and clear decisiveness by which it is contradistinguished from the German, and in sympathy with the languages of Greece and Rome: so that to limit an English translator of Homer to words of Saxon origin is to deprive him of one of his special advantages for translating Homer. In Voss's well-known translation of Homer, it is precisely the qualities of his German language itself, something heavy and trailing both in the structure of its sentence and in the words of which it is composed, which prevent his translation, in spite of the hexameters, in spite of his fidelity, from creating in us the impression created by the Greek. Mr. Newman's prescription, if followed, would just strip the English translator of the advantage which he has over Voss.

Homer is rapid in his movement, Homer is plain in his words and style, Homer is simple in his ideas, Homer is noble in his manner. Cowper renders him ill because he is slow in his movement, and elaborate in his style; Pope renders him ill because he is artificial both in his style and his words; Chapman renders him ill because he is fantastic in his ideas; Mr. Newman renders him ill because he is odd in his words and ignoble in his manner... Mr. Newman's movement, grammatical style, and ideas, are a thousand times in strong contrast with Homer's; still it is by the oddness of his diction and the ignobleness of his manner that he contrasts with Homer the most violently.

...

(The translator) will find one English book and one book only, where, as in *The Iliad* itself, perfect plainness of speech is allied with perfect nobleness; and that book is the Bible. No one could see this more clearly than Pope saw it: 'This pure and noble simplicity', he says, 'is nowhere in such perfection as in the Scripture and Homer': yet even with Pope a woman is a 'fair', a father is a 'sire' and an old man a 'reverend sage', and so on through all the phrases of that pseudo-Augustan, and most unbiblical, vocabulary. The Bible, however, is undoubtedly the grand mine of diction for the translator of Homer; and, if he knows how to discriminate truly between what will suit him and what will not, the Bible may afford him also invaluable lessons of style."

...

I must repeat what I said in beginning, that the translator of Homer ought steadily to keep in mind where lies the real test of the success of his translation, what judges he is to try to satisfy. He is to try to satisfy *scholars*, because scholars alone have the means of really judging him. A scholar may be a pedant, it is true, and then his judgment will be worthless; but a scholar may also have poetical feeling, and then he can judge him truly; whereas all the poetical feeling in the world will not enable a man who is not a scholar to judge him truly. For the translator is to reproduce Homer, and the scholar alone has the means of knowing that Homer who is to be reproduced. He knows him but imperfectly, for he is separated from him by time, race, and language; but he alone knows him at all. Yet people speak as if there were two real tribunals in this matter, -- the scholar's tribunal, and that of the general public. They speak as if the scholar's judgment was one thing, and the general public's judgment another; both with their shortcomings, both with their liability to error; but both to be regarded by the translator. The translator who makes verbal literalness his chief care 'will', says a writer in the *National Review* whom I have already quoted,

'be appreciated by the scholar accustomed to test a translation rigidly by comparison with the original, to look perhaps with excessive care to finish in detail rather than boldness and general effect, and find pardon even for a version that seems bare and bald, so it be scholastic and faithful.'

But, if the scholar in judging a translation looks to detail rather than to general effect, he judges it pedantically and ill. The appeal, however, lies not from the pedantic scholar to the general public, which can only like or dislike Chapman's version, or Pope's, or Mr. Newman's, but cannot judge them; it lies from the pedantic scholar to the scholar who is not pedantic, who knows that Homer is Homer by his general effect, and not by his single words, and who demands but one thing in a translation, — that it shall, as nearly as possible, reproduce for him the general effect of Homer. This, then, remains the one proper aim of the translator: to reproduce on the intelligent scholar, as nearly as possible, the *general effect* of Homer. Except so far as he reproduces this, he loses his labor, even though he may make a spirited *Iliad* of his own, like Pope, or translate Homer's *Iliad* word for word, like Mr. Newman. If his proper aim were to stimulate in any manner possible the general public, he might be right in following Pope's example; if his proper aim were to help schoolboys to construe Homer, he might be right in following Mr. Newman's. But it is not: his proper aim is, I repeat it yet once more, to reproduce on the intelligent scholar, as nearly as he can, the general effect of Homer ..."

And then the following is taken from *Homeric Translation in Theory and Practice* (1861), a reply to Matthew Arnold, by Francis W. Newman.

"Scholars are the tribunal of Erudition, but of Taste the educated but unlearned public is the only rightful judge; and to it I wish to appeal…Where I differ in taste from Mr. Arnold, it is very difficult to find 'the scholars' tribunal,'…but as regards Erudition, this difficulty does not occur, and I shall fully reply to the numerous dogmatisms by which he settles the case against me.

(Regarding hexameters:) The method could not be profitably used for translating Homer or Virgil, plainly because it is impossible to say for whose service such a translation would be executed. Those who can read the original will never care to read through any translation; and the unlearned

look on all, even the best hexameters, whether from Southey, Lockhart or Longfellow, as odd and disagreeable prose…'Homer is popular,' is one of the very few matters of fact in this controversy on which Mr. Arnold and I are agreed. 'English hexameters are not popular', is a truth so obvious, that I do not yet believe he will deny it. Therefore, 'Hexameters are not the metre for translating Homer.'

At length I come to the topic of Diction, where Mr. Arnold and I are at variance not only as to taste, but to the main facts of Greek literature. I had called Homer's style quaint and garrulous; and said that he rises and falls with his subject, being prosaic when it is tame and low when it is mean. I added no proof; for I did not dream that it was needed. Mr. Arnold not only absolutely denies all this, and denies it without proof; but adds that these assertions prove my incompetence, and account for my total and conspicuous failure.

It is not to be expected, that one who is blind to superficial facts so very prominent as those which I have recounted, should retain any delicate perception of that highly colored, intense, and very eccentric diction of Homer, even if he has ever understood it, which he forces me to doubt."

And the next following part is taken from *Last Words on Translating Homer*, a reply to Francis W. Newman by Matthew Arnold (1862).

"I think that in England, partly from the want of an Academy, partly from a national habit of intellect to which that want of an Academy is itself due, there exists too little of what I may call a public force of correct literary opinion, possessing within certain limits a clear sense of what is right and wrong, sound and unsound, and sharply recalling men of ability and learning from any flagrant misdirection of these their advantages.

Mr. Newman errs by not perceiving that the question is not one of scholarship, but of a poetical translation of Homer. This, I say, should be perfectly simple and intelligible…That the poetical translation, in his rendering of them, is to give us a sense of the difficulties of the scholar, and so is to make his translation obscure…It may even be affirmed that everyone who reads Homer perpetually for the sake of enjoying his poetry (and no one who does not so read him will ever translate him well), comes at last to form a perfectly clear sense in his own mind for every important word in Homer, whatever the scholar's doubts about the word maybe. And this sense is present to his mind with perfect clearness and fullness, whenever the word recurs, although as a scholar he may know that he cannot be sure whether this sense is the right one or not. But poetically he feels clearly about the word, although philologically he may not.

Perplexed by his knowledge of the philological aspect of Homer's language, encumbered by his own learning, Mr. Newman, I say, misses the poetical aspect, misses that with which alone we are here concerned… He talks of my 'monomaniac fancy that there is nothing quaint or antique in Homer.' Terrible learning, I cannot help in my turn exclaiming, terrible learning, which discovers so much!"

 2 Exercises

(1) What are the main differences between Newman's and Arnold's attitudes towards the translation of Homer?

(2) What is your main point of view toward the translation of classics?

3 References and Further Readings

(1) PETER F, KENNETH H. The Oxford History of Literary Translation in English (Volume 4) [M]. Oxford: Oxford University Press, 2006.

(2) SIMEON U. English Translators of Homer: From George Chapman to Christopher Logue [M]. Plymouth: Northcote House, 1998.

(3) WEISSBORT D, EYSTEINSSON A. Translation — Theory and Practice [M]. London: Oxford University Press, 2006.

Chapter Eight

Edward Fitzgerald and His Translation of
The Rubáiyát

1   An Introduction to Edward Fitzgerald

Edward Fitzgerald (1809–1883) is a poet, a prolific letter-writer, and the renowned translator of *The Rubáiyát of Omar Khayyám*, which, though it is a very free adaptation and selection from the Persian poet's verses, stands on its own as a classic of English literature. It is one of the most frequently quoted of lyric poems, and many of its phrases, such as "A jug of wine, a loaf of bread, and thou" and "The moving finger writes," have passed into common currency.

Fitzgerald was educated at Trinity College, Cambridge, where he formed a lifelong friendship with William Makepeace Thackeray. Soon after graduating in 1830, he retired to the life of a country gentleman in Woodbridge. Though he lived chiefly in seclusion, he had many intimate friends, including Alfred, Lord Tennyson and Thomas Carlyle, with whom he kept up a steady correspondence.

A slow and diffident writer, Fitzgerald published a few works anonymously, then freely translated *Six Dramas of Calderón* (1853) before learning Persian with the help of his Orientalist friend Edward Cowell. In 1857 Fitzgerald "mashed together," as he put it, material from two different manuscript transcripts (one from the Bodleian Library, the other from Kolkata / Calcutta to create a poem whose "Epicurean Pathos" consoled him in the aftermath of his brief and disastrous marriage.

In 1859 the *Rubáiyát* was published in an unpretentious, anonymous little pamphlet. The book attracted no attention until, in 1860, it was discovered by Dante Gabriel Rossetti and soon after by Algernon Swinburne. Today, Fitzgerald is famous among students of translation for his pithy aphorisms in favor of free translation: "Better a live sparrow than a stuffed eagle" and "the live dog better than the dead lion".

② Fitzgerald's Translation of *The Rubáiyát*

The word Rubai (Rubáiyát -- plural), meaning "quatrain," comes from the word al-Rabi, the number four in Arabic. It refers to a four-lined stanza that became popular in Persian poetry for the simplicity of its style and its short length which allows an aphorism to be delivered effectively. A Rubai consists of two hemistiches for a total of four parts. Whereas in the early period of Persian literary tradition the four parts often rhymed, by the time of Khayyám, only the first, second and fourth lines rhymed, providing the poet with a greater degree of freedom.

The historical Omar Khayyám (1048–1131), a Persian mathematician, is hardly one of the great poets of the Persian tradition. His four-line epigrams might now be forgotten except for Edward Fitzgerald's transposition and indeed transmogrification of *Material Poetica* that Omar provided.

In 1857, amid marital troubles, Fitzgerald found that Omar Khayyám "breathes a sort of consolation!" He jokingly signed his name, in letters to Cowell, "Edward FitzOmar." A stanza crystallized in his mind fairly early, and, in a letter to Cowell in 1857, he wrote, "I see how a very pretty Eclogue might be tessellated out of his scattered Quatrains." He became obsessed with the translation, but was of course aware of its outrageous nature, publishing the work in 1859, anonymously, in a limited edition. He had turned these spontaneous occasional short poems into a continuous, dramatically unified sequence, sometimes compressing more than one poem into one of his own quatrains. In a letter in January 1858, he sent the manuscript to his publisher, and later again to Parker, and on the 3rd September, 1858, he wrote to Cowell:

"As to my Omar, I gave it to Parker in January, I think: he saying Fraser was agreeable to take it. Since then I have heard no more; so as, I suppose, they don't care about it; and may be quite right. Had I thought that they would be so long, however, I would have copied it out and sent it to you; and I will still do so from a rough and imperfect copy I have (though not now at hand), in case they show no signs of printing me. My translation will interest you from its form, and also in many respects in its detail, very unliteral as it is. Many quatrains are mashed together and something lost, I doubt, of Omar's simplicity, which is so much a virtue in him. But there it is, such as it is. I purposely said in the very short notice I prefixed to the poem that it was so short because better information might be furnished in another paper which I thought you would undertake. So it rests."

On the 2nd November he wrote again to Cowell:

"As to Omar, I hear and see nothing of it in Eraser yet; and so I suppose they don't want it. I told Parker he might find it rather dangerous among his Divines; he took it, however, and keeps it. I really think I shall take it back; add some stanzas, which I kept out for fear of being too strong; print fifty copies and give away; one to you, who won't like it neither. Yet it is most ingeniously tesselated into a sort of Epicurean eclogue in a Persian garden."

And on the 27th of April, 1859, having printed his Quatrains, he wrote to Cowell:

"I sent you poor old Omar, who has his kind of consolation for all these things. I doubt you will regret you ever introduced him to me. And yet you would have me print the original, with many worse things than I have translated... I hardly know why I print any of these things, which nobody buys; and I scarce now see the few I give them to. But when one has done one's best, and is sure that that best is better than so many will take pains to do, though far from the best that might be done, one likes to make an end of the matter by print. I suppose very few people have ever taken such pains in translation as I have, though certainly not to be literal. But at all cost, a thing must live, with a transfusion of one's own worse life if one can't retain the original's better. Better a live sparrow than a stuffed eagle. I shall be very well pleased to see the new MS. of Omar."

His *Rubáiyát of Omar Khayyám* was first issued anonymously on January 15, 1859, but it caused no great stir, and, half-forgotten, was reintroduced to the notice of the literary world in the following year by Rossetti, and, in this connection, it is curious to note to what a large extent Rossetti played the part of a literary Lucina. Fitzgerald, Blake and Wells are all indebted to him for timely aid in the reanimation of offspring, that seemed doomed to survive but for a short time the pangs that gave them birth. Mr. Swinburne and Lord Houghton were also impressed by its merits, and its fame slowly spread. Eight years elapsed, however, before the publication of the second edition.

It was only after some time, once it had been discovered by Rossetti, Swinburne, and Ruskin, that the poem became widely known, achieving its heights, in fact, only after the translator's death, and it was not until 1869 that the American scholar Charles Eliot Norton reviewed it in the most flattering terms: "He is to be called 'translator' only in default of a better word, one which should express the poetic transfusion of a poetic spirit from one language to another, and the representation of the ideas and images of the original in a form not altogether diverse from their own but perfectly adapted to the new conditions of time, place, custom, and habit of mind in which they reappear." Norton, with whom Fitzgerald corresponded, added, in a manner which the 17th-century exponents of what Dryden called Imitation might have echoed: "It is the work of a poet inspired by the work of a poet; not a copy, but a reproduction, not a translation, but the redelivery of a poetic inspiration." Fitzgerald himself, however, writing to Cowell in 1858, expressed perhaps certain unease: "My Translation will interest you from its Form, and also in many respects in its Detail: very un-literal as it is. Many Quatrains are mashed together and something lost, I doubt, of Omar's Simplicity, which is so much a Virtue in him."

The success of the poem may be explained in terms of Khayyám's evident rebellion against bigotry and religious dogmatism. The translation addressed several prevalent concerns: divine justice versus hedonism; science versus religion; as well as catering to the taste for eastern art and bric-a-brac. The only consolation, in a puzzling life, was physical pleasure. The "skeptical" *Rubáiyát* seemed appropriately published in the same year as *Origin of Species*, although Fitzgerald himself was no atheist or agnostic. He felt a kinship with Omar, tinged with guilt, whereas Cowell himself openly disapproved of Omar's pessimism about life and especially about the certainty of a Hereafter.

Like Ruskin, Fitzgerald found himself out of step with the "March of progresses, lamenting the spoliation of nature and, in fact, turning for relief to the less vulnerable sea. He produced translations of plays by Calderon (1853), Aeschylus (*The Agamemnon*, 1876), and Sophocles. His other translations from Persian included Attar-ut-Tair's 13th-century text *The Bird Parliament* (1859), a kind of ornithological Pilgrim's Progress, affirming in this case the benevolence of God, and Jami's *Salaman and Absal* (1856). A critic, while regretting Fitsgerald's somewhat deficient Persian, seemed to approve his work in general, writing that "As a first attempt, however, to make Jami accessible to the English reader, this little volume is deserving of commendation.' "

③ Fitzgerald's Approach to Translation

Fitzgerald's approach to translation in general was typified by the freedom he felt appropriate in his treatment of Omar. In a letter to Cowell (1859) he famously wrote, "I suppose very few People have ever taken such pains in translation as I have: though certainly not to be literal. But at all costs a thing must live: with a transfusion for one's own life if one can't retain the original's better. Better a live Sparrow than a stuffed Eagle." In a letter to James Russell Lowell, the American poet, essayist, and editor, he underlined this sentiment, writing explicitly of his approach to translation:

"I am persuaded that, to keep Life in the Work (as Drama must) the Translator (however inferior to his Original) must re-cast that original into his own Likeness, more or less: the less like

his original, so much the worse: but still, the live Dog better than the dead Lion; in Drama, I say... Another shot have I made at Faust in Bayard Taylor's Version: but I do not even get on with him as with Hayward, hampered as he (Taylor) is with his allegiance to original metres, etc. His Notes I was interested in: but I shall die ungoethed."

Probably the original rose of Omar was, so to speak, never a rose at ally but only petals toward the making of a rose; and perhaps Fitzgerald did not so much bring Omar's rose to bloom again as make it bloom for the first time. The petals came from Persia but it was an English magician who charmed them into a living rose.

The following part is taken from Edward Fitzgerald's *Introduction to the Rubáiyát of Omar Khayyám* (1859).

With regard to the present Translation. The original *Rubáiyát* (as, missing an Arabic Guttural, these Tetrastichs are more musically called), are independent Stanzas, consisting each of four lines

of equal, though varied, Prosody, sometimes all rhyming, but oftener (as here attempted) the third line suspending the Cadence by which the last atones with the former Two. Something as in the Greek Alcaic, where the third line seems to lift and suspend the Wave that falls over in the last. As usual with such kind of Oriental Verse, the *Rubáiyát* follow one another according to Alphabetic Rhyme -- a strange Farrago of Grave and Gay. Those here selected are strung into something of an Eclogue, with perhaps a less than equal proportion of the 'Drink and make-merry', which (genuine or not) recurs over-frequently in the Original. For Lucretian as Omar's Genius might be, he cross'd that darker Mood with much of Oliver de Basselin Humour. Anyway, the Result is sad enough: saddest perhaps when most ostentatiously merry: any way, fitter to move Sorrow than Anger towards the old Tentmaker, who after vainly endeavouring to unshackle his Steps from Destiny, and to catch some authentic Glimpse of tomorrow, fell back upon today (which has out-lasted so many Tomorrows!) as the only Ground he got to stand upon, however momentarily slipping from under his Feet."

His translation idea is consistent in his other translations. In the preface of his translation of *Agamemnon*, he said:

"I suppose that a literal version of this play, if possible, would scarce be intelligible. Even were the dialogue always clear, the lyric Choruses, which make up so large a part, are so dark and abrupt in themselves, and therefore so much the more mangled and tormented by copyist and commentator, that the most conscientious translator must not only jump at a meaning, but must bridge over a chasm; especially if he determine to complete the antiphony of Strophe and Antistrophe in English verse.

Thus, encumbered with forms which sometimes, I think, hang heavy on Aeschylus himself; struggling with indistinct meanings, obscure allusions, and even with puns which some have tried to reproduce in English; this grand play, which to the scholar and the poet, lives, breathes, and moves in the dead language, has hitherto seemed to me to drag and stifle under conscientious translation into the living; that is to say, to have lost that which I think the drama can least afford to lose all the world over. And so it was that, hopeless of succeeding where as good versifiers, and better scholars, seem to me to have failed, I came first to break the bounds of Greek tragedy; then to swerve from the Master's footsteps; and so, one license drawing on another to make all of a piece, arrived at the present anomalous conclusion. If it has succeeded in shaping itself into a distinct, consistent, and animated whole, through which the reader can follow without halting, and not without accelerating interest from beginning to end, he will perhaps excuse my acknowledged transgressions, unless as well or better satisfied by some more faithful Interpreter, or by one more entitled than myself to make free with the original."

4　A Case Study of *The Rubáiyát* Translation

In illustration of Fitzgerald's capacity for conveying the spirit rather than the very words of the original, comparison of the Ousely MS. of 1460 AD, in the Bodleian Library at Oxford, with *The Rubáiyát* as we know it, is of great interest.

The MS. runs thus:

> For a while, when young, we frequented a teacher;
>
> For a while we were contented with our proficiency;

> Behold the foundation of the discourse! — What happened to us?
>
> We came in like Water, and we depart like Wind.

In Fitzgerald's version the verses appear thus:

> Myself when young did eagerly frequent
>
> Doctor and Saint , and heard great Argument
>
> About it and about: but evermore
>
> Came out by the same Door as in I went.
>
> With them the Seed of Wisdom did I sow
>
> And with my own hand labour'd it to grow:
>
> And this was all the Harvest that I reap'd —
>
> "I came like Water, and like Wind I go."

Similar examples may be found elsewhere, thus:

> From the Beginning was written what shall be
>
> Unhaltingly the Pen writes, and is heedless of good and bad;
>
> On the First Day He appointed everything that must be,
>
> Our grief and our efforts are vain,

develops into:

> The Moving Finger writes; and, having writ,
>
> Moves on: nor all thy Piety nor Wit
>
> Shall lure it back to cancel half a Line,
>
> Nor all thy Tears wash out a Word of it.

Perhaps the most famous one is number 12. Fitzgerald's translation goes like this:

> A Book of Verses underneath the Bough,
>
> A Jug of Wine, a Loaf of Bread — and Thou
>
> Beside me singing in the Wilderness —
>
> Oh, Wilderness were Paradise now!

However, the original two are the following:

> If a loaf of wheaten bread be forthcoming,
>
> A gourd of wine, and a thigh-bone of mutton.

> And then, if thou and I be sitting in the wilderness, —
>
> That were a joy not within the power of any Sultan.
>
> I desire a flask of ruby wine and a book of verses
>
> Just enough to keep me alive and half a loaf is needful,
>
> And then, that thou and I should sit in the wilderness,
>
> Is better than the kingdom of a Sultan.

So several images are lost in this translation, several altered, and some added. This is perhaps why Prof. Qian Zhongshu commented that this translation, a combination of the original two, and better than the original poems.

 5 Exercises

Appreciate the following lines from The Rubáiyát:

I

Awake! For Morning in the Bowl of Night

Has flung the Stone that puts the Stars to Flight:

And Lo! The Hunter of the East has caught

The Sultán's Turret in a Noose of Light.

VII

Come, fill the Cup, and in the Fire of Spring

The Winter Garment of Repentance fling:

The Bird of Time has but a little way

To fly — and Lo! The Bird is on the Wing.

XXVI

Oh, come with old Khayyám, and leave the Wise

To talk; one thing is certain, that Life flies;

One thing is certain, and the Rest is Lies;

The Flower that once has blown for ever dies.

XXIX

Into this Universe, and why not knowing,

Nor whence, like Water willy-nilly flowing:

And out of it, as Wind along the Waste,

I know not whither, willy-nilly blowing.

6 References and Further Readings

(1) DANIEL K. Rubáiyát of Omar Khayyám [M]. London and New York: Oxford University Press, 2009.

(2) 邵斌. 诗歌创意翻译研究: 以《鲁拜集》翻译为个案 [M]. 杭州: 浙江大学出版社, 2011.

Chapter Nine

Linguistic Theory of Translation: Jakobson and Catford

① Roman Jakobson

Roman Jakobson (1896–1982), literary theorist and linguist, was born and educated in Moscow. He was associated with a number of Futurist painters and poets, and he experimented with "superconscious" poems. Jakobson was co-founder of both the Moscow Linguistic Circle, in 1915, and the Prague Linguistic Circle, in 1926, and was thus a key figure both in the development of Russian Formalism and Czech Structuralism. In 1916, he had collaborated with Petersburg literary scholars in establishing a formalist group, called the Society for the Study of Poetic Language. Jakobson came to the USA in 1941, teaching at Harvard and MIT. His essay "On Linguistic Aspects of Translation" extends the significance of translation to include intralingual and intersemiotic translation. It first appeared in Reuben Brower's landmark volume, *On Translation* (1959). Jakobson's emphasis on the functional role of linguistic elements in the translated text had a positive effect on the work of poetry translators. Regarding poetry by definition as untranslatable, Jakobson believed in the inevitability of 'creative transposition'.

The following part is excerpts from "On Linguistic Aspects of Translation."

"According to Bertrand Russell, 'no one can understand the word 'cheese' unless he has a nonlinguistic acquaintance with cheese'. If, however, we follow Russell's fundamental precept and place our "emphasis upon the linguistic aspects of traditional philosophical problems," then we are obliged to state that no one can understand the word cheese unless he has an acquaintance with the meaning assigned to this word in the lexical code of English. Any representative of a cheese-less culinary culture will understand the English word *cheese* if he is aware that in this language it means 'food made of pressed curds' and if he has at least a linguistic acquaintance with *curds*. We never consumed ambrosia or nectar and have only a linguistic acquaintance with the words *ambrosia*, *nectar*, and *gods* — the name of their mythical users; nonetheless, we understand these words and know in what contexts each of them may be used.

The meaning of the words *cheese, apple, nectar, acquaintance, but, mere*, and of any word or phrase whatsoever is definitely a linguistic — or to be more precise and less narrow — a semiotic fact. Against those who assign meaning (signatum) not to the sign, but to the thing itself, the simplest and truest argument would be that nobody has ever smelled or tasted the meaning of *cheese* or *apple*. There is no *signatum* without *signum*. The meaning of the word 'cheese' cannot be inferred from a nonlinguistic acquaintance with cheddar or with camembert without the assistance of the verbal code. An array of linguistic signs is needed to introduce an unfamiliar word. Mere pointing will not teach us whether 'cheese' is the name of the given specimen, or of any box of camembert, or of camembert in general or of any cheese, any milk product, any food, any refreshment, or perhaps any box irrespective of contents. Finally, does a word simply name the thing in question, or does it imply a meaning such as offering, sale, prohibition, or malediction? (Pointing actually may mean male diction; in some cultures, particularly in Africa, it is an ominous gesture.)

For us, both as linguists and as ordinary word-users, the meaning of any linguistic sign is its translation into some further, alternative sign, especially a sign 'in which it is more fully developed', as Peirce, the deepest inquirer into the essence of signs, insistently stated. The term 'bachelor' may be converted into a more explicit designation, 'unmarried man', whenever higher explicitness is required. We distinguish three ways of interpreting a verbal sign: it may be translated into other signs of the same language, into another language, or into another, nonverbal system of symbols. These three kinds of translation are to be differently labeled:

(1) Intralingual translation or *rewording* is an interpretation of verbal signs by means of other signs of the same language.

(2) Interlingual translation or *translation proper* is an interpretation of verbal signs by means of some other language.

(3) Intersemiotic translation or *transmutation* is an interpretation of verbal signs by means of signs of nonverbal sign systems.

The intralingual translation of a word uses either another, more or less synonymous, word or resorts to a circumlocution. Yet synonymy, as a rule, is not complete equivalence: for example, 'every celibate is a bachelor, but not every bachelor is a celibate'. A word or an idiomatic phrase word, briefly a code-unit of the highest level, may be fully interpreted only by means of an equivalent combination of code-units, i.e., a message referring to this code-unit: 'every bachelor is an unmarried man, and every unmarried man is a bachelor', or 'every celibate is bound not to marry, and everyone who is bound not to marry is a celibate.'

Likewise, on the level of interlingual translation, there is ordinarily no full equivalence between code-units, while messages may serve as adequate interpretations of alien code units or messages. The English word 'cheese' cannot be completely identified with its standard Russian heteronym *syr* because cottage cheese is a cheese but not a *syr*. Russians say: *prinesi syru i tvorogu*, (bring cheese and [sic] cottage cheese). In standard Russian, the food made of pressed curds is called *syr* only if ferment is used.

Most frequently, however, translation from one language into another substitutes messages in one language not for separate code-units but for entire messages in some other language. Such a translation is a reported speech; the translator recodes and transmits a message received from another source. Thus translation involves two equivalent messages in two different codes.

Equivalence in difference is the cardinal problem of language and the pivotal concern of linguistics. Like any receiver of verbal messages, the linguist acts as their interpreter. No linguistic specimen may be interpreted by the science of language without a translation of its signs into other signs of the same system or into signs of another system. Any comparison of two languages implies an examination of their mutual translatability; widespread practice of interlingual communication, particularly translating activities, must be kept under constant scrutiny by linguistic science. It is difficult to overestimate the urgent need for and the theoretical and practical significance of differential bilingual dictionaries with careful comparative definition of all the corresponding units in their intension and extension. Likewise differential bilingual grammars should define what unifies and what differentiates the two languages in their selection and delimitation of grammatical concepts."

All cognitive experience and its classification is conveyable in any existing language. Whenever there is deficiency, terminology may be qualified and amplified by loan-words or loan-translations, neologisms or semantic shifts, and finally, by circumlocutions. Thus in the newborn literary language of the Northeast Siberian Chukchees, "screw" is rendered as "rotating nail," "steel" as "hard iron," "tin" as "thin iron," "chalk" as "writing soap," "watch" as "hammering heart." Even seemingly contradictory circumlocutions, like "electrical horse-car", the first Russian name of the horseless street car, or "flying steamship" (jena paragot), the Koryak term for the airplane, simply designate the electrical analogue of the horse-car and the flying analogue of the steamer and do not impede communication, just as there is no semantic "noise" and disturbance in the double oxymoron — "cold beef-and-pork hot dog."

No lack of grammatical device in the language translated into makes impossible a literal translation of the entire conceptual information contained in the original. The traditional conjunctions "and," "or" are now supplemented by a new connective — "and / or" — which was discussed a few years ago in the witty book *Federal Prose — How to Write in and/or for Washington*. Of these three conjunctions, only the latter occurs in one of the Samoyed languages. Despite these differences in the inventory of conjunctions, all three varieties of messages observed in "federal prose" may be distinctly translated both into traditional English and into this Samoyed language. Federal prose: (1) John and Peter, (2) John or Peter, (3) John and / or Peter will come. Traditional English: (3) John and Peter or one of them will come. Samoyed: (1) John and/or Peter both will come, (2) John and/or Peter, one of them will come.

In poetry, verbal equations become a constructive principle of the text. Syntactic and morphological categories, roots, and affixes, phonemes and their components (distinctive features) — in short, any constituents of the verbal code — are confronted, juxtaposed, brought into contiguous relation according to the principle of similarity and contrast and carry their own autonomous signification. Phonemic similarity is sensed as semantic relationship. The pun, or to use a more erudite, and perhaps more precise term — paronomasia, reigns over poetic art, and whether its rule is absolute or limited, poetry by definition is untranslatable. Only creative transposition is possible: either intralingual transposition — from one poetic shape into another, or interlingual transposition — from one language into another, or finally intersemiotic transposition—from one system of signs into another, e.g., from verbal art into music, dance, cinema, or painting.

② J. C. Catford

J. C. Catford was born in Edinburgh in 1917. He died in Seattle in 2009. His contribution to phonetic studies was one of indisputable greatness. He did very important work on the phonetics of Caucasian languages, Applied Linguistics and instrumental and taxonomic phonetics. He was very deeply concerned with producing a systematic universal phonetic taxonomy, and also with the aerodynamic aspects of speech and with the development of proprioceptive insights into its motor aspects. These were the principal topics of his long-gestated perhaps most important book *Fundamental Problems in Phonetics* published in 1977. From 1964 to his retirement in 1985 he was at the University of Michigan where he was the Director of its English Language Institute. He always continued to travel very widely in search of his data. His very last book was the very aptly named *Practical Introduction to Phonetics* (1988). He was well liked personally and hugely admired as a teacher.

A Linguistic Theory of Translation was published in 1965, in which Catford studies translation from the linguistic perspective. He pointed out, "since translation has to do with language, the analysis and description of translation processes must make considerable use of categories set up for the description of languages. It must, in other words, draw upon a theory of language -- a general linguistics theory." The book was originally intended for an audience of students already fairly well-informed about general linguistics.

I Catford's Translation Ideas

Catford's contribution of translation is reflected in the following aspects.

The Definition of Translation

Translation is the replacement of textual material in one language (SL) by equivalent textual material in another language (TL).

Two lexical items in it call for comment. These are "textual material" and "equivalent." The use of the term "textual material" underlines the fact that in normal conditions it is not the entirety of a SL text which is translated, that is, replaced by TL equivalents. At one or more levels of language there may be simple replacement, by non-equivalent TL material: for example, if we translate the English text *what time is it*? into Chinese as 现在几点？There is replacement of SL grammar and lexis by equivalent TL grammar and lexis. There is also replacement of SL graphology by TL graphology—but the TL graphological form is by no means a translation equivalent of the SL graphological form.

The term "equivalent" is a key term. The central problem of translation practice is that of finding TL translation equivalents. A central task of translation theory is that of defining the nature and conditions of translation equivalence.

The General Types of Translation

Catford saw language as a set of systems operating at different levels. This view allowed him to describe broad translation types using three sets of criteria:

(1) In terms of the extent of translation, Catford distinguished between full translation, where the entire text is submitted to the translation process and "every part of the SL text is replaced by TL text material," and partial translation, where "some part or parts of the SL text are left untranslated." This is not a technical distinction but one which Catford adopted in order to avoid confusion between the nontechnical sense of partial and the technical way in which he used the term restricted translation.

(2) In terms of the levels of language involved in translation, a distinction is drawn between total translation and restricted translation. In total translation, which is what is generally meant by translation, all the linguistic levels of the source text (phonology, graphology, grammar and lexis) are replaced by target-language material. EQUIVALENCE in this type of translation is normally only achieved at the level of grammar and lexis, and Catford therefore defined total translation as the "replacement of SL grammar and lexis by equivalent TL grammar and lexis with consequential replacement of SL phonology/graphology by (nonequivalent) TL phonology/graphology." In restricted translation, on the other hand, there is "replacement of SL textual material by equivalent TL textual material at only one level. There are two main types of restricted translation: phonological translation and graphological translation. Restricted translation at the grammatical level or lexical level only is "difficult if not impossible" because of the interdependence of grammar and lexis. Catford also stressed that there can be no restricted translation at the interlevel of context because "there is no way in which we can replace SL 'contextual units' by equivalent TL 'contextual units' without simultaneously replacing SL grammatical/lexical units by equivalent TL grammatical/lexical units."

(3) In terms of the grammatical or phonological rank at which translation equivalence is established, Catford distinguished between rank-bound translation, which involves a deliberate attempt to consistently select TL equivalents at the same rank in the hierarchy of grammatical units, for example at the rank of morpheme, word, group, clause or sentence, and unbounded translation, where equivalences "shunt up and down the rank scale, but tend to be at the higher ranks -- sometimes between larger units than the sentence."

Formal Correspondence and Textual Equivalence

Catford made an important distinction between formal correspondence and textual equivalence. A formal correspondent is "any TL category (unit, class, element of structure, etc.) which can be said to occupy, as nearly as possible, the 'same' place in the 'economy' of the TL as the given SL category occupies in the SL." A textual equivalent is "any TL text or portion of text which is observed on a particular occasion... to be the equivalent of a given SL text or portion of text." Textual equivalence is thus tied to a particular ST-TT pair, while formal equivalence is a more general system-based concept between a pair of languages. When the two concepts diverge, a translation shift is deemed to have occurred. In Catford's own words, translation shifts are thus "departures from formal correspondence in the process of going from the SL to the TL."

Catford considers two kinds of shift: (a) shift of level and (b) shift of category.

(1) A level shift would be something that is expressed by grammar in one language and lexis in another; this could, for example, be: aspect in Russian being translated by a lexical verb in English: e.g. igrat (to play) and sigrat (to finish playing).

(2) Most of Catford's analysis is given over to category shifts. These are subdivided into four kinds:

a) Structural shifts: These are said by Catford to be the most common form of shift and to involve mostly a shift in grammatical structure. For example, the subject pronoun + verb + direct object structures of *I like jazz* and *j'aime le jazz* in English and French are translated by an indirect object pronoun + verb + subject noun structure in Spanish (me gusta el jazz) and in Italian (mi piace il jazz).

b) Class shifts: These comprise shifts from one part of speech to another. An example given by Catford is the English *a medical student* and the French *UN étudiant en médecine*, where the English premodifying adjective medical is translated by the adverbial qualifying phrase *en médecine*.

c) Unit shifts or rank shifts: These are shifts where the translation equivalent in the TL is at a different rank to the SL. "Rank" here refers to the hierarchical linguistic units of sentence, clause, group, word and morpheme.

d) Intra-system shifts: These are shifts that take place when the SL and TL possess approximately corresponding systems but where "the translation involves selection of a non-corresponding term in the TL system." Examples given between French and English are number and article systems, where, although similar systems operate in the two languages, they do not always correspond. Thus, *advice* (singular) in English becomes *des conseils* (plural) in French.

The Limits of Translatability

The limits of translatability in total translation are, however, much more difficult to state. Indeed, translatability here appears, intuitively, to be a cline rather than a clear-cut dichotomy. SL texts and items are more or less translatable than absolutely translatable or untranslatable. In total translation, translation equivalence depends on the interchangeability of the SL and TL text in the same situation — ultimately, that is, on relationship of SL and TL texts to the same relevant features of situation-substance.

Translation fails — or untranslatability occurs — when it is impossible to build functionally relevant features of the situation into the contextual meaning of the TL text. Broadly speaking, the cases where this happens fall into two categories: those where the difficulty is linguistic, and those where it is cultural.

In linguistic untranslatability the functionally relevant features include some which are in fact formal features of the *language* of the SL text. If the TL has no formally corresponding features, the text, or the item, is (relatively) untranslatable.

Linguistic untranslatability occurs in cases where an ambiguity peculiar to the SL text is a functionally relevant features — e.g. in SL puns. Ambiguities arise from two main sources: (a) *shared exponence* of two or more SL grammatical or lexical item, (b) *polysemy* of an SL item with no corresponding TL polysemy. By *shared exponence* we mean those cases where two or more distinct grammatical or lexical item is expounded in one and the same phonological or graphological form.

A grammatical example in English is the shared exponence of the two distinct morphemes

"plural" and "(verbal) third person single present" both of which are frequently expounded graphologically by-s, as in *cats* and *eats*. In most cases, there in no ambiguity, since the co-text indicates clearly which item is being expounded, and the translation equivalent is then not in doubt. But cases of ambiguity can arise, an example is *Time flies*. It can mean "time passes quickly" or something like "make observations on the speed of flies."

A lexical example might be *bank*, which is the graphological exponent of two distinct lexical items in English. This normally presents no problem in translation; the co-text normally shows whether, for example, the French translation equivalent should be *banquet* or *rive*. But *bank* is untranslatable when the ambiguity is itself a functionally relevant feature, as in Ogden and Richard's punning fable about Amoeba, which begins:

"'Realize you, Amoeba dear', said Will; and Amoeba realized herself, and there was no Small Change but many Checks on the Bank wherein the wild Time grew and grew and grew."

Here it is clear that the reader is expected to relate the graphological form *Bank* to both the lexical items which it expounds. This is impossible in French, where the translation equivalent must be either *banquet* or *rive* and not both at once.

II Catford and Translation Shifts

The word "shift," in discussing translation shift, seems to originate in Catford's *A Linguistic Theory of Translation*, where he devoted a chapter to the subject. Catford followed the Firthian and Hallidayan linguistic model, which analyses language as communication, operating functionally in context and on a range of different levels (e.g., phonology, graphology, grammar, lexis) and ranks (sentence, clause, group, word, morpheme, etc.).

As far as translation is concerned, Catford made an important distinction between formal correspondence and textual equivalence, which was later to be developed by Koller. Catford's book is an important attempt to apply to translation advances in linguistics in a systematic fashion. However, his analysis of intra-system shifts betrays some of the weaknesses of his approach. From his comparison of the use of French and English article systems in short parallel texts, Catford concluded that French "le/la/les" "will have English 'the' as its translation equivalent with probability supporting his statement that 'translation equivalence does not entirely match formal correspondence'." This kind of scientific-like statement of probability, which characterizes Catford's whole approach and was linked to the growing interest in machine translation at the time, was later heavily criticized by, amongst others, Delisle for its static contrastive linguistic basis. Henry (1984), revisiting Catford's book twenty years after publication, considered the work to be "by and large of historical academic interest" only. He did, however, point out the usefulness of Catford's final chapter, on the limits of translatability. Of particular interest is Catford's assertion that translation equivalence depends on communicative features such as function, relevance, situation and culture rather than just on formal linguistic criteria. However, as Catford himself notes, deciding what is "functionally relevant" in a given situation is inevitably "a matter of opinion."

③ Exercises

(1) Is translation a technique and process of linguistic transfer?

(2) Please comment on the difference between linguistic untranslatability and cultural untranslatability with the following examples.

1) –Where is Washington ?

  –He's dead.

  –I mean, the capital of the United States.

  –They loaded it all to Europe.

  –Now do you promise to support the constitution?

  –Me? How can I? I've got a wife and five children to support.

2) A: What kind of tree has hands?

  B: Palm tree.

  A: "If April showers bring May flowers, what do May flowers bring?"

  B: Pilgrims.

  A: "What is the worst kind of fish?"

  B: Selfish.

  A: "What do you call a country where the people drive only pink cars?"

  B: Pink carnation.

  A: Which is the longest word in English?"

  B: Smiles.

3) Here the Red Queen began again. 'Can you answer useful questions?' she said. 'How is bread made?" "I know THAT!' Alice cried eagerly. 'You take some flour —' 'Where do you pick the flower?' the White Queen asked. 'In a garden, or in the hedges?' 'Well, it isn't PICKED at all,' Alice explained: 'it's GROUND —''How many acres of ground?' said the White Queen. 'You mustn't leave out so many things. (Lewis Carroll: *Alice in Wonderland*)

4) If you shed tears when you miss the sun, you also miss the stars. (Rabindranath Tagor: *Stray Birds*)

Version 1: 如果你为思念太阳而落泪，那你也会思念群星。(周策纵译)

Version 2: 如果你因失去了太阳而流泪，那么你也将失去群星了。(郑振铎译)

4 References and Further Readings

(1) JAKOBSON R. On Linguistic Aspects of Translation [M] // R. Schulte, et al. Theories of Translation: An Anthology of Essays from Dryden to Derrida. Chicago and London: The University of Chicago Press, 1992.

(2) CATFORD J C. A Linguistic Theory of Translation [M]. London: Oxford University Press, 1965.

Chapter Ten

Theodore Savory and *The Art of Translation*

① An Introduction to Theodore Savory

Theodore H. Savory was born in London in 1896 and was educated at Alderham and St. John's, Cambridge. He was Science Master at Malvern College from 1920 to 1951 and was appointed Senior Biology Master at Haberdashers Aske's Hampstead School in 1951. Savory specialized for more than forty years in the study of spiders and is one of the few men in Britain who can justifiably call themselves arachnologists. Besides this specialization Savory was also interested in literature and authored *The Language of Science* and *Words of Science* in the 1950s. In *The Language of Science* (1953) he devoted a page or so to contrasting the ease of making good translations of scientific writing with the difficulty of making translations of literature and later decided to make a fuller study of translation. Four years later (1957), *The Art of Translation* was published and established his reputation in the field of translation.

② Translation Is an Art of Choice

To Savory, translation is an art which has a long history. No one who is interested in language can for long confine his interest to his native language only and from the moment that his thoughts are turned to the words and phrases used in other countries he is brought face to face with the problems of translation. Actually, translation is almost as old as original authorship and has a history as honorable and as complex as that of any other branch of literature.

Translation, Savory observes, "is made possible by an equivalence of thought which lies behind the different verbal expressions of a thought. No doubt this equivalence is traceable to the fact that men of all nations belong to the same species. When an Englishman is thinking of the woman whom he describes as 'my mother,' a Frenchman is thinking of '*ma mere*,' and a German of '*meine Mutter*.'

Among normal people these three thoughts will be very similar and will recall the same memories of tenderness, loving care and maternal pride. In consequence 'my mother' can be perfectly translated by '*ma mere*' or '*meine Mutter.*' Why then is translation so difficult as often to be described as impossible? Why is it said that translation is an art?"

Savory points out that the idea that for every word in any one language there is another accurately equivalent to it in every other language is not in accordance with the facts and the assumption of a dictionary of the type X=Y is essentially fallacious. Indeed, as we all know, a good dictionary usually offers its reader two, three or more "translations" of any word, and the reader is left to choose, as well as he can, the one that best suits his purpose. In his search for the equivalent of a word the translator meets many difficulties, among which the following three are the most obvious ones:

I Illusory Correspondence

This is the commonest pitfall that lies in the path of the translator. For instance, translators often, without pausing to think, translate "*luridi Flores*" into "lurid flowers". But actually, "lurid" here should be replaced by "yellow." A word often has several meanings, and the translator should take the context into consideration when choosing an appropriate word in the target language to translate it.

II Gaps in Languages Which Cannot Be Filled in Translating

This difficulty arises because "for a word that may be quite familiar in one language there is no equivalent in another." Savory remarks that "this kind of difficulty is frequent in the translation of all kinds of writings where the two nations whose languages are concerned may have different customs, different games and amusements, and different degrees of technical development."

III Idioms, Idiomatic Phrases and Proverbial Expressions

Every language has its own unique way of sayings, including idioms, idiomatic phrases and proverbial expressions, which add to the translators' difficulties. Savory uses the proverb "*Mit Wolfen muss man heulen*" as an example to illustrate this point. The translator may translate it directly into "Among wolves one must howl." But the critic may say that it's nonsense and it should be translated into "When in Rome do as the Romans do." However, the translator then argues, "That is not the author wrote." "No," says the critic, "but it is what he meant." And so the translator faces the question as to whether his function is to record the words of the original or to report on their meaning.

At all times and in all places the purpose of translation is to "remove the barrier that is placed by a difference in languages between the writer and the reader". At the primitive stage of translation literal translation is the dominant method. However, "as soon as a translator requires himself, or is required, to produce a better translation, he faces all the problems involved in the choosing of words. In this his task is much harder than that of the original author. If the latter seeks a word with which to express a thought or describe an experience, he has available many words in his own language and can without much difficulty or delay choose the one that suits him best and pleases him most. The translator of the word thus chosen has to decide on the nearest equivalent, taking into consideration the probable thoughts of the author, the probable feelings of the author's readers and of his own readers, and of the period in history in which the author lived. It follows then that at every pause the translator makes a choice, and that his choice is not between alternative yet exact equivalents, but between a numbers of equivalents, possibly all more or less inexact. Such a choice depends in large part on the personality of the translator and that it is essentially an aesthetic choice cannot be denied."

Savory suggests that the translator should ask himself the following three questions before making a choice: (1) What does the author say? (2) What does he mean? (3) How does he say it? This method of analysis may be applied to the paragraph, to the sentence, or even to the phrase. Savory maintains that the existence of possible alternatives between which the translator must make his choice is the essence of his art. The writing of the original author may be blunt or subtle, hesitant or fluent, sober or cheerful, majestic or paltry; and the translation may be any of these according to the wit and skill of the translator.

Savory points out that the task of translation has much in common with the universally acknowledged arts of painting and drawing. Both aim at nothing more than a clear, succinct expression of fact. "The wrong color or wrong thickness of line is the equivalent of the wrong word; a mistake in drawing, in perspective, is the same as a mistake in the meaning of a phrase." Savory compares scientific translations to the work of the photographer, for "both translation and photography are affected by the technical knowledge of the operator."

If translation is an art, what kind of man is the artist? Savory divides translators into three classes: the good, the bad and the indifferent. He argues that a good translator's knowledge of the translated language must be wide and it must also be critically applied so that no detail is likely to be missed. However, "linguistic knowledge and literary capacity will not by themselves ensure the best translation. A degree of sympathy and a higher degree of familiarity with the subject of the work that is being translated are almost essential. In the translation of verse or of any purely literary piece of prose, sympathy with the feelings of the author is naturally expected, for in the absence of such sympathy the translator is unlikely ever to have felt an inclination to undertake his task; but in the translation of informative, scientific or philosophical works knowledge of the subject makes the translating very much easier. More than this, it often ensures an avoidance of errors which ignorance would allow to pass unnoticed."

Savory remarks that a translator who adequately fulfills the requirements outlined above and who is able to attain a faultless standard of translation is obviously not to be found easily. Thus the art of translation ought to be highly valued and the translator adequately rewarded for his work. But this is not always the case. The critics seem to agree that the translator is undertaking a hopeless, almost an impossible, task, in return for which he will not receive a proportionate reward. The translator's reward is the pleasure that flows from intellectual exercise. If it were not so, translation would be one of the rarest of arts.

③ Categories of Translation

Savory divides translation into four categories: (1) perfect translation; (2) adequate translation; (3) composite translation; (4) translation of learned, scientific, technical and practical matter.

Perfect translation refers to "the translation of all purely informative statements such as are encountered by the traveler or used by the advertiser." Savory takes the notice boards at an international airport as an example. They are written in different languages, yet are in every respect identical. The perfection of the translations is a result of the nature of the original message. It is direct

and unemotional and is made in plain words to which no very intense associations are attached. Therefore, the translations can be very easily made, without very much hesitation on the part of the translator, and be correctly understood by all the readers.

In adequate translation, matter is more important than manner. That is to say, so long as the translations are satisfactory in practice, a grumble at words or phrases here and there may be dismissed as a quibble. "Into this second category fall the very much almost characterless translations made for 'the general reader,' who may use them without giving a thought to the fact that what he is reading was not originally written in his own language." These include all the translations of Dumas's *Black Tulip*, Boccaccio's *Decameron*, Cervantes's *Don Quixote* and Tolstoy's *Anna Karenina* and so on. The general reader of this kind of translations "may know little or nothing of the language of the original, and possibly have no interest at all in such linguistic problems as translation abundantly raises, so that the translator, realizing this, is justified in wasting no time in deliberation over the words and phrases that he uses. He may omit words, or even whole sentences, which he finds obscure; he can freely paraphrase the original meaning whenever it suits him to do so." Savory maintains that there is no reason why the translator should not do so, as long as the readers want nothing but the story.

Composite translation includes the translation of prose into prose, of poetry into prose and of poetry into poetry. This kind of translation is made by scholars for serious students, and for all earnest readers who seek in their reading something more than mere entertainment. Savory points out that in composite translation the manner is at least as important as the matter and may far surpass it. "It is in this category only that the theoretical impossibility of perfect translation can have so serious an effect that the conscientious translator may spend a very long time on his work. The time may, indeed, be so long that the commercial value of the translation is wholly neglected and all that is gained is the intellectual exercise and the keen intellectual pleasure that results from the effort. A great quantity of translation is in fact made, printed and published for no other reason than this -- that the translator has enjoyed the reading of some passage or poem, has felt the urge to try to render or express it in English, and has fallen under the spell of task to such a degree that he has wished to share his pleasure with others."

In the fourth and last category is included the translation of all learned, scientific, technical and practical matter. "Translation of this sort may appear not to be very different from those in the second category, in which perhaps they might have been included in a special sub-group; and it is certainly true that in them the matter is of the first importance and the manner of no significance whatever. Scientific and technical translating has, however, important characteristics of its own. First, these translations are made solely because of the intrinsic importance of the original work, an importance which is strictly confined to the practical business of living... Again, scientific and technical translation is peculiar in that it is almost a necessity that the translator shall have a reasonable knowledge of the science or the technique about which the original was written."

4 The Principles of Translation

The fourth chapter of *The Art of Translation* is devoted to the discussion of the principles of translation in which Savory puts forward twelve principles in contrasting pairs, as follows.

(1) A translation must give the words of the original.

(2) A translation must give the ideas of the original.

(3) A translation should read like an original work.

(4) A translation should read like a translation.

(5) A translation should reflect the style of the original.

(6) A translation should possess the style of the translator.

(7) A translation should read as a contemporary of the original.

(8) A translation should read as a contemporary of the translator.

(9) A translation may add to or omit from the original.

(10) A translation may never add to or omit from the original.

(11) A translation of verse should be in prose.

(12) A translation of verse should be in verse.

Savory maintains that the translator may choose different principles based on his own preference, the original text, the translated text and the needs of the readers. He analyzes these principles as follows:

"The pair of alternatives at the head of the list given above can be easily recognized as giving one form of expression to the distinction between the literal or faithful translation and the idiomatic or free translation. There has always been support for the literal translation because people generally agree that it is the duty of a translator to be faithful to his original. No translator would wish to incur the charge of being unfaithful. But we should first of all make clear what faithfulness implies and in what faithfulness consists. It does not mean a literal, a word-to-word translation, for this is the most primitive type of translating, fit only for the most mundane and prosaic of matters; and even if faithfulness could be taken to mean this, there would remain the unavoidable fact that any one word in any language cannot invariably be translated by the same word in any other language...

The reason for the advocacy of faithfulness is that the translator has never allowed himself to forget that he is a translator. He is not, he recognizes, the original author, and the work in hand is never his own; he is an interpreter, one whose duty it is to act as a bridge or channel between the mind of the author and the minds of his readers. He must efface himself and allow Rome or Berlin to speak directly to London or Paris. If he feels that he has done this, he may well be proud of achievement. 'My chief boast,' said William Cowper, in writing of his *Homer*, 'is that I have adhered closely to the original.'

But the translator who accepts this principle soon runs into difficulties, which have never been better described than in the words of Rossetti, 'The work of the translator is one of some self-denial. Often would he avail himself of any special grace of his own idiom and epoch, if only his will belonged to him; often would some cadence serve him but for his author's structure — some structure but for his author's cadence... Now he would slight the matter for the music, and now the music for the matter, but no, he must deal with each alike. Sometimes too a flaw in the work galls him, and he would fain remove it, doing for the poet that which his age denied him; but no, it is not in the bond.'

A reading of this paragraph would leave most of us in no doubt that a literal translation is too difficult a task to be performed efficiently, and would make us decide to turn at once into the ways of freedom. This is why Postgate was moved to say that the principle of faithfulness was set up as a merit off true translation 'by general consent, though not by universal practice.' Much that has been written in support of freedom in translation gives just this impression — the translator has shirked the labor of a close approach to the original, and lacks the discipline of self-denial described by Rossetti, whereupon he seeks to discover or to invent a 'principle' to which he can appeal, justifying his own actions and salving his own conscience.

In consequence we are told, often enough, that it is entirely legitimate to include in a translation any idiomatic expression that the original may seem to suggest, or that the first requisite of an English translation is that it shall be English, or that a translation ought to be able to pass itself off

as an original and show all the features of an original composition. These instructions all add up to a general implication that a translation must be such as may be read with ease and pleasure, with the suggestion that if it is not easy and pleasant it will never be read and might as well never have been made.

The risks lie in the extent of the latitude which the translator permits himself.

The limit is found, perhaps, in the casual words of our linguistic friends when we appeal to them for help with an almost illegible postcard just received from a foreign correspondent. Amused, they scan the document with an air of superior wisdom, and say, 'I can't make it out, exactly, but roughly speaking what it means is...' We have all, surely, had this experience and that the only thing to do is to examine the card with a magnifying glass and decipher it word for word with a dictionary. Our friend's free translation is too often quite valueless.

A more careful discussion of the characteristics of a translation which is both free and acceptable will bring to light three important points. First, the too brief and dogmatic statement that a translation must read like an original may be supported by a show of reason. The original reads like an original: hence it is only right that a translation of it should do so too. Common sense suggests that this is so; and the logical development of the notion is that from the translation alone it should not be possible for the reader to determine whether it had been translated from French or Greek, from Arabic or Russian. Whether this is important or not seems to depend solely on the reader and on his reasons for using the translation.

Secondly, while it may be admitted that there is a distinction between the original author and the translator, and that the latter must constantly remember his debt to the former, it is equally true that a translation is the result of the original work and thought by the translator. The original author has equally a debt to the translator, who is in a recognizable degree the proprietor of the translation as such. This proprietorship may be assumed to permit, without further question, the introduction of departures from the phrasing of the original, and the only doubt left is the extent of the departure. This doubt is resolved not by the wishes of the translator, but by the nature of his language: the latitude may be sufficient to make of the translation an example of the translator's language correct in idiom, expression and structure, but it should not be more than this.

Thirdly, there is the fact that, unlike the author, a translator is often one of a number, perhaps a large number, of writers who have preceded him at his task, and a translator of Goethe or Maupassant works in the knowledge that he is the latest of a series of writers who in the past have tried to find solutions to the problems he is now meeting. This raises a question of some delicacy. If he has conceived a phrase which, he believes, exactly expresses his author's meaning, and if he then finds that one or more of his predecessors have used it already, what should he do? Authority has spoken, not for the first time, with divided opinion. There have been those who have said that a translation, once made, must not be improved by a comparison with its forerunners and those who have gone further and asserted that such a comparison must be made for the purpose of removing any 'fortuitous coincidences". This, if strictly applied, is nonsense...

A more acceptable point of view, put forward by Postgate, gives a diametrically opposite opinion. If a translator who has done his best finds that some phrases of his have been used before by others, he should in no way feel obliged to alter them. On the contrary, he has 'one more reason for their retention'.

A translation may include any of the idiomatic expressions which are peculiar to its language and which the translator sees fit to adopt; but it need not, because of this, possess the style which the reader may expect. Style is the essential characteristic of every piece of writing, the outcome of the writer's personality and his emotions at the moment, and no single paragraph can be put together without revealing in some degree the nature of its author. What is true of the author is true also of the translator. The author's style, natural or adopted, determines his choice of a word, and, as has been, the translator is often compelled to make a choice between alternatives. The choice he makes cannot be uninfluenced by his own personality, cannot but reflect, though dimly, his own style. What does the reader expect? What does the critic demand?

One of the reasons for a preference for a literal translation is that it is likely to come nearer to the style of the original. It ought to be more accurate; and any copy, whether of a picture or a poem, is likely to be judged by its accuracy. Yet it is a fact that in making an attempt to reproduce the effect of the original, too literal a rendering is a mistake and it may be necessary to alter even the construction of the author's sentences in order to transfer their effects to another tongue. As Dr. E. V. Rieu says, in introducing his translation of *Odyssey*, 'In Homer, as in all great writers, matter and manner are inseparably blended…and if we put Homer straight into English words neither meaning nor manner survives.'

This is the unescapable fact, which advocates of precise, accurate and literal translation cannot gainsay. The ideal that the translator may set before himself has been so admirably described by Ritchie and Moore that their words must be quoted: 'Suppose that we have succeeded in writing a faithful translation of a characteristic page of Ruskin, and that we submit it for criticism to two well-educated French friends, one of whom has but little acquaintance with English, while the other has an intimate knowledge of our language. If the first were to say 'A fine description! Who is the author?' and the second 'Surely that is Ruskin, though I do not remember the passage,' then we might be confident that in respect of style our translation did not fall too far short of our ideal. We should have written French that was French, while it still kept the flavor of the original.'

…

Style is influenced both by the personality of the writer and also by the period of history in which he lives; and translation includes the bridging of time as well as the bridging of space. Chaucer is usually said to have written English, yet many a reader finds the *Canterbury Tales* to be incomprehensible, and is glad to read them in "translation" or a version in contemporary English…

Cervantes published *Don Quixote* in 1605; should that story be translated into contemporary English, such as he would have used at that time had he been an Englishman, or into the English of today? There can, as a rule, be very little doubt as to the answer, and in most cases the reader is justified in expecting the kind of language that he himself is accustomed to use. If a function of translation is to produce in the minds of its readers the same emotions as those produced by the original in the minds

of readers, the answer is clear. Yet there is need to notice in passing the possibility of an exception when the original author is read more for his manner than for his matter. We may read the speeches of Cicero to appreciate his eloquence. Today the most eloquent speaker of English is Sir Winston Churchill, yet Churchill's style is not Cicero's style. Should a speech by Cicero be so translated as to sound as if it has been delivered by Churchill? No.

...

Part of the explanation is no doubt to be found in normal variability of the human mind, and this alone is enough to account for a preference by some readers for a literal translation and a preference by others for a free one; for a preference by some for continual reminders that they are reading a translation, and a preference by others for no such thing. But this is not enough to account for the whole of the diversity.

The most probable reason is neglect by the critic of the reader's point of view. Readers of translations do not differ only in their personal preferences, they differ also — and most significantly — in the reasons for which they are reading translation at all.

...

For whom, then, are translations intended? At least four groups can be distinguished.

The first is the reader who knows nothing at all of the original language; who reads either from curiosity or from a genuine interest in a literature of which he will never be able to read one sentence in its original form. The second is the student who is learning the language of the original, and does so in part by reading its literature with the help of a translation. The third is the reader who knew the language in the past but who, because of other duties and occupations, has now forgotten almost the whole of his early knowledge. The fourth is the scholar who knows it still.

These four types of readers are obviously using translation for recognizably different purposes, and it must follow from this that, since different purposes are usually achieved by different methods and with the help of different tools, the same translation cannot be equally suited to them all. In other words, the concept of reader-analysis will show that each form of translation has its own function, which it adequately fulfills when used by the type of reader for which it was intended.

...

The ignoramus is happy with the free translation; it satisfies his curiosity and he reads it easily, without the pains of thought. The student is best helped by the most literal translation that can be made in accurate English; it helps him to grasp the implications of the different constructions of the language that he is studying and points out the correct usage of its familiar words. The third prefers the translation that sounds like a translation; it brings back more keenly the memories of his early scholarship and gives him a subconscious impression that almost he is reading the original language. And the fourth, who knows both the matter and style of the original, may perhaps find pleasure in occasional touches of scholarship, though it must be admitted that his comments are more likely to be caustic or critical."

5   The Translation of Poetry

Savory devotes the sixth chapter of *The Art of Translation* to the discussion of the translation of poetry. How should poetry be translated? Experts differ in their opinions. Postgate states in his book *Translations and Translators* as a cardinal principle that prose should be translated by prose, and verse by verse. Matthew Arnold argues that a prose translation of poetry may still be highly poetical, but Carlyle, Leigh Hunt and Archbishop Whately agree that poetry is incomplete without the aesthetic effects of meter. Lord Woodhouselee observes that a prose translation is the most absurd of all such ventures and that none but a poet should translate a poem; whereas Hilaire Belloc states dogmatically that "translation of verse is nearly always better rendered in prose."

Savory first discusses the arguments in favor of verse translation. He quotes a sentence from Sir John Denham's preface to the second book of the *Aeneid*: "The business is not alone to translate language into language, but poesie into poesie, and poesie is of so subtle a spirit that in the pouring out of one language into another it will all evaporate, and if a new spirit is not added in the transfusion there will remain nothing but a *caput mortuum*." Savory points out that there is undeniably the fact that verse translation more closely resembles the form of the original. A verse translation gives at least an opportunity to indulge in figures of speech and to adopt the varied word order which the original contained, and which some translators wish to preserve whenever possible. In general the power of verse to stir the emotions is greater than the power of prose, so that to choose to make a prose translation of a poem is to impose a handicap on the translator and ask him to sacrifice a portion of his effect before he has begun.

Experienced translators such as Archer and Lenard have found that in verse they could be more exact, more accurate, than in prose, thus the principle of "verse for verse" is established beyond a doubt. But why should prose translations have been considered at all by translators, and why does in some collections the proportion of prose translations actually exceed the verse? One answer is soon discovered by any translator who tries to put a few lines of Greek, Latin or French poetry into English verse. His first step is to make a prose translation, to be quite sure, perhaps, that he knows what he is going to say and then to convert his prose into verse. But verse, satisfying verse, as Savory points out, "does not normally rise to the lips or flow from the pen unbidden; and the translator finds himself

devoting thought and sacrificing time in the effort to find the best words and secure the best result." This clearly demonstrates that a verse translation demands more effort and more skill than a prose one.

Savory remarks that rhyme imposes a constraint upon the writer, "a constraint which bears most heavily on the essential feature of the translator's art, his choice of words." He writes, "It is scarcely possible to find a rhymed translation of a lyric which does not contain evidence of this, as shown either by the omission of something that the original author wrote, or the inclusion of something that he did not. Why should a translator wish to omit anything that his author has said, unless it be from laziness or from a wish to hide his own ignorance of what has been written, and why, still less, should a translator have the impertinence to put into his author's mouth words that he has never spoken? The only possible answer to these questions is that the translator has been forced to do so because he has handicapped himself with the tyranny of rhyme."

But by some writers these enormities are concealed or condoned by the establishment of a principle of "compensation." If a translator finds himself forced to omit something, he may be excused if he offers something else in its place. Yet this is a practice that involves a risk and is liable to be misused. Modern opinion scarcely condones it. Rhyme has lost much of the inevitability that tradition had given it, with results that cannot easily be exaggerated when the translation of poetry is in question. The contemporary writers of prose-poetry or poetic prose are bound neither to the tyranny of rhyme nor even to the exactitude of stress and accent insisted on by past generations, and they have thus gained for themselves the opportunity of giving in translation both the meaning and the movement, the matter and the manner of a poem from another language."

Another feature of poetic translation is the matter of relative length. "As soon as faithfulness in translation is abandoned in favor of freedom, a translation tends to become a paraphrase, and one of the normal features of a paraphrase is that it is longer than its original. In prose this is of small importance; in poetry, where the quantity, the mere number of words, is a part of the nature of the poem, the importance is greater. A translator ought not to neglect this fact." Savory cites the English translations of the *Aeneid* as an example. The first English version of the poem occupies 756 lines, James Rhoades needs 947 and Dryden 1065.

So when it is agreed that the translation of a poem is not necessarily expected to be faithful, when it may be in rhyme where the original rhymed not, when excuses will be found for omissions and when additions will be condoned, and when the consensus of opinion is that the work is impossible and the ideal unattainable, a reasonable conclusion as to the nature of a poem in translation, Savory argues, is that "the translation is not the original poem in any but the primitive sense of a transcription of its meaning: it is a new product, the result of new intellectual effort." It is just "something like the original", and it is "perhaps the strongest possible incentive to a study of the original language, so that in the original form the poem may be read and appreciated."

6 Exercises

(1) Why does Savory maintain that translation is an art?

(2) How do you understand Savory's twelve principles of translation?

(3) Do you agree with Savory that in his translation the translator should take the reader's point of view into consideration? Why or why not?

(4) What is your view about the translation of poetry?

7 Reference and Further Reading

(1) SAVORY T. The Art of Translation [M]. London: The Alden Press, 1957.

(2) 廖七一, 等. 当代英国翻译理论 [M]. 武汉：湖北教育出版社，2001.

Chapter Eleven

Eugene Nida's Translation Theory

1 An Introduction to Eugene Nida

Eugene A. Nida (1914–2011) was a distinguished American translator as well as a linguist. His works on translation set off the study of modern translation as an academic field, and he is regarded as the patriarch of translation study and the founder of the discipline.

Born in 1914, in Oklahoma City, Eugene Nida and his family moved to Long Beach, California when he was 5 years old. He began studying Latin in high school and was already looking forward to being able to translate Scripture as a missionary. He became a Christian at a young age, when he responded to the altar call at his church to accept Christ as his Saviour. By the time he received his Bachelor's degree in 1936 from the University of California at Los Angeles, he was well on his way. After graduating he attended Camp Wycliffe, where Bible translation theory was taught. He ministered for a short time among the Tarahumara Indians in Mexico, until health problems due to an inadequate diet and the high altitude forced him to leave. Sometime in this period, Nida became a founding charter member of Wycliffe Bible Translators, a sister organization of the Summer Institute of Linguistics. Having earned his degree in Greek, summa cum laude, he enrolled in the Summer Institute of Linguistics (SIL) and studied the works of such linguists as Edward Sapir and Leonard Bloomfield. In 1937, Nida undertook studies at the University of Southern California, where he obtained a Master's Degree in New Testament Greek in 1939. In 1941 he began a Ph.D. in Linguistics at the University of Michigan. In 1943, he completed his Ph.D. and was ordained in the Northern Baptist Convention. He began his career as a linguist with the American Bible Society (ABS) and was quickly promoted to Associate Secretary for Versions, then he worked as Executive Secretary for Translations, providing practical service for missionary Bible translators, including counseling them how to translate better and, sometimes, providing them with a model of translation, etc.

Eugene Nida's main academic works include *Morphology: The Descriptive Analysis of Words* (1946), *Toward a Science of Translating* (1964), *The Theory and Practice of Translation* (1968, with Charles R. Taber), *From one Language to Another* (1986, with Jan de Waard), and *Language and Culture Contexts in Translating* (2001). Besides, he founds the journal *The Bible Translator* and served as its editor in 1949.

Upon joining the ABS staff, Dr. Nida immediately set out on a series of extended field trips in Africa and Latin America. These site visits led him to see that his most important role for ABS Translations' interests would not be limited to checking translations for publication, but of educating translators, and providing them with better models, resources, training, and organization for efficiency. This he managed to do through on-site visits, teaching and training workshops, and through building a translations network and organizational structure that became the global United Bible Societies Translations Program through which work in hundreds of indigenous languages is constantly in process around the world.

Nida was determined to produce cross-denominational Bibles in translations across the globe. His book *Toward a Science of Translating* (1964), and later *The Theory and Practice of Translation* (1969, with C. R. Taber) helped him achieve this objective. These two very influential books are his first book-length efforts to expound his theory on what he called dynamic equivalence translation, later to be called functional equivalence. How significant, revolutionary, and convincing this new approach proved to be can be seen in the fact that hundreds of Bible translations have now been effectively carried out with this methodology. In essence, this approach enables the translator to capture the meaning and spirit of the original language text without being bound to its linguistic structure.

Nida's work with indigenous language translations had shown that in order to reach people who bring no prior knowledge to their encounter with the Bible, the translation needs to place the highest priority on clear communication in easily-understood language and style. In 1968, the United Bible Societies (UBS) and the Vatican entered into a joint agreement to undertake hundreds of new inter-confessional Bible translation projects around the world, using functional equivalence principles. Nida was one of the principals on this collaborative work.

A scholar, teacher, leader, influencer, conceptualizer, innovator, and influential theoretician, Eugene A. Nida is very possibly unsurpassed in the history of the Bible Society movement in terms of global impact. His work, his organization, his ideas and the organization he put into place represent a watershed for the movement and for Bible translation.

 ## 2 Nida's Main Translation Ideas

I Two Basic Orientations in Translating

In the study of Bible translation, Nida identified two basic orientations in translating based on two different types of equivalence: Formal Equivalence and Dynamic Equivalence. Formal Equivalence focuses attention on the message itself, in both form and content. In such a translation one is concerned with such correspondences as poetry to poetry, sentence to sentence, and concept to concept. Viewed from this formal orientation, one is concerned that the message in the receptor language should match as closely as possible the different elements in the source language. This means, for example, that the message in the receptor culture is constantly compared with the message in the source culture to determine standards of accuracy and correctness.

The type of translation which most completely typifies this structural equivalence might be called a "gloss translation," in which the translator attempts to reproduce as literally and meaningfully as possible the form and content of the original. Such a translation might be a rendering of some Medieval French text into English, intended for students of certain aspects of early French literature and thus not requiring knowledge of the original language of the text. Their needs call for a relatively close approximation to the structure of the early French text, both in form (e.g. syntax and idioms) and in content (e.g. themes and concepts). Such a translation would require numerous footnotes in order to make the text fully comprehensible.

In contrast, a translation which attempts to produce a dynamic rather than a formal equivalence is based upon the principle of equivalent effect. In such a translation one is not so concerned with matching the receptor-language message with the source-language message, but with the dynamic relationship, that the relationship between receptor and message should be substantially the same as that which existed between the original receptors and the message. The message has to be tailored to the receptor's linguistic needs and cultural expectation and aims at the complete naturalness of expression. "Naturalness" is a key requirement for Nida. Indeed, he defines the goal of dynamic equivalence as seeking the closest natural equivalent to the source-language message.

Dynamic Equivalence attempts to convey the thought expressed in a source text (if necessary, at the expense of literalness, original word order, the source text's grammatical voice, etc.), while Formal Equivalence attempts to render the text word-for-word (if necessary, at the expense of natural expression in the target language). The two approaches represent emphasis, respectively, on readability and on literal fidelity to the source text. Broadly, dynamic and formal equivalence represent a spectrum of translation approaches with no sharp boundary. Nida coined the two terms in terms of how to produce an acceptable translation. Although it was originally coined to describe ways of translating the Bible, it is applicable to any translation. Between the two poles of translating (i.e. between strict formal equivalence and complete dynamic equivalence) there are a number of intervening grades, representing various acceptable standards of literary translation. During the past fifty years, however, there has been a marked shift of emphasis from the formal to the dynamic dimension. A recent summary of opinion on translating by literary artists, publishers, educators, and professional translators indicates clearly that the present direction is toward increasing emphasis on dynamic equivalences. Nida also distanced himself from the Formal-Equivalence and preferred the term Dynamic-Equivalence.

II Principles Governing a Translation Oriented Toward Formal Equivalence

A formal-equivalence (or F-E) translation is basically source-oriented; that is, it is designed to reveal as much as possible of the form and content of the original message.

In doing so, an F-E translation attempts to reproduce several formal elements, including:

> (1) grammatical units, (2) consistency in word usage, and (3) meanings in terms of the source context. The reproduction of grammatical units may consist in: (a) translating nouns by nouns, verbs by verbs, etc.; (b) keeping all phrases and sentences intact (i.e. not splitting up and readjusting the units); and (c) preserving all formal indicators, e.g. marks of punctuation, paragraph breaks, and poetic indentation.

In attempting to reproduce consistency in word usage, an F-E translation usually aims at so-called concordance of terminology; that is, it always renders a particular term in the source language document by the corresponding term in the receptor document. Such a principle may, of course, be pushed to an absurd extent, with the result being relatively meaningless strings of words. On the other hand, a certain degree of concordance may be highly desirable in certain types of F-E translating. An F-E translation may also make use of brackets, parentheses, or even italics for words added to make sense in the translation, but missing in the original document.

In order to reproduce meanings in terms of the source context, an F-E translation normally attempts not to make adjustments in idioms, but rather to reproduce such expressions more or less literally, so that the reader may be able to perceive something of the way in which the original document employed local cultural document to convey meanings.

A consistent F-E translation will obviously contain much that is not readily intelligible to the average reader. One must therefore usually supplement such translations with marginal notes, not only to explain some of the formal features which could not be adequately represented, but also to make intelligible some of the formal equivalents employed, for such expressions may have significance only in terms of the source language or culture.

The more the source language differs from the target language, the more difficult it may be to understand a literal translation. On the other hand, formal equivalence can sometimes allow readers familiar with the source language to see how meaning was expressed in the original text, preserving untranslated idioms, rhetorical devices (such as chiastic structures in the Hebrew Bible), and diction.

Formal equivalence is often more goal than reality, if only because one language may contain a word for a concept which has no direct equivalent in another language. In such cases, a more dynamic translation may be used or a neologism may be created in the target language to represent the concept (sometimes by borrowing a word from the source language).

III Principles Governing a Translation Oriented Toward Dynamic Equivalence

Nida's most notable contribution to translation theory is Dynamic Equivalence, which is often held in opposition to the views of philologists who maintain that an understanding of the source text (ST) can be achieved by assessing the inter-animation of words on the page, and that meaning is self-contained within the text (i.e. much more focused on achieving semantic equivalence).

Dynamic-Equivalence theory, along with other theories of correspondence in translating, are elaborated in Nida's essay "Principles of Correspondence," where Nida begins by asserting that given that "no two languages are identical, either in the meanings given to corresponding symbols or in the ways in which symbols are arranged in phrases and sentences, it stands to reason that there can be no absolute correspondence between languages. Hence, there can be no fully exact translations." While the impact of a translation may be close to the original, there can be no identity in detail.

Aiming at complete "naturalness" of expression, a Dynamic-Equivalence translation is directed primarily towards equivalence of response rather than equivalence of form. The essence of it is a receptor-centered theory of translation that aims at achieving a "dynamic equivalence between the effect obtained from respective readers of the original text and the translated version, which requires that translators view from the angle of the sense and spirit of the original instead of rigidly adhering to language structures of it. That is, not rigidly adhering to formal equivalence. The relationship between the target language receptor and message should be substantially the same as that which existed between the original (source language) receptors and the message.

Because dynamic equivalence eschews strict adherence to the grammatical structure of the original text in favor of a more natural rendering in the target language, it is sometimes used when the readability of the translation is more important than the preservation of the original grammatical structure. Thus a novel might be translated with greater use of dynamic equivalence so that it may read well, while in diplomacy or in some business settings people may insist on formal equivalence because they believe that fidelity to the grammatical structure of the language equals greater accuracy.

One way of defining a D-E translation is to describe it as "the closest natural equivalent to the source-language message." This type of definition contains three essential terms:

> (1) equivalent, which points towards the source language message, (2) natural, which points towards the receptor language, and (3) closest, which binds the two orientations together on the basis of the highest degree of approximation.

However, since a D-E translation is directed primarily toward equivalence of response rather than equivalence of form, it is important to define more fully the implication of the word "natural" as applied to such translations. Basically, the word "natural" is applicable to three areas of the communication process; for a natural rendering must fit (1) the receptor language and culture as a whole, (2) the context of the particular message, and (3) the receptor-language audience.

It is inevitable that when source and receptor languages represent very different cultures there should be many basic themes and accounts which cannot be "naturalized" by the process of translating. Nevertheless, these cultural discrepancies offer less difficulty than might be imagined, especially when footnotes are used to point out the basis for the cultural diversity; for all people recognize that other people behave differently from themselves.

In addition to being appropriate to the receptor language and culture, a natural translation must be in accordance with the context of the particular message. The problem is thus not restricted to gross grammatical and lexical features, but may also involve such detailed matters as intonation and sentence rhythm. A truly natural translation can in some respects be described more easily in terms of what it avoids than in what it actually states; for it is the presence of serious anomalies, avoided in a successful translation, which immediately strike the reader as being out of place in the context.

A translation which aims at dynamic equivalence inevitably involves a number of formal adjustments, for one cannot have his formal cake and eat it dynamically too. In general, this limitation involves three principal areas: (1) special literary form, (2) semantically exocentric expressions, and (3) intraorganismic meanings.

IV Principles Governing a Translation Oriented Toward Functional Equivalence

Nida held that the term "dynamic" has been misunderstood by some persons as referring to something that has impact. Accordingly, many individuals have been led to think that if a translation has considerable impact, then it must be a correct example of dynamic equivalence. Because of this misunderstanding and in order to emphasize the concept of function, it has seemed much more satisfactory to use the expression "functional equivalence" in describing the degrees of adequacy of a translation. "The terms 'function' and 'functional' seem to provide a much sounder basis for talking about translation as a form of communication, since the focus is on what a translation dose or performs."

In his book *Language, Culture and Translating,* Nida stated that translating means communicating, and this process depends on what is received by persons hearing or reading a translation. Judging the validity of a translation cannot stop with a comparison of corresponding comparison of corresponding lexical meanings, grammatical classes, and rhetorical devices. What is important is the translated text. Accordingly, it is essential that functional equivalence be stated primarily in terms of a comparison of the way in which the original receptors understand and appreciate the text and the way in which the receptors of the translated text understand and appreciate the translated text.

Nida tried to list a number of relevant principles governing the kinds and degrees of adjustment which may be necessary in order to produce a satisfactory functional equivalent of a source text. If a more or less literal correspondence is functionally equivalent in both designative and associative meaning, then obviously no adjustment in form is necessary. But if this is not the case, then the following principles may be helpful in deciding what should be done in order to produce the closest natural equivalence:

(1) If a close, formal translation is likely to result in a misunderstanding of the designative meaning, (a) certain changes must be introduced into the text of the translation or (b) the literal translation may be retained and a footnote explaining the likely misunderstanding must be added.

(2) If a close, formal translation makes no sense, i.e. is totally obscure in designative meaning, certain changes may be introduced into the text unless the source text is purposely obscure, in which case the obscurity may be retained, and a footnote explaining the nature of the obscurity may be very useful and in most instances fully justified.

(3) If a close, formal translation is so semantically and syntactically difficult that the average person for whom the translation is being made is very likely to give up trying it, certain changes are warranted, although it may be useful to indicate the nature of such changes in an introduction or in footnotes.

(4) If a close, formal translation is likely to result in serious misunderstanding of the associative meanings of the source text or in a significant loss in a proper appreciation for the stylistic value of the source text, it is important to make such adjustments as are necessary to reflect the associative values of the source text.

(5) The manner in which the translation is to be used has a significant influence upon the extent to which adjustments are to be made. For example, the translation of a drama to be read in the quiet of one's home is generally quite different from one which is designated to be acted on the stage. The former type of translation can afford to have relatively close, formal correspondences, since significant differences or problems in understanding can be explained in footnotes. But there is no time or place for footnotes in a stage performance.

(6) The fact that the source text must be translated in such a way as to occur with accompanying codes usually requires a number of adjustments on all levels: phonology, lexicon, syntax, and discourse.

③ Exercises

(1) Is translation a science or an art?

(2) Is Nida's translation theory only applicable in Bible translation? Make a brief comment on his theory.

(3) What is your understanding of the term "equivalence" in translation?

4 **References and Further Readings**

(1) NIDA E A. Language, Culture, and Translating [M]. Shanghai: Shanghai Foreign Language Education Press, 1999.

(2) NIDA E A. Language and Culture [M]. Shanghai: Shanghai Foreign Language Education Press, 2001.

(3) NIDA E A. Toward a Science of Translating [M]. Shanghai: Shanghai Foreign Language Education Press, 2004.

(4) STINE P. Let the Words Be Written: The Lasting Influence of Eugene A. Nida [M]. Leiden: Brill Academic Publishers, 2005.

(5) 谭载喜. 新编奈达论翻译 [M]. 北京: 中国对外翻译出版公司, 1999.

Chapter Twelve

Peter Newmark's Translation Theory

① An Introduction to Peter Newmark

Peter Newmark (1916–2011) was an English professor of translation at the University of Surrey. He got a BA and Ph.D. in Biochemistry from Oxford University. He joined *Nature* as Biology Editor in 1974 and left as Deputy Editor in 1990 to join the *Current Science Group*. There he managed the *Current Opinion* review journals and founded and edited the journal *Current Biology*. In 1997, he moved with these journals to *Elsevier Science* and became responsible also for the *Trends* review journals. In 2000, he returned to the *Current Science Group* as Biology Editorial Director for BioMed Central, the pioneering open-access publisher.

From the early 1980s, Professor Newmark was associated with the founding and development of the Centre for Translation Studies at Surrey. He was chair of the editorial board of the *Journal of Specialized Translation*. He also wrote "Translation Now" bimonthly for *The Linguist* and was an Editorial Board Member of the Institute of Linguists.

Professor Newmark cared passionately about language, civilization, and respect for great texts. His views were generally conservative, but always offered in the spirit of lively public debate. He was one of the main figures in the founding of translation studies in the English-speaking world from the 1980s. He was also very influential in the Spanish-speaking world. He is widely read through a series of accessible and occasionally polemical works, the titles of which are as straightforward as the man himself: *A Textbook of Translation* (1988), *Paragraphs on Translation* (1989), *About Translation* (1991), *More Paragraphs on Translation* (1998).

2 Communicative Translation and Semantic Translation

The concepts of communicative and semantic translation represent Peter Newmark's main contribution to general translation theory. In his book *Approaches to Translation*, two chapters contribute to the elaboration on these two methods.

In the pre-linguistics period of writing on translation, opinion swung between literal and free, faithful and beautiful, exact and natural translation, depending on whether the bias was to be in favor of the author or the reader, the source or the target language of the text. Since the rise of the modern linguistics, the general emphasis, supported by communication-theorists as well as by non-literary translators, has been placed on the reader — on informing the reader effectively and appropriately, notably in Nida, Firth, Koller and the Leipzig School. Newmark held that the conflict of loyalties, the gap between emphasis on source and target language will always remain as the overriding problem in translation theory and practice. However, the gap could perhaps be narrowed if the previous terms were replaced as follows (Figure 2.12.1):

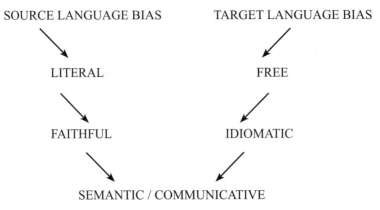

Figure 2.12.1 Semantic / Communicative

Communicative translation attempts to produce on its readers an effect as close as possible to that contained on the readers of the original. Semantic translation attempts to render, as closely as the semantic and syntactic structures of the second language allow, the exact contextual meaning of the original.

In theory, there are wide differences between the two methods. Communicative translation addresses itself solely to the second reader, who does not anticipate difficulties or obscurities, and would expect a generous transfer of foreign elements into his own cultures as well as his language where necessary. Semantic translation remains within the original culture and assists the reader only in its connotations if they constitute the essential human message of the text. One basic difference between the two methods is that where there is a conflict, the communicative must emphasize the "force" rather than the content of the message. Generally, a communicative translation is likely to be smoother, simpler, clearer, more direct, more conventional, conforming to a particular register of language, tending to undertranslate. A semantic translation tends to be more complex, more awkward, more detailed, more concentrated, and pursues the thought-processes rather than the intention of the transmitter. It tends to overtranslate, to be more specific than the original, to include more meanings in its search for one nuance of meaning.

Communicative and semantic translation may well coincide — in particular, where the text conveys a general rather than a culturally (temporally and spatially) bound message and where the matter is as important as the manner — notably in the translation of the most important religious, philosophical, artistic and scientific texts, assuming second readers as informed and interested as the first. Further, there are often sections in one text that must be translated communicatively and others semantically. There is no one communicative or one semantic method of translating a text — these are in fact widely overlapping bands of methods. A translation can be more, or less, semantic — more, or less, communicative — even a particular section or sentence can be treated more communicatively or less semantically. Each method has a common basis in analytical or cognitive translation which is built up both proposition by proposition and word by word, denoting the empirical factual knowledge of the text, but finally respecting the convention of the target language provided that the thought-content of the text has been reproduced. The translation emerges in such a way that the exact meaning or functions of the words only become apparent as they are used. The translator may have to make interim decisions without being able at the time to visualize the relation of words with the end product. Communicative and semantic translation bifurcate at a later stage of analytical or cognitive translation which is a pre-translation procedure which may be performed on the source-language text to convert it into the source or the target language — the resultant versions will be closer to each other than the original text and the final translation.

Newmark assumes that whilst a semantic translation is always inferior to its original, since it involves loss of meaning, a communicative translation may be better, since it may gain in force and clarity what it loses in semantic content. In communicative translation the translator is trying in his own language to write a little better than the original, unless he is reproducing the well-established formulate of notices or correspondence. In communicative translation one has the right to correct or improve the logic; to replace clumsy with elegant, or at least functional, syntactic structures; to remove obscurities; to eliminate repetition and tautology; to exclude the less likely interpretations of an ambiguity; to modify and clarify jargon (e.g. reduce loose generic terms to rather more concrete components), and to normalize bizarreries of idiolect, i.e. wayward uses of language. Further, one has the right to correct mistakes of facts and slips, normally stating what one has done in a footnote. (All such corrections and improvements are usually inadmissible in semantic translation.)

In some sense, communicative translation, by adapting and making the thought and cultural content of the original more accessible to the reader, gives semantic translation another dimension. The Leipzig School has referred to this as the "pragmatic" element, but Newmark thought this is a little misleading and he would prefer to avoid the use of the term "pragmatic" and to regard both communicative and semantic as  divergent refinements or revisions of cognitive translation. In both cases, the cognitive element may soon have to be abandoned, since the TL view of the same referent may differ from the SL. The transition to semantic translation normally reduces the unit of translation, and brings the text closer to the figurative and formal elements of the original. Therefore, the text becomes more idiosyncratic and "sensitive." Length of sentences, however long or short, position and integrity of clauses, word position for emphasis, are preserved, unless the divergence between the relevant norms of the source and target languages is extensive. The transition to communicative translation normally makes the text smoother, lighter, more idiomatic and easier to read. Syntax is remodeled, and more common collocations and more usual words are found. Semantic translation is basically addressed to one "reader" only, namely, the writer of the SL text, with the assumption that he can read the TL and will be the best arbiter of the translation's quality.

It is not always possible to state which is the better method to use for a particular text. In a mainly informative text, the section containing recommendations, instructions, value-judgements, etc., may be translated more communicatively than the descriptive passages. Where language is used to accompany action or as its symbol (speech-acts), it is treated communicatively, whilst definitions, explanations, etc., are semantic. "Standardized language" must be translated communicatively, whether a standardized equivalent exists or not, even if it appears in a novel or a quotation, unless the term is used descriptively rather than operatively in the original text.

A semantic translation attempts to recreate the precise flavor and tone of the original: the words are "sacred," not because they are more important than the content, but because form and content are one. The thought-processes in the words are as significant as the intention behind the words in a communicative translation. Thus, a semantic translation is out of time and local space (but has to be done again every generation, if still "valid"), where a communicative translation is ephemeral and rooted in its context. A semantic translation attempts to preserve its author's idiolect, his peculiar form of expression, in preference to the "spirit" of the source or the target language. Communicative translation responds to the representational and vocative functions. In semantic translation, every word translated represents some loss of meaning, where in communicative translation the same words similarly translated lose no meaning at all. The syntax in semantic translation which gives the text its stresses and rhythm — the "foregrounding" as the Prague School calls it — is as sacred as the words, being basically subject only to the standard transpositions or shifts from one language to another. There is a constant temptation, which should be resisted, to transcribe the terms for key-concepts or theme words.

The distinction between semantic and communicative translation, which a behaviorist might deny, shows how closely translation theory relates not only to philosophy of language, but even to philosophy in an old sense of the term, when it meant perhaps "interpretation of the meaning of life." Thus, an affirmative attitude to translation would perhaps stem from a belief in rationalism, in the communicability, and renewal of common experience, in "innate" human nature and even in natural law.

Normally, one assumes that a semantic translation is briefer and "more literal" than a communicative translation. This is usually, but not always so. If the original is rich in metaphor, has simultaneously abstract as well as physical meanings and is concerned with say religion, ritual magic, witchcraft or other domains of discourse which have covert categories, a prose translation with explanatory power (the interpretation must be within the translation, not follow it) is likely to be longer than the original. It has to reproduce the full meaning of the original, not simply one of its functions.

The following is an example of semantic translation and communicative translation, and the differences are self-evident.

The original text: "携你到那昌明隆盛之邦、诗礼簪缨之族、花柳繁华地、温柔富贵乡那里去走一遭"。(曹雪芹《红楼梦》)

Semantic translation:

> "Then we can take you to some civilized and prosperous realm, to a cultured family of official status, a place where flowers and willows flourish, the home of pleasure and

Communicative translation:

"After that I shall take you to certain

Brilliant

Successful

Poetical

Cultivated

Aristocratic

Elegant

Delectable

Luxurious

Opulent

Locality on a little trip."

③ Exercises

(1) What is the main difference between semantic translation and communicative translation?

(2) What is Peter Newmark's main contribution to translation theory?

(3) How do you comment on Newmark's translation theory?

(4) Please comment on the following translation from the perspective of Peter Newmark's translation theory.

一双丹凤三角眼，两弯柳叶吊梢眉，身量苗条，体格风骚。粉面含春威不露，丹唇未启笑声闻。(曹雪芹《红楼梦》)

She had the almond-shaped eyes of a phoenix, slanting eyebrows as long and drooping as willow leaves. Her figure was slender and her manner vivacious. The springtime charm of her powdered face gave no hint of her latent formidability. And before her crimson lips parted, her laughter rang out.

She had, moreover,

eyes like a painted phoenix,

eyebrows like willow-leaves,

a slender form,

seductive grace,

the ever-smiling summer face

of hidden thunders showed no trace;

the ever-bubbling laughter started

almost before the lips were parted.

4 References and Further Readings

(1) NEWMARK P. Approaches to Translation [M]. Shanghai: Shanghai Foreign Language Education Press, 2001.

(2) NEWMARK P. A Textbook of Translation [M]. Shanghai: Shanghai Foreign Language Education Press, 2001.

(3) MUNDAY J. Introducing Translation Studies: Theories and Applications [M]. New York: Routledge, 2001.

Chapter Thirteen

Susan Bassnett and Cultural Translation

① An Introduction to Susan Bassnett

Susan Bassnett (1945–) is one of the leading international translation theorists and scholars of comparative literature. She was educated in several European countries, which gave her grounding in diverse languages and cultures. She began her academic career in Italy and has lectured in universities around the world including Belgium, Brazil, Canada, Germany, and the United States prior to the University of Warwick in Great Britain where she is currently professor of comparative literature. In 2007, she was elected a Fellow at the Royal Society of Literature -- the United Kingdom's premium literary association.

Susan Bassnett is the author of over 20 books, and her Translation Studies, which first appeared in 1980, has remained consistently in print and has become the most important textbook around the world in the expanding field of Translation Studies. Her Comparative Literature: A Critical Introduction (1993) has also become an internationally renowned work and has been translated into several languages. Other books include Translation, History and Culture (1990) and Constructing Cultures (1998) written with Andre Lefevere, and Post-Colonial Translation (1999) co-edited with Harish Trivedi. Besides her academic research, Susan Bassnett writes poetry. Her latest collection is Exchanging Lives (2002). She also writes for several national newspapers.

② Bassnett's Translation Ideas

I Translation Studies Is a Discipline in Its Own Right

Translation has a very long history. Many people have assumed that such a discipline as translation studies came into existence long ago in view of the widespread use of the term "translation." But in fact the systematic study of translation is still in swaddling bands. The name

Translation Studies was first adopted by André Lefevere in 1978 to refer to the discipline that concerns itself with "the problems raised by the production and description of translations." Bassnett keeps this name and maintains that "translation studies is indeed a discipline in its own right: not merely a minor branch of comparative literary study, nor yet a specific area of linguistics, but a vastly complex field with may far-reaching ramifications."

II Four Categories of Translation Studies

According to Bassnett, translation studies can be roughly divided into four general areas of interest, each with a degree of overlap. Two are product-oriented, in that the emphasis is on the functional aspects of the TL text in relation to the SL text, and two of them are process-oriented, in that the emphasis is on analyzing what actually takes place during translation.

The first category involves the *History of Translation* and is a component part of literary history. The type of work involved in this area includes investigation of the theories of translation at different times, the critical response to translations, the practical processes of commissioning and publishing translations, the role and function of translations in a given period, the methodological development of translation and, by far the most common type of study, analysis of the work of individual translators.

The second category, *Translation in the TL culture*, extends the work on single texts or authors and includes work on the influence of a text, author or genre, on the absorption of the norms of the translated text into the TL system and on the principles of selection operating within that system.

The third category *Translation and Linguistics* includes studies which place their emphasis on the comparative arrangement of linguistic elements between the SL and the TL text with regard to phonemic, morphemic, lexical, syntagmatic and syntactic levels. Into this category come studies of the problems of linguistic equivalence, of language-bound meaning, of linguistic untranslatability, of machine translation, etc., and also studies of the translation problems of non-literary texts.

The fourth category, loosely called *Translation and Poetics*, includes the whole area of literary translation, in theory and practice. Studies may be general or genre-specific, including investigation of the particular problems of translating poetry, theatre texts or libretti and the affiliated problem of translation for the cinema, whether dubbing or sub-titling. Under this category also come studies of the poetics of individual, translators and comparisons between them, studies of the problems of formulating a poetics, and studies of the interrelationship between SL and TL texts and author–

translator–reader. Above all in this section come studies attempting to formulate a theory of literary translation.

Bassnett points out that work in categories 1 and 3 is more widespread than work in categories 2 and 4, although there is little systematic study of translation history and some of the work on translation and linguistics is rather isolated from the mainstream of translation study. It is important for the student of translation to be mindful of the four general categories, even while investigating one specific area of interest, in order to avoid fragmentation.

Bassnett holds that the question of evaluation is the final great stumbling block waiting for the person with an interest in Translation Studies: For if a translator perceives his or her role as partly that of "improving" either the SL text or existing translations, and that is indeed often the reason why we undertake translations, an implicit value judgement underlies this position. All too often, in discussing their work, translators avoid analysis of their own methods and concentrate on exposing the frailties of other translators. Critics, on the other hand, frequently evaluate a translation from one or other of two limited standpoints: from the narrow view of the closeness of the translation to the SL text (an evaluation that can only be made if the critic has access to both languages) or from the treatment of the TL text as a work in their  own language. And whilst this latter position clearly has some validity — it is, after all, important that a play should be playable and a poem should be readable — the arrogant way in which critics will define a translation as good or bad from a purely monolingual position again indicates the peculiar position occupied by translation vis-à-vis another type of metatext (a work derived from, or containing another existing text), literary criticism itself.

Bassnett believes that it is pointless to argue for a definitive translation, because translation is intimately tied up with the context in which it is made. She proposes that there is no universal canon according to which texts may be assessed. There are whole sets of canons that shift and change and each text is involved in a continuing dialectical relationship with those ties. There can no more be the ultimate translation than there can be the ultimate poem or the ultimate novel, and any assessment of a translation can only be made by taking into account both the process of creating it and its function in a given context.

III Central Issues of Translation Studies

In Section One of *Translation Studies*, Bassnett discusses the following central issues of translation studies:

Language and Culture

Bassnett argues that although translation has a central core of linguistic activity, it belongs most properly to semiotics, the science that studies sign systems or structures, sign processes and sign functions. Beyond the notion stressed by the narrowly linguistic approach, that translation involves the transfer of "meaning" contained in one set of language signs into another set of language signs through competent use of the dictionary and grammar, the process involves a whole set of extra-linguistic criteria also. She agrees with the Soviet semiotician Juri Lotman that no language can exist unless it is steeped in the context of culture; and no culture can exist which does not have at its center, the structure of natural language. Language is the heart within the body of culture, and it is the interaction between the two that results in the continuation of life-energy. In the same way that the surgeon, operating on the heart, cannot neglect the body that surrounds it, so the translator treats the text in isolation from the culture at his peril.

Types of Translation

Roman Jakobson distinguishes three types of translation in his article "*On Linguistic Aspects of Translation*":

(1) Intralingual translation, or rewording (an interpretation of verbal signs by means of other signs in the same language);

(2) Interlingual translation or translation proper (an interpretation of verbal signs by means of some other language);

(3) Intersemiotic translation or transmutation (an interpretation of verbal signs by means of signs of nonverbal sign systems)

Of these three types, Bassnett points out, the second describes the process of transfer from SL to TL. She agrees with Jakobson that there is ordinarily no full equivalence through translation. Even apparent synonymy does not yield equivalence, and the translator has to resort to a combination of units in order to find an appropriate equivalent.

Decoding and Recoding

Bassnett holds that the translator operates criteria that transcend the purely linguistic, and a process of decoding and recoding takes place. In determining what to use in TL, the translator must:

(1) Accept the untranslatability of the SL phrase in the TL on the linguistic level;

(2) Accept the lack of a similar cultural convention in the TL;

(3) Consider the range of TL phrases available, having regard to the presentation of class, status, age, sex of the speaker, his relationship to the listeners and the context of their meeting in the SL;

(4) Consider the significance of the phrase in its particular context — i.e. as a moment of high tension in the dramatic text;

(5) Replace in the TL the invariant core of the SL phrase in its two referential systems (the particular system of the text and the system of culture out of which the text has sprung).

Bassnett is supportive of Levý's view that any contracting or omitting of difficult expressions in translating is immoral. The translator has the responsibility of finding a solution to the most daunting of problems, and the functional view must be adopted with regard not only to meaning but also to style and form.

She argues that the emphasis always in translation is on the reader or listener, and the translator must tackle the SL text in such a way that the TL version will correspond to the SL version. The nature of that correspondence may vary considerably but the principle remains constant. Hence Albrecht Neubert's view that Shakespeare's Sonnet *"Shall I compare thee to a summer's day?"* cannot be semantically translated into a language where summers are unpleasant is perfectly proper, just as the concept of God the Father cannot be translated into a language where the deity is female. To attempt to impose the value system of the SL culture onto the TL culture is dangerous ground, and the translator should not be tempted by the school that pretends to determine the original intentions of an author on the basis of a self-contained text. The translator cannot be the author of the SL text, but as the author of the TL text has a clear moral responsibility to the TL readers.

Problems of Equivalence

Bassnett believes that the problem of equivalence, a much-used and abused term in Translation Studies, is of central importance. As to the definition of equivalence, translation theorists have given different answers.

In his definition of translation equivalence, Popovič distinguishes four types:

(1) Linguistic equivalence, where there is homogeneity on the linguistic level of both SL and TL texts, i.e. word for word translation;

(2) Paradigmatic equivalence, where there is equivalence of "the elements of a paradigmatic expressive axis," i.e. elements of grammar, which Popovič sees as being a

higher category than lexical equivalence;

(3) Stylistic (translational) equivalence, where there is "functional equivalence of elements in both original and translation aiming at an expressive identity with an invariant of identical meaning";

(4) Textual (syntagmatic) equivalence, where there is equivalence of the syntagmatic structuring of a text, i.e. equivalence of form and shape.

Bassnett maintains that translation involves far more than replacement of lexical and grammatical items between languages and, as can be seen in the translation of idioms and metaphors, the process may involve discarding the basic linguistic elements of the SL text so as to achieve Popovič's goal of "expressive identity" between the SL and TL texts. But once the translator moves away from close linguistic equivalence, the problems of determining the exact nature of the level of equivalence aimed for begin to emerge.

Eugene Nida distinguishes two types of equivalence, formal and dynamic, where formal equivalence "focuses attention on the message itself, in both form and content. In such a translation one is concerned with such correspondence as poetry to poetry, sentence to sentence, and concept to concept." Nida calls this type of translation a "gloss translation", which aims to allow the reader to understand as much of the SL context as possible. Dynamic equivalence is based on the principle of equivalent effect, i.e. that the relationship between receiver and message should aim at being the same as that between the original receivers and the SL message. But Bassnett argues that Nida's categories can actually be in conflict with each other as the principle of equivalent effect involves us in areas of speculation and at times can lead to very dubious conclusions.

Bassnett points out that if a dozen translators tackle the same poem, they will produce a dozen different versions. This is an established fact in Translation Studies. And yet somewhere in those dozen versions there will be what Popovič calls the "invariant core" of the original poem. This invariant is represented by stable, basic and constant semantic elements in the text, existing in common between all existing translations of a single work. So the invariant is part of a dynamic relationship and should not be confused with speculative arguments about the "nature", the "spirit" or "soul" of the text.

Bassnett is in favor of Neubert's and Peirce's view that translation equivalence must be considered a semiotic category, comprising a syntactic, semantic and pragmatic component. These components are arranged in a hierarchical relationship, where semantic equivalence takes priority over syntactic equivalence, and pragmatic equivalence conditions and modifies both the other elements. Equivalence overall results from the relation between signs themselves, the relationship between signs and what they stand for, and the relationship between signs, what they stand for and those who use them.

Bassnett observes that the question of defining equivalence is being pursued by two lines of development in Translation Studies. The first, rather predictably, lays an emphasis on the special problems of semantics and on the transfer of semantic content from SL to TL. With the second, which explores the question of equivalence of literary texts, the work of the Russian Formalists and the Prague Linguists, together with more recent developments in discourse analysis, have broadened the problem of equivalence in its application to the translation of such texts. James Holmes, for example, feels that the use of the term equivalence is "*perverse*," since to ask for sameness is to ask too much, while Durišin argues that the translator of a literary text is not concerned with establishing equivalence of natural language but of artistic procedures. And those procedures cannot be considered in isolation, but must be located within the specific cultural-temporal context within which they are utilized.

Bassnett concludes that equivalence in translation should not be approached as a search for sameness, since sameness cannot even exist between two TL versions of the same text, let alone between the SL and the TL version. Popovič's four types offer a useful starting point and Neubert's three semiotic categories point the way towards an approach that perceives equivalence as dialectic between the signs and the structures within and surrounding the SL and TL texts.

Loss and Gain

Since sameness cannot exist between two languages, it is inevitable for the question of loss and gain to arise in the translation process. Bassnett remarks that much time has been spent on discussing what is lost in the transfer of a text from SL to TL whilst ignoring what can also be gained, for the translator can at times enrich or clarify the SL text as a direct result of the translation process. Moreover, what is often seen as "lost" from the SL text may be replaced in the TL context.

Untranslatability

With regard to the question of untranslatability in the translation process, Bassnett is more supportive of Popovič's view. Popovič distinguishes two types. The first is defined as "a situation in which the linguistic elements of the original cannot be replaced adequately in structural, linear, functional or semantic terms in consequence of a lack of denotation or connotation." The second type refers to "a situation where the relation of expressing the meaning, i.e. the relation between the creative subject and its linguistic expression in the original does not find an adequate linguistic expression in the translation." Bassnett points out that more attention should be given to the actual problems that the translator has to deal with rather than the problem of untranslatability. She acknowledges that translation is a dialectic process that can be accomplished with relative success and it is the task of the translator to find a solution to even the most daunting of problems.

Science or "Secondary Activity"?

According to Bassnett, the purpose of translation theory is to reach an understanding of the processes undertaken in the act of translation and not, as is so commonly understood, to provide a set of norms for effecting the perfect translation. She argues that any debate about the existence of a science of translation is out of date: there already exists, with Translation Studies, a serious discipline investigating the process of translation, attempting to clarify the question of equivalence and to examine what constitutes meaning within that process. The myth of translation as a secondary activity with all the associations of lower status implied in the assessment, can be dispelled once the extent of the pragmatic element of translation is accepted, and once the relationship between author/ translator/ reader is outlined. A diagram of the communicative relationship in the process of translation shows that the translator is both receiver and emitter, the end and the beginning of two separate but linked chains of communication:

Author — Text — Receiver = Translator — Text — Receiver

She agrees with Octavio Paz's remark that "every translation, up to a certain point, is an invention and as such it constitutes a unique text".

IV The Cultural Turn in Translation Studies and the Translation Turn in Cultural Studies

In 1990, Susan Bassnett edited a collection of essays entitled *Translation, History and Culture* with André Lefevere. In "Introduction" of the book, which they intended as a kind of manifesto of what they saw as a major change of emphasis in translation studies, they argue that the study of the practice of translation has moved on from its formalist phase and is beginning to consider broader issues of context, history and convention:

"Once upon a time, the questions that were always being asked were 'How can translation be taught?' and 'How can translation be studied?' Those who regarded themselves as translators were often contemptuous of any attempts to teach translation, whilst those who claimed to teach often did not translate, and so had to resort to the old evaluative method of setting one translation alongside another and examining both in a formalist vacuum. Now, the questions have changed. The object of study has been redefined; what is studied is the text embedded in its network of both source and target cultural signs and in this way Translation Studies has been able both to utilize the linguistic approach and to move out beyond it."

They call this shift of emphasis "the cultural turn" in translation studies, and suggest that a study of the processes of translation combined with the praxis of translating could offer a way of understanding how complex manipulative textual processes take place: how a text is selected for translation, for example, what role the translator plays in that selection, what role an editor, publisher or patron plays, what criteria determine the strategies that will be employed by the translator, how a text might be received in the target system. For a translation always takes place in a continuum, never in a void, and there are all kinds of textual and extratextual constraints upon the translator. These constraints, or manipulatory processes involved in the transfer of texts have become the primary focus of work in translation studies, and in order to study those processes, translation studies has changed its course and has become both broader and deeper.

Bassnett proposes four suggestions: first, translation should take culture as the translation unit, not always linger on the discourse level; second, translation is not a simple process of decoding and recoding, but an activity of communication; third, translation should not be restricted as the description of the source text, but viewed as the functional equivalence in the target language culture; fourth, translation will have different principles and norms in different times in order to meet different needs. Translation, in a word, is to satisfy the needs of different culture and the needs of different groups in a certain culture.

In *Constructing Cultures* (1998) co-edited with André Lefevere, Susan Bassnett putS forward a new concept: the translation turn in cultural studies.

Bassnett first traces the evolution of cultural studies. The field of study is generally held to have begun in the 1960s, initiated by the publication of a series of texts by British academics who had worked in universities and in adult education. Richard Hoggart's *The Uses of Literacy* appeared in 1957, followed by Raymond Williams' *Culture and Society* and by E.P. Thompson's *The Making of the English Working Class* in 1963. Hoggart set up the Centre for Contemporary Cultural Studies at the University of Birmingham in 1964. In the early years of cultural studies, as the subject sought to establish itself within the academy, the principle concern was to reevaluate oral culture

and working class culture, to reclaim the word "culture" for a mass public rather than an elite minority. Under the leadership of Hoggart's successor, Stuart Hall, the Binningham Centre moved to considerations of race and gender also, and became less specifically English, drawing more upon theoretical work from the continent of Europe.

In his 1997 essay entitled "But What Is Cultural Studies?" Anthony Easthope argued that cultural studies have undergone three phases: the Culturalist phase of the 1960s, the Structuralist phase of the 1970s and the Post-structuralist / Cultural Materialist phase of the 1980s and 1990s. These three phases correspond to different stages in the establishment of the subject as an academic discipline. The culturalist phase records the period when the principal challenge was to the appropriation of the term "culture" by an elite minority, and the goal was to broaden concepts of "culture" to include other than canonical texts. The structuralist phase marks the period when attention shifted to an investigation of the relationship between textuality and hegemony, and the third stage reflects the recognition of cultural pluralism.

Bassnett holds that this tripartite distinction, which traces in broad brush strokes a series of profoundly significant shifts of emphasis that have affected the study of literature just as much as the study of culture, could just as well apply to translation studies over the last twenty years or so. In translation studies, the culturalist phase would describe the work of Nida and probably also of Peter Newmark, as well as the work of scholars such as Catford or Georges Mounin. The value of their attempts to think culturally, to explore the problem of how to define equivalence, to wrestle with notions of linguistic versus cultural untranslatability is undeniable.

The polysystems phase may also be described as a structuralist phase, for systems and structures dominated thinking in the field for a time. We may have used figurative language and talked about "mapping" (Holmes) labyrinths (Bassnett) or even refractions (Lefevere) but what we were concerned with was a more systematic approach to the study and practice of translation. While translation studies took on polysystems theory, cultural studies delved more deeply into gender theory and the study of youth cultures. It also began to move away from the specifically English focus, and in the 1980s cultural studies expanded rapidly in many parts of the world, notably in the United States and Canada and Australia, changing and adapting as it moved. Questions of cultural identity, multiculturalism, linguistic pluralism became part of the agenda, shifting the emphasis away from those specifically British concerns of the early years.

Cultural studies in its new internationalist phase turned to sociology, to ethnography and to history. And likewise, translation studies turned to ethnography and history and sociology to deepen the methods of analyzing what happens to texts in the process of what we might call "intercultural transfer," or translation. In short, a cultural study has moved from its very English beginnings towards increased internationalisation, and has discovered the comparative dimension necessary for what we might call "intercultural analysis." Translation studies has moved away from an anthropological notion of culture (albeit a very fuzzy version) and towards a notion of cultures in the plural. In terms of methodology, cultural studies has abandoned its evangelical phase as an oppositional force to traditional literary studies and is looking more closely at questions of hegemonic relations in text production. Similarly, translation studies has moved on from endless debates about "equivalence" to discussion of the factors involved in text production across linguistic boundaries.

Both cultural studies and translation studies practitioners recognize the importance of understanding the manipulatory processes that are involved in textual production. A writer does not just write in a vacuum: he or she is the product of a particular culture, of a particular moment in time, and the writing reflects those factors such as race, gender, age, class, and birthplace as well as the stylistic, idiosyncratic features of the individual. Moreover, the material conditions in which the text is produced, sold, marketed and read also have a crucial role to play.

Bassnett quotes Lawrence Venuti (1995) to show that translation, wherever, whenever and however it takes place, is always to some extent circumscribed:

"Every step in the translation process — from the selection of foreign texts to the implementation of translation strategies to the editing, reviewing and reading of translations — is mediated by the diverse cultural values that circulate in the target language, always in some hierarchical order."

Translation as a sign of fragmentation, of cultural destabilization and negotiation is a powerful image for the late twentieth century. As English extends its international influence, so more and more people outside the English-speaking world actively participate in translational activity. Both translation studies and cultural studies have come of age. Both interdisciplines have entered a new internationalist phase, and have been moving for some time away from their more overtly parochial and Eurocentric beginnings, towards a more sophisticated investigation of the relationship between the local and the global. Both are now vast wide-ranging fields, within which there is no consensus. Bassnett points out that there are now clearly several areas that would lend themselves fruitfully to greater cooperation between practitioners of both interdisciplines.

(1) There needs to be more investigation of the acculturation process that takes place between cultures and the way in which different cultures construct their image of writers and texts.

(2) There needs to be more comparative study of the ways in which texts become cultural capital across cultural boundaries.

(3) There needs to be greater investigation of what Venuti has called "the ethnocentric violence of translation" and much more research into the politics of translating.

(4) There needs to be a pooling of resources to extend research into intercultural training and the implications of such training in today's world.

Bassnett concludes that both cultural studies and translation studies have tended to move in the direction of the collaborative approach, with the establishment of research teams and groups, and with more international networks and increased communication. What we can see from both cultural studies and translation studies today is that the moment of the isolated academic sitting in an ivory tower is over, and indeed in these multifaceted interdisciplines, isolation is counterproductive. Translation is, after all, dialogic in its very nature, involving as it does more than one voice. The study of translation, like the study of culture, needs a plurality of voices. And, similarly, the study of culture always involves an examination of the processes of encoding and decoding that comprise translation.

③ Exercises

(1) What is the significance of the cultural turn in translation studies and the translation turn in cultural studies?

(2) Please briefly comment on Bassnett's translation ideas.

④ References and Further Readings

(1) BASSNETT S. Translation Studies [M]. 3rd ed. Shanghai: Shanghai Foreign Language Education Press, 2004.

(2) BASSNETT S, LEFEVERE A. Constructing Cultures: Essays on Literary Translation [M]. Shanghai: Shanghai Foreign Language Education Press, 2001.

(3) BASSNETT S. Ways through the Labyrinth: Strategies and Methods for Translating Theatre Texts. [M] // Theo Hennans. The Manipulation of Literature. London: Croom Helm, 1985.

Chapter Fourteen

Lawrence Venuti's Translation Theory

① An Introduction to Lawrence Venuti

Lawrence Venuti (1953–) is a distinguished American translation theorist, translation historian and translator from Italian, French and Catalan. Born in Philadelphia, Venuti got his B.A. from Temple University in 1974 and Ph.D. from Columbia University in 1980. He now works as a professor of English at Temple University. He also delivers lectures in creative writing at the Lewis Center for the Arts, Princeton University.

Lawrence Venuti is one of the world's best known experts on translation and translation theory. With such canonical publications as The Translator's Invisibility: A History of Translation (1995) and The Scandals of Translation: Towards an Ethics of Difference (1998), his ideas have had a broad influence beyond the boundaries of the discipline. He is also the editor of the anthology of essays, Rethinking Translation: Discourse, Subjectivity, Ideology (1992) and The Translation Studies Reader (2000), a survey of translation theory from antiquity to the present, which has become a standard reference book for courses on translation theory. His articles have appeared in journals such as Harvard Advocate, Times Literary Supplement, Translation and Literature, Words Without Borders, and Yale Journal of Criticism. Venuti is a member of the editorial advisory boards of various journals, including Palimpsestes, Reformation: The Journal of Tyndale Society, The Translator: Studies in Intercultural Communication, and Translation Studies.

Venuti's translation criticism is based on his translation practice. His translations include *Restless Nights: Selected Stories of Dino Buzzati* (1983), I. U. Tarchetti's *Fantastic Tales* (1992), Juan Rodolfo Wilcock's collection of real and imaginary biographies, *The Temple of Iconoclasts* (2000), *Antonia Pozzi's Breath: Poems and Letters* (2002), the anthology *Italy: A Traveler's Literary Companion* (2003), Melissa P.'s fictionalized memoir, *100 Strokes of the Brush Before Bed* (2004), and Massimo Carlotto's crime novel *The Goodbye Kiss* (2006). His translation projects have won awards and grants from the PEN American Center (1980), the Italian government (1983), the National Endowment for the Arts (1983; 1999), and the National Endowment for the Humanities (1989). In 1999, he held a Fulbright Senior Lectureship in translation studies at the Universitat de Vic (Spain). In 2007–2008, he held a Guggenheim Fellowship. For his version of Catalan poet Ernest Farrés's book *Edward Hopper* he received the 2008 Robert Fagles Translation Prize.

② Venuti's Translation Ideas

I Invisibility of the Translator

In his influential work *The Translator's Invisibility: A History of Translation*, Venuti traces the history of translation into English from the 17th century to the present day and reveals that the translator's situation and activity are actually "invisible" in contemporary Anglo-American culture. He points out that the prevailing practice in the United Kingdom and the United States, among other cultures, is that a translated text, whether prose or poetry, fiction or nonfiction, is judged acceptable by most publishers, reviewers, and readers when it reads fluently, when the absence of any linguistic or stylistic peculiarities makes it seem transparent, giving the appearance that it reflects the foreign writer's personality or intention or the essential meaning of the foreign text — the appearance, in other words, that the translation is not in fact a translation, but the "original."

This illusion of transparency is an effect of fluent discourse, of the translator's effort to insure easy readability by adhering to current usage, maintaining continuous syntax, fixing a precise meaning. Venuti criticizes that this illusory effect conceals the numerous conditions under which the translation is made, starting with the translator's crucial intervention in the foreign text. The more fluent the translation, the more invisible the translator, and, presumably, the more visible the writer or meaning of the foreign text.

The dominance of fluency in English-language translation becomes apparent in sampling of reviews from newspapers and periodicals. On those rare occasions when reviewers address the translation at all, their brief comments usually focus on its style, neglecting such other possible questions as its accuracy, its intended audience, its economic value in the current book market, its relation to literary trends in English, its place in the translator's career. And over the past fifty years the comments are amazingly consistent in praising fluent discourse while damning deviations from it, even when the most diverse range of foreign texts is considered. Thus under the regime of fluent translation, the translator usually works to make his or her work "invisible," producing the illusory effect of transparency that simultaneously masks its status as an illusion: the translated text seems "natural," i.e., not translated.

Venuti states straightly that the motive of his book is to make the translator more visible so as to resist and change the conditions under which translation is theorized and practiced today, especially in English-speaking countries. His first step is to present a theoretical basis from which translations can be read as translations, as texts in their own right, permitting transparency to be demystified, seen as one discursive effect among others.

II Foreignizing Translation Strategy

Venuti defines translation as a process by which the chain of signifiers that constitutes the source-language text is replaced by a chain of signifiers in the target language which the translator provides on the strength of an interpretation. Because meaning is an effect of relations and differences among signifiers along a potentially endless chain (polysemous, intertextual, subject to infinite linkages), it is always differential and deferred, never present as an original unity. Both foreign text and translation are derivative: both consist of diverse linguistic and cultural materials that neither the foreign writer nor the translator originates, and that destabilize the work of signification, inevitably exceeding and possibly conflicting with their intentions. As a result, a foreign text is the site of many different semantic possibilities that are fixed only provisionally in any one translation, on the basis of varying cultural assumptions and interpretive choices, in specific social situations, in different historical periods. Meaning is a plural and contingent relation, not an unchanging unified essence, and therefore a translation cannot be judged according to mathematics-based concepts of semantic equivalence or one-to-one correspondence.

Thus translation wields enormous power in the construction of national identities for foreign cultures, and hence it potentially figures in ethnic discrimination, geopolitical confrontations, colonialism, terrorism, war. On the other hand, translation enlists the foreign text in the maintenance or revision of literary cannons in the target-language culture, inscribing poetry and fiction, for example, with the various poetic and narrative discourses that compete for cultural dominance in the target language. Translation also enlists the foreign text in the maintenance or revision of dominant conceptual paradigms, research methodologies, and clinical practices in target-language disciplines and professions, whether physics or architecture, philosophy or psychiatry, sociology or law. Therefore, translation can be called a cultural political practice, constructing or critiquing ideology-stamped identities for foreign cultures, affirming or transgressing discursive values and institutional limits in the target-language culture. The violence wreaked by translation is partly inevitable, inherent in the translation process, partly potential, emerging at any point in the production and reception of the translated text, varying with specific cultural and social formations at different historical moments.

Foreignizing translation signifies the difference of the foreign text, yet only by disrupting the cultural codes that prevail in the target language. Venuti suggests that insofar as foreignizing translation seeks to restrain the ethnocentric violence of translation, it is highly desirable today, a strategic cultural intervention in the current state of world affairs, pitched against the hegemonic English-language nations and the unequal cultural exchanges in which they engage their global others. Foreignizing translation in English can be a form of resistance against ethnocentrism and racism, cultural narcissism and imperialism, in the interests of democratic geopolitical relations. Venuti points out that as a theory and practice of translation, the foreignizing method is specific to certain European countries at particular historical moments: formulated first in German culture during the classical and romantic periods, it has recently been revived in a French cultural scene characterized by postmodern developments in philosophy, literary criticism, psychoanalysis, and social theory that have come to be known as "poststructuralism." Anglo-American culture, in contrast, has long been dominated by domesticating theories that recommend fluent translating. By producing the illusion of transparency, a fluent translation masquerades as true semantic equivalence when it in fact inscribes the foreign text with a partial interpretation, partial to English- language values, reducing if not simply excluding the very difference that translation is called on to convey.

Venuti observes that this ethnocentric violence is evident in the translation theories put forth by the prolific and influential Eugene Nida, whose concept of "dynamic" or "functional equivalence" in translation "aims at complete naturalness of expression" and "tries to relate the receptor to modes of behavior relevant within the context of his own culture." The phrase "naturalness of expression" signals the importance of a fluent strategy to this theory of translation, and in Nida's work it is obvious that fluency involves domestication. When Nida asserts that "an easy and natural style in translating, despite the extreme difficulty of producing it is nevertheless essential to producing in the ultimate receptors a response similar to that of the original receptors," he is in fact imposing the English-language valorization of transparent discourse on every foreign culture, masking a basic disjunction between the source- and target-language texts which puts into question the possibility of eliciting a "similar" response.

Venuti states that to advocate translation in opposition to the Anglo-American tradition of domestication is not to do away with cultural political agendas — such an advocacy is itself an agenda. The point is rather to develop a theory and practice of translation that resists dominant target-language cultural values so as to signify the linguistic and cultural difference of the foreign text. Such a translation strategy can be best called "resistancy," not merely because it avoids fluency, but because it challenges the target-language culture even as it enacts its own ethnocentric violence on the foreign text.

By writing *The Translator's Invisibility*, Venuti hopes to force translators and readers to reflect on the ethnocentric violence of translation and hence to write and read in ways that seek to recognize the linguistic and cultural difference of foreign texts. However, Venuti also points out that what he is advocating is not an indiscriminate valorization of every foreign culture or a metaphysical concept of foreignness as an essential value. Indeed, the foreign text is privileged in a foreignizing translation only insofar as it enables a disruption of target-language cultural codes, so that its value is always strategic, depending on the cultural formation into which it is translated. The point is rather to elaborate the theoretical, critical, and textual means by which translation can be studied and practiced as a locus of difference, instead of the homogeneity that widely characterizes it today.

Venuti states that by resorting to techniques that make the translated text strange and estranging in the target-language culture, resistancy seeks to free the reader of the translation, as well as the translator, from the cultural constraints that ordinarily govern their reading and writing and threaten to overpower and domesticate the foreign text, annihilating its foreignness. Resistancy makes English-language translation a dissident cultural politics today, when fluent strategies and transparent discourse routinely perform that mystification of foreign texts. He believes that his translations resist the hegemony of transparent discourse in English-language culture, and they do this from within, by deterritorializing the target language itself, questioning its major cultural status by using it as the vehicle for ideas and discursive techniques which remain minor in it, which it excludes. If the resistant strategy effectively produces an estranging translation, then the foreign text also enjoys a momentary liberation from the target-language culture, perhaps before it is reterritorialized with the reader's articulation of a voice — recognizable, transparent — or of some reading amenable to the dominant aesthetic in English. The liberating moment would occur when the reader of the resistant translation experiences, in the target language, the cultural differences which separate that language and the foreign text.

Venuti argues that translation is a process that involves looking for similarities between languages and cultures — particularly similar messages and formal techniques — but it does this only because it is constantly confronting dissimilarities. It can never and should never aim to remove these dissimilarities entirely. A translated text should be the site where a different culture emerges, where a reader gets a glimpse of a cultural other, and resistancy, a translation strategy based on an aesthetic of discontinuity, can best preserve that difference, that otherness, by reminding the reader of the gains and losses in the translation process and the unbridgeable gaps between cultures. In contrast, the notion of *simpatico*, by placing a premium on transparency and demanding a fluent strategy, can be viewed as a cultural narcissism: it seeks an identity, a self-recognition, and finds only the same culture in foreign writing, only the same self in the cultural other.

According to Venuti, every step in the translation process — from the selection of foreign texts to the implementation of translation strategies to the editing, reviewing, and reading of translations — is mediated by the diverse cultural values that circulate in the target language, always in some hierarchical order. The translator, who works with varying degrees of calculation, under continuous self-monitoring and often with active consultation of cultural rules and resources (from dictionaries and grammars to other texts, translation strategies, and translations, both canonical and marginal), may submit or resist dominant values in the target language, with either course of action susceptible to ongoing redirection. Submission assumes an ideology of assimilation at work in the translation process, locating the same in a cultural other, pursuing a cultural narcissism that is imperialistic abroad and conservative, even reactionary, in maintaining canons at home. Resistance assumes an ideology of autonomy, locating the alien in a cultural other, pursuing cultural diversity, foregrounding the linguistic and cultural differences of the source-language text and transforming the hierarchy of cultural values in the target language.

III Identity-forming Power of Translation

In Chapter 4 of *The Scandals of Translation: Towards an Ethics of Difference* (1998), Venuti discusses the power of translation in the formation of cultural identity from the perspective of ethics.

He argues that translation is a double-edged sword in the process of identity formation:

"As translation constructs a domestic representation for a foreign text and culture, it simultaneously constructs a domestic subject, a position of intelligibility that is also an ideological position, informed by the codes and canons, interests and agendas of certain domestic social groups. Circulating in the church, the state, and the school, a translation can be powerful in maintaining or revising the hierarchy of values in the translating language. A calculated choice of foreign text and translation strategy can change or consolidate literary canons, conceptual paradigms, research methodologies, clinical techniques, and commercial practices in the domestic culture. Whether the effects of a translation prove to be conservative or transgressive depends fundamentally on the discursive strategies developed by the translator, but also on the various factors in their reception, including the page design and cover art of the printed book, the advertising copy, the opinions of reviewers, and the uses made of the translation in cultural and social institutions, how it is read and taught. Such factors mediate the impact of any translation by assisting in the positioning of domestic subjects, equipping them with specific reading practices, affiliating them with specific cultural values and constituencies, reinforcing or crossing institutional limits."

Venuti uses several translation projects from different periods, past and present, to illustrate how translation forms particular cultural identities and maintains them with a relative degree of coherence and homogeneity, as well as how it creates possibilities for cultural resistance, innovation, and change at any historical moment. He then moves on to discuss the ethics of translation as follows:

"A translation ethics, clearly, can't be restricted to a notion of fidelity. Not only does a translation constitute an interpretation of the foreign text, varying with different cultural situations at different historical moments, but canons of accuracy are articulated and applied in the domestic culture and therefore are basically ethnocentric, no matter how seemingly faithful, no matter how linguistically correct. The ethical values implicit in such canons are generally professional or institutional, established by agencies and officials, academic specialists, publishers, and reviewers and subsequently assimilated by translators, who adopt varying attitudes towards them, from acceptance to ambivalence to interrogation and revision. Any evaluation of a translation project must include a consideration of discursive strategies, their institutional settings, and their social functions and effects.

Institutions, whether academic or religious, commercial or political, show a preference for a translation ethics of sameness, translating that enables and ratifies existing discourses and canons, interpretations and pedagogies, advertising campaigns and liturgies — if only to ensure the continued and unruffled reproduction of the institution. Yet translation is scandalous because it can create different values and practices, whatever the domestic setting. This is not to say that translation can ever rid itself of its fundamental domestication, its basic task of rewriting the foreign text in domestic cultural terms. The point is rather that a translator can choose to redirect the ethnocentric movement of translation so as to decenter the domestic terms that a translation project must inescapably utilize. This is an ethics of difference that can change the domestic culture."

Venuti also points out that "a translation ethics of difference reforms cultural identities that occupy dominant positions in the domestic culture, yet in many cases this reformation subsequently issues into another dominance and another ethnocentrism".

"A translation practice that rigorously redirects its ethnocentrism is likely to be subversive of domestic ideologies and institutions. It too would form a cultural identity, but one that is simultaneously critical and contingent, constantly assessing the relations between a domestic culture and its foreign others and developing translation projects solely on the basis of changing assessments. This identity will be truly intercultural, nor merely in the sense of straddling two cultures, domestic and foreign, but crossing the cultural borders among domestic audiences. And it will be historical, distinguished by an awareness of domestic as well as foreign cultural traditions, including traditions of translation."

Venuti concludes that translation concerned with limiting its ethnocentrism does not necessarily risk unintelligibility and cultural marginality. "A translation project can deviate from domestic norms to signal the foreignness of the foreign text and create a readership that is more open to linguistic and cultural differences — yet without resorting to stylistic experiments that are so estranging as to be self-defeating. The key factor is the translator's ambivalence toward domestic norms and the institutional practices in which they are implemented, a reluctance to identify completely with them coupled with a determination to address diverse cultural constituencies, elite and popular. In attempting to straddle the foreign and domestic cultures as well as domestic readerships, a translation practice cannot fail to produce a text that is a potential source of cultural change."

③ Exercises

(1) What does Venuti think of the invisibility of the translator

(2) What is Venuti's Resistancy in translation?

(3) How does Venuti assess the power of translation in the formation of cultural identity?

(4) What are the similarities and differences between Lu Xun's and Venuti's translation ideas?

4 References and Further Readings

(1) VENUTI L. The Translator's Invisibility: A History of Translation [M]. London: Routledge, 1995.

(2) VENUTI L. The Scandals of Translation: Towards an Ethics of Difference [M]. London: Routledge, 1998.

(3) VENUTI L. 译者的隐形——翻译史论 [M]. 张景华, 白立平, 蒋骁华, 主译. 北京: 外语教学与研究出版社, 2009.

(4) 张景华. 翻译伦理: 韦努蒂翻译思想研究 [M]. 上海: 上海交通大学出版社, 2009.

Chapter Fifteen

Functionalist Approaches to Translation and Skopostheorie

① Introduction to Functionalist Approaches

Functionalist approaches to translation are another influential trend in modern translation studies. They are developed in Germany in the late 1970s. Katharina Reiss, Justa Holz-Manttari, Hans J. Vermere and Christiane Nord are prominent figures of this school. Working at translator-training institutions in universities, these scholars have noticed that there are cases where equivalence is not called for at all in professional practice. In *Translation Criticism: The Potentials & Limitations* (2004), Reiss, while arguing for an "objective approach to translation criticism" based on the functional equivalence between source texts and target texts, finds that there are two exceptions from the general purpose of achieving equivalence.

(1) When the target text is intended to achieve a purpose or function other than that of the original (e.g., adaptations of prose texts for the stage, translating Shakespeare's play for foreign language class), functionality (i.e. adequacy to the intended function) takes precedence over equivalence.

(2) When the target text addresses an audience which is different from the intended readership of the original (e.g. translating *Gulliver's Travels* for children, purification motivated by religious, ideological, ethical reasons), reader-orientedness takes precedence over equivalence.

Since the then prevalent equivalence-based linguistic translation theorists held the view that any target text that is not equivalent as far as possible to the corresponding source text is a non-translation, the German functionalists became increasingly dissatisfied with the relationship between translation theory and practice. Drawing on practical experience of the translation profession, they proposed their own functionalist approaches to translation. Here functionalist means focusing on the function or functions of texts and translations, and functionalism is a broad term for various translation theories that approach translation in this way. Vermeer's skopos theory, for example, is an attempt to bridge the gap between theory and practice. He considers translation as a type of human action, which is intentional, purposeful behavior that takes place in a given situation.

② Skopos Theory

Hans J. Vermeer, who had been trained as an interpreter by Reiss, was dissatisfied with the linguistic-oriented translation theory, because in his view translation was "not merely and not even primarily a linguistic process". Instead, translation (including interpreting) was only "a type of transfer where communicative verbal and non-verbal signs are transferred from one language into another". Hans J. Vermeer's general theory of translation, which he calls Skopostheorie, is a theory of purposeful activity. The theory is explained in detail in the book co-authored by Vermeer and Reiss in 1984. In the framework of this theory, one of the most important factors determining the purpose of a translation is the addressee, who is the intended receiver or audience of the target text with their culture-specific world-knowledge, their expectation and their communicative needs. Every translation is directed at an intended audience, since to translate means "to produce a text in a target setting for a target purpose and target addressees in target circumstances."

In Skopostheorie, the status of the source is clearly much lower than in equivalence-based theories. While Reiss declared that the source text is the measure of all things in translation (Reiss, 1988:70), Vermeer regarded it as an "offer of information" that is partly or wholly turned into an "offer of information" for the target audience.

The Greek word "skopos," which was introduced into translation theory by Vermere in the 1970s, is a technique term for the goal and purpose of a translation. The Skopostheorie holds that the way the target text eventually shapes up is determined to a great extent by the function, or "skopos," intended for in the target context. According to Skopostheorie, the prime principle determining any translation process is the purpose (skopos) of the overall translation action. This fits in with intentionality being part of the very definition of any action.

Vermeer puts forward three basic rules in the Skopostheorie, with the skopos rule being the primary guideline and the other two, the intratextual coherence rule and the intertextual coherence rule, being subordinate to it. The top-ranking rule for any translation is the "skopos rule," which says that a translational action is determined by its skopos; that is, "the end justifies the means." Vermeer explained the skopos rule in the following way:

"Each text is produced for a given purpose and should serve this purpose. The skopos rule thus reads as follows: translate / interpret / speak / write in a way that enables your text /translation to function in the situation in which it is used and with the people who want to use it and precisely in the way they want it to function."

Most translational actions allow a variety of skopos, which may be related to each other in a hierarchical order. The translator should be able to justify their choice of a particular skopos in a given translational situation.

This rule is intended to solve the eternal dilemmas of free vs faithful translation, dynamic vs formal equivalence, good interpreters vs slavish translators, and so on. It means that the skopos of a particular translation task may require a "free" or a "faithful" translation, or anything between these two extremes, depending on the purpose for which the translation is needed. As Vermeer put it, "What the skopos state is that one must translate, consciously and consistently, in accordance with some principle respecting the target text. The theory does not state what the principle is: this must be decided separately in each specific case."

Then who decides what the principle is? As we know, translation is normally done by assignment. A client needs a text for a particular purpose and calls upon the translator for a translation, thus acting as the initiator of the translation process. In an ideal case, the client would give as many details as possible about the purpose, explaining the addressee, time, place, occasion and medium of the intended communication and the function the text is intended to have. This information would constitute an explicit translation brief.

The translation brief specifies what kind of translation is needed. This is why the initiator or the person playing the role of initiator (who might also be the translator) actually decides on the translation skopos, even though the brief as such may not be explicit about the conditions.

Evidently, skopos has to be negotiated between the client and the translator, especially when the client has only a vague or even incorrect idea of what kind of text is needed for the situation in question. Clients do not normally bother to give the translator an explicit translation brief; not being expert in intercultural communication, they often do not know that a good brief spells a better translation.

Note that the translation brief does not tell the translator how to go about their translating job, what translation strategy to use, or what translation type to choose. These decisions depend entirely on the translator's responsibility and competence. If the client or the translator disagree as to what kind of target text would serve the intended purpose best, the translator may either refuse the assignment or refuse any responsibility for the function of the target text and simply do what the client asks for. In many cases, however, an experienced translator is able to infer the skopos from the translational situation itself.

In terms of Skopostheorie, the viability of the brief depends on the circumstances of the target culture, not on the source culture. Since we have defined translation as a translational action involving a source text, the source is usually part of the brief. The agents (sender, receiver, initiator, translator) play the most important part and it is problematic to speak of "the source text" unless we really only mean source language words or sentence structures. The meaning or function of a text is not something inherent in the linguistic signs; it cannot simply be extracted by anyone who knows the code. A text is made meaningful by its receiver and for its receiver. Different receivers (or even the same receiver at different times) find different meanings in the same linguistic material offered by the text. We might even say that a "text" is as many texts as there are receivers.

This dynamic concept of text meaning and function is common enough in modern theories of literary reception. Vermeer summed it up by saying that any text is just an "offer of information" from which each receiver selects the items they find interesting and important. Applying this concept to translation, we could say that a target text is an offer of information formulated by a translator in a target culture and language about an offer of information formulated by someone else in the source culture and language.

This concept does not allow us to speak of the meaning of the source text being transferred to the target receivers. Guided by the translation brief, the translator selects certain items from the source-language offer of information (originally meant for source-language addressees) and processes them in order to form a new offer of information in the target language, from which the target-culture addressees can in turn select what they consider to be meaningful in their own situation. In these terms, the translation process is irreversible.

What the translator can do, and should do, is to produce a text that is at least likely to be meaningful

to target-culture receivers. In Vermeer's terms, the target text should conform to the standard of "intratextual coherence." This means that the receiver should be able to understand it; it should make sense in the communicative situation and culture in which it is received. A communicative interaction can only be regarded as successful if the receiver interprets it as being sufficiently coherent with their situation. Accordingly, another important rule of Skopostheorie, the "coherence rule," specifies that a translation should be acceptable in a sense that it is coherent with the receiver's situation. Being "coherent with" is synonymous with being "part of" the receiver's situation.

However, since a translation is an offer of information about a proceeding offer of information, it is expected to bear some kind of relationship with the corresponding source text. Vermeer calls this relationship "intertextual coherence" or "fidelity". This is postulated as a further principle, referring to the "fidelity rule." Again, as in the case of the skopos rule, the important point is that intertextual coherence should exist between source and target text, while the form it takes depends both on the translator's interpretation of the source text and on the translation skopos. Intertextual coherence is considered subordinate to intratextual coherence, and both are subordinate to the skopos rule. If the skopos requires a change of function, the standard will no longer be intertextual coherence with the source text but adequacy or appropriateness with regard to the skopos. And if the skopos demand intratextual incoherence (as in the theatre of the absurd), the standard of intratextual coherence is no longer valid.

③ Functionality Plus Loyalty

For many years, it was usually the source text or some of its features that were declared to be responsible for the change in strategy. It was the source text that required faithfulness, even with regard to punctuation in some literary or legal translations, and it was the source text, too, that demanded adaptation of some examples or culture-bound concepts to target-culture conventions or expectations in other translations such as newspaper texts.

In Skopostheorie, not only did it account for different strategies in different translation situations, in which source texts are not the only factor involved, but it also coincided with a change of paradigm in quite a few disciplines, among them linguistics, which had developed a stronger focus on communication as a social, culture-bound occurrence, on the individuals involved, on the spatiotemporal conditions of communication, and on communicative intentions and functions. Skopostheorie seemed to be exactly the translational model that was needed. It is:

(1) pragmatic, accounting for the situational conditions of communicative interaction and, accordingly, for the needs and expectations of the addressees or prospective receivers

of the target text and even making the target receiver the most important yardstick of translational decisions;

(2) culture-oriented, giving consideration to the culture-specific forms of verbal and nonverbal behavior involved in translation;

(3) consistent, able to establish a coherent theoretical and methodological framework that could serve as a guideline for an intersubjective justification of the translator's decisions in any type or form of translation task, permitting any translation procedures that would lead to a functional target text;

(4) practical, accounting for all the forms of transcultural communication needed in professional translation practice;

(5) normative, in the sense of giving the translator a guideline as to the best or safest ways to attain a particular translation purpose;

(6) comprehensive, because target function was considered to be the main standard for any translation process, one possible function being the presentation of a target text whose communicative effects were equivalent to those of the source text; and

(7) expert, in the sense that it attributed to the translator the prestige of being an expert in their field, competent to make purpose-adequate decisions with full responsibility to their partners.

Like the concept of equivalence, Skopostheorie claims to be a general or universal model of translation. Although Vermeer allowed for a relationship of "intertextual coherence" or fidelity to hold between the source and target texts, the demand for fidelity is subordinate to the skopos rule. As we have seen, the main idea of Skopostheorie could be paraphrased as "the translation purpose justifies the translation procedures." Now, this seems acceptable whenever the translation purpose is in line with the communicative intentions of the original author. But what happens if the translation brief requires a translation whose communicative aims are contrary to or incompatible with the author's opinion or intention? In this case, the skopos rule could easily be interpreted as "the end justifies the means," and there would be no restriction to the range of possible ends.

In Christiane Nord's (1943–) *Translating as a Purposeful Activity: Functionalist Approaches Explained* (1997), she advocates "functionality plus loyalty". Here she adds a new concept "loyalty" to the functional approach to translation. Nord called "loyalty" the responsibility translators have toward their partners in translational interaction. Loyalty commits the translator bilaterally to the source and the target sides. It must not be mixed up with fidelity or faithfulness, concepts that usually refer to a relationship holding between the source text and the target texts. Loyalty refers to the interpersonal relationship between translator, source text author, target text reader and translation initiator. Loyalty is an interpersonal category referring to a social relationship between people.

In this context, loyalty means that the target-text should be compatible with the original author's intentions. This may not be a problem where the sender's intentions are evident from the communicative situation in which the source text is or was used, as with operating instructions or commercial advertisements. In these cases we may speak of "conventional" intentions linked with certain text types. In other cases, the analysis of extratextual factors such as author, time, place, or medium may shed some light on what may have been the sender's intentions. However, it can be difficult to elicit the sender's intentions in cases where we don't have enough information about the original situation (as is the case with ancient texts) or where the source-text situation is so different from the target-text situation that there is no way of establishing a direct link between the source-text author and the target-text readers. In these cases, a documentary translation may be the only way to solve the dilemma. Sometimes a thorough analysis of intratextual function markers helps the translator to find out about the communicative intentions that may have guided the author.

Nord's version of the functionalist approach thus stands on two pillars: function plus loyalty. It is precisely the combination of the two principles that matters, even though there may be cases where they seem to contradict each other. Function refers to the factors that make a target text work in the intended way in the target situation. Loyalty refers to the interpersonal relationship between the translator, the source-text sender, the target-text addressees and the initiator. Loyalty limits the range of justifiable target-text functions for one particular source-text and raises the need for a negotiation of the translation assignment between translators and their clients.

The function-plus-loyalty model is also an answer to those critics who argue that the functional approach leaves translators free to do whatever they like with any source text, or worse, what their clients like. The loyalty principle takes account of the legitimate interests of the three parties involved: initiators (who want a particular type of translation), target receivers (who expect a particular relationship between original and target texts) and original authors (who have a right to demand respect for their individual intentions and expect a particular kind of relationship between their text and its translation.) If there is any conflict between the interests of the three partners of the translator, it is the translator who has to mediate and, where necessary, seek the understanding of all sides.

If a text is regarded as a combination of communicative signs exchanged between the sender and the receiver, we can analyze the text function from either the sender's or the receiver's point of view. The sender intends to achieve purpose and therefore chooses certain strategies of text production considered appropriate for this purpose, using structural features in order to "signal" their intention to the addressee. But as is known to all, the best of intentions does not guarantee a perfect result. It is the receiver who "completes" the communicative action by deciding to receive the text in a particular function. When referring to "function" in this context, Nord means function or set of functions because texts are rarely intended for one function only. Various functions usually form a hierarchy of functions, subfunctions, etc.

Text function is, therefore, a pragmatic quality assigned to a text by the receiver in a particular situation and not something attached to, or, inherent in, the text. Thus, it seems only logical that the function of the source text is specific to the original situation and cannot be left invariant or "preserved" through the translation process. The function of the target text, on the other hand, is specific to the target situation, and it is an illusion that a target text should have automatically the same function as the original. Vermeer seeks to distinguish three related concepts as follows: the intention is what the client wants to do; the skopos is what the translation is for; and the function is the text purpose as inferred, ascribed by recipient. Function, in particular, remains an unclear concept. The conceptual and terminological confusion here has not been resolved.

There are several models of text functions which could be used as a frame of reference for functional analysis. Nord established four basic textual functions.

(1) Referential function (i.e. reference to objects and phenomena of the world). Some subfunctions: informative function (object: e.g. a traffic accident), metalinguistic function (object: e.g. a particular use of language), instructive function (object: e.g. the correct way of handling a washing machine), teaching function (object: e.g. Geography), etc.

(2) Expressive function (i.e. expression of the sender's attitude or feeling towards the objects and phenomena dealt with in the text). Some subfunctions: emotive function (expression of feelings, e.g. in interjections), evaluative function (expression of evaluation, e.g. in a political commentary).

(3) Appellative function (i.e., appealing to the receiver's experience, feeling, knowledge, sensibility, etc., in order to induce him/her to react in a specific way). Some subfunctions: illustrative function (intended reaction: recognition of something known), persuasive function (intended reaction: adopt the sender's viewpoint), imperative function (intended reaction: do what the sender is asking for), pedagogical function (intended reaction: learn certain forms of behavior), advertising function (intended function: buy the product).

(4) Phatic function (i.e. establishing, maintaining or finishing contact). Some subfunction: salutational function, "small-talk" function, "peg" function (e.g. text introductions).

While the function of the original is defined with regard to its own referent and situation, the function of the translation has to be first defined with regard to the source text. According to Nida's two translation "types," which have split translation theories into two camps since the days of Cicero, the translation can be:

(1) a *document* of the situation in which an SC sender communicates with SC receivers via the source text, which are often reproduced in the target language, and (2) an *instrument* in a new TC situation in which the ST sender communicates with TC receivers via the target text which has been produced under TT conditions using the source text as a kind of model.

In a documentary translation, certain aspects of the source text-in-situation are reproduced for the target receivers, who are conscious of "observing" a communicative interaction of which they are not a part. If the focus is on the morphological, lexical or syntactic features of the source language system as present in the source text, we speak of a word-to-word translation or an interlineal version. If a documentary translation is intended to reproduce the words of the original, adapting syntactic structures and idiomatic use of vocabulary to the target language norms, we speak of a literal or grammar translation, which is frequently used in foreign language teaching, but also in news texts when the utterance of a foreign politician is rendered literally. If the target text reproduces the source text rather literally, adding, however, the necessary cultural or linguistic information in footnotes or glossaries, we speak of philological or learned translation. This form is frequently used with classical texts. Another form of documentary translation, which is the conventional form of literary translations in many cultures today, is called "exoticizing translation" because the "setting" of the story is left unchanged, producing an "exotic" effect on the target readers where the original readers found their own culture reflected in the text. If the function of the target text is the same as that of the original, we can speak of an "equifunctional translation." This form is normally used for technical texts, computer manuals, instructions for use, and the like. If the function or a set of functions cannot be reproduced as a whole or in the same hierarchy of functions, we could speak of a "heterofunctional" translation. Another form of instrumental translation is what Nord calls "homologous translation." It is intended to achieve a homologous effect by reproducing in the TC literary context the function the source text has in its own SC literary context. This form is often found in the translation of poetry. It is called "semiotic transformation" by Ludskanov or creative transposition in Jakobson's terms.

In reading an instrumental translation, the reader is not supposed to become aware of reading a translation at all. Therefore, the form of the text is usually adapted to TC norms and conventions of text type, genre, register, tenor, etc.

④ Exercises

(1) How do you define "translational action" and "translation brief"?

(2) What are the basic translation criteria of Skopostheorie?

(3) Please make a brief comment on Functionalist Approaches.

⑤ References and Further Readings

(1) NORD C. Translating as a Purposeful Activity: Functionalist Approaches Explained [M]. Shanghai: Shanghai Foreign Language Education Press, 2001.

(2) REISS K. Translation Criticism: The Potentials & Limitations [M]. Shanghai: Shanghai Foreign Language Education Press. 2004.

Chapter Sixteen

Pierre Bourdieu and *The Field of Cultural Production*

① An Introduction to Pierre Bourdieu

Pierre Bourdieu (1930–2002), one of the most internationally influential philosophers in contemporary France, was a professor at the Paris Higher School of Studies and an academician of the French Academy. As early as 1972, Bourdieu published the classic sociological work *Outline of a Theory of Practice*. In 1975, he founded the *Actes de la Recherche en Sciences Sociales*, a journal that acted as a vehicle for Bourdieu's shorter articles. In 1993, he published *The Field of Cultural Production*, which was one of his most important writings on arts, literature and aesthetics.

Born in France in 1930, Bourdieu's early academic career was mostly riveted on structuralism, in which he tried to develop a "universal cultural theory" based on Saussure's theories. Later, he critically rethought Saussure's theoretical propositions and began to explore a theory of cultural practice. He concluded that only when the analysis goes beyond the traditional antagonism and dichotomy, can the development of the theory become possible.

Bourdieu's work is almost encyclopedic, looking over the disciplinary fence to cover almost everything in social sciences from anthropology, sociology, and pedagogy to history, linguistics, political science, philosophy, aesthetics to literary studies. At the heart of his work lies the three key concepts: "field," "habitus" and "capital," which are often interconnected to each other in Bourdieu's studies as a whole.

2 The Field of Cultural Production

I The Three Key Concepts in *The Field of Cultural Production*

Field

Field is not only an important concept in Bourdieu's theory of practice, but also an elementary unit of research in his sociological studies. The concept of "field," originated from the term "magnetic field" in physical sciences, is related to a high degree of differentiation in modern society. For Bourdieu, fields denote arenas of production, circulation, and appropriation and exchange of goods, services, knowledge, or status, and the competitive positions held by actors in their struggle to accumulate, exchange, and monopolize different kinds of power resources (capitals). The field can be understood as a structural space with specific functions and rules. First, different from its literal meaning in physics, the concept of "field" proposed

by Bourdieu is a relatively independent space, which has a certain social nature. Since society is composed of human activities, the field is also the sum of social activities and social relations. In modern society, the division of labor between social classes and fields is clear: all kinds of people always play a specific role in one or more specific fields. Therefore, the fields that exist in society also have different categories, such as "economic fields," "literature field," "art field," "translation field" and "power field."

Bourdieu clearly pointed out that fields follow their specific logic and needs. They exist independently of an individual's will, but are closely related to the individual's behaviors of various kinds. Take the "art field" as an example: the individuals in the field are artists and people of relevant industries; hence, most of the activities in this social network center on aesthetic pursuits and artistic values. By contrast, in the economic field, the individuals in the network relationship target material interests and capital accumulation. Yet, it is worth stressing that the independent status of each field is not absolute, but relative in nature. In the art field, for instance, the role of the patron becomes more and more prominent in the field over time. In the nineteenth century, the art field required complete autonomy, in which artists were not restricted by patrons. However, patrons nowadays have almost dominant controls and restrictions on artists. It follows therefore that the composition of a field and the relationship between different individuals within the field are not static. With the development of society, the relationship between different internal and/or external elements within a field is ever changing just like the time itself.

Furthermore, different fields of the society are believed to be interconnected, upon which the entire society is shaped by the interweaving of fields. Bourdieu holds that connections of different elements in society are not interactions between actors or subjective connections between individuals, but rather existing relationships, which are the consciousness and will of independent individuals.

Habitus

"Habitus" is a concept initially proposed by Plato and later developed by Aristotle in the ancient Greek. In modern times, scholars such as Norbert Elias has used the concept to study the development of European history and arts. However, it was Bourdieu who first used the concept of habitus to discuss sociological issues, which has brought forth the academia a fresh dimension to understand systematically varied issues and phenomena in human society.

Bourdieu first put forward the concept of "situation", which he believes can better convey the meaning of habitus. He defines the concept as the result of an organized behavior, which is close to the structural meaning. "Situation" is also a kind of existence, a habitual state of the body and mind.

Based on "situation", Bourdieu developed the concept of habitus in his book *Gothic Architecture and Scholasticism*, and later used it to explain varied social activities. To Bourdieu, people learn and understand social rules through such social activities as personal growth, family education, school learning, work and social interaction. In the process of growing up, for instance, people will form a systematic and relatively fixed mode of thinking and rules of activity. Meanwhile, as individuals in society, people will embed certain social rules into their own thoughts and activities, where different rules of action will affect the development and changes of surrounding environment. The formation of individual habitus came from practical experiences of individuals in society. In this process, the external structure is continuously internalized in the accumulation of experience, which, together with some previous social experience finally develops into the habitus of the individual.

In 1966, however, Bourdieu updated the definition of "habitus", which is then defined as "a continuous and convertible system, which integrates past experience and functions as a matrix of perception, appreciation, and behavior of all times. With the conversion of this framework, habitus allows a variety of different tasks to be completed. Therefore, it was later defined as a "sustainable and convertible system, which tends to make the structured structure function as a structure with structural capabilities. This is to say that in the updated definition, "habitus" is meant to play the role of generating and organizing practices and expressions. These practices and expressions are compatible with each other and with their outcomes, but are at the same time detached from conscious goals or necessary methods that help achieve these goals.

Overall, habitus is not only a kind of acquisition in the process of human growth, but also accumulation of human experience. As a structure that has been constructed, habitus is not an automatically acquired capability; instead, it is gradually developed and possessed by an individual in the process of social life. At the same time, with the development of habitus, specific actions that reflect social and economic conditions will be derived.

Capital

Bourdieu viewed social capital as a property of the individual rather than the collective. Social capital, derived primarily from a person's position and social status, allows him/her to exercise power over the very individual or collective who mobilizes resources. For Bourdieu, social capital isn't consistently accessible to individuals of a group, but available to those who give endeavors to procure it by accomplishing positions of power and status and by creating goodwill. Therefore, social capital is irreducibly attached to class and other forms of stratification, which are in turn connected to various forms of benefit or advancement.

To Bourdieu, capital is also accumulated labor, either in materialized or "consolidated," "concrete form." Capital has three manifestations: first, economic capital, which can be directly converted into money and can be institutionalized in the form of property rights; second, cultural capital, which can be transformed into economic capital under certain circumstances; the third is social capital, which is composed of social relations, which can likewise be transformed into economic capital under certain circumstances and can be institutionalized in the form of noble names. Bourdieu pointed out that as long as capital is connected with cognition and knowledge, it becomes a kind of socialized capability, regardless of its specific forms.

In terms of cultural capital, Bourdieu believes that cultural capital can exist in three forms: (1) The state of reification, that is, the long-term fixed form of the body and mind. (2) The state of objectification, which is the very form of cultural products (pictures, books, dictionaries, tools, machines, etc.). It is the trace or manifestation of a theory or theoretical criticism of various problems. (3) The institutionalized state, which must be distinguished from materialized forms, because it transforms the original assets into cultural capital, as with the example of academic qualifications. Of the forms of capital, reification is an external manifestation of the spirit and mind; objectification is the objective existence of things, such as literary works, clothing and other cultural capital that must be exchanged for economic capital; institutionalization is about different institutionalized forms of culture, including but not limited to such forms as academic qualifications, professional qualifications, etc.

II The Three Key Concepts and Translation Practices

Field and Translation

One of the most noticeable features of "field" is competition. Participants in the field bring their own habitus and capital to pursue their own interests. They compete for a higher position, and continue to promote the development of the field. However, in the field of translation, participants often use capital in other fields to compete. Participants struggle to obtain recognition in the field. According to the logic of field, recognition gained through participants and institutions in the field is more decisive than external recognition gained by the market. For instance, the identity and works of writers in the literary field can undoubtedly have a great effect on their struggle in the field, but for translators this is not the case at all. Their professional structure is very weak, as translation is often regarded as a secondary profession. Hence, all these have negatively affected the activities of translators in the field, making them often use capital in other fields for competition.

In the field of translation, every translator will bring his own habitus and capital to engage in translation activities, even though their subordination is believed to prevail over their limited subjectivity in the process. Consequently, a translator is often regarded as just the intercultural mediator between two languages. The formation of the "translation field" is only possible under certain circumstances, and the reason for these restrictions lies in the submissive behavior of a translator as well as the consequent low status of this translator in the field. Over the centuries, translation has been internalized as a kind of submissive behavior, so it has not brought much social prestige to the translator. With the development of history and society, translators' subjugation to this norm has, in turn, a decisive influence on the subordinate nature of their translation activities.

In Bourdieu's point of view, translations will be regarded as original works in the target country. In the translation field, however, as the original work and its author are in a relatively active position, the very translation strategy adopted by the translator in the translation process is affected by the field of this original literary and cultural capital. As a result, despite the translator has the habitus in translation, he/she cannot use it to fight for his/her deserved rights, due largely to the influence of cultural capital.

Habitus and Translation

One of the earliest scholars who applied Bourdieu's theory to translation studies was Daniel Simeoni. In his highly cited *The Pivotal Status of the Translator's Habitus*, he attempted to reinterpret Even-Zohar's Polysystem Theory, in order to introduce the concept of habitus into translation. For Simeoni, translation norms are a part of habitus, where the main difference between the two is that habitus has the double dimension of "structuring and structured" function. However, Simeoni did not want to use habitus to replace norms, because he did not discuss habitus in Bourdieu's entire social theory or the field theory. He claimed that for half a century, a translator's habitus may bring forth the internalization of a submissive behavior (i.e., obedience to the author or the source text), which in turn gives rise to the relatively invisible status of the translator. Consequently, a translator has no choice but to accept translation norms with limitations, which leads to the secondariness of the translation behavior. Simeoni emphasized the important role of internalization has played in the "translation field". He tried to combine the domain of a translator's habitus with the Polysystem Theory to restructure Toury's theory of translation norm. Simeoni views translation habitus as a process in which participants in translation are such culturally constructed in advance as to play a constructive role in the coordination of cultural products in translation processes.

Jean-Marc Gouanvic distinguishes the difference between a translator's habitus and the specific habitus. The former is the translator's habitus as a result of his or her practice, and the latter a specific habitus, which is constructed while the cultures involved encounter one another during the transfer process. Therefore, according to his philosophy, the use of translation strategies in general is not a deliberate act catering to or breaking the norm; instead, it is the habitus of a translator, which, together with the habitus of other participants, constructs a specific field in translation. It is through the habitus of participants in translation that the illusion of a translator can be realized. Here, the so-called illusion refers to the aesthetic pleasure a translator obtains when he / she participates in the power competition between the source and target languages / cultures, and between various participants in translation. Therefore, the habitus of a translator is expected to run through the whole translation practices, which also affects his/her translation behavior and reconstructs the social trajectory of the translator.

Capital and Translation

Among various forms of capital, symbolic capital is most closely related to translation. Gouanvic believes that in the literary field, the author obtains symbolic capital through social recognition of his work. If each individual relationship in the literary field is universally recognized, then the symbolic capital acquired by his works will be relatively strong and difficult to lose. However, in the field of translation, the translator, as a relatively passive role in the field, must use translation strategies to translate and recreate the original work, so that the original work can be recognized as much as possible in the target country in order to obtain symbolic capital. Hence, in translation, the process of capital accumulation relies on the original work.

The study of translation from a sociological perspective does not only study the text itself from the perspective of the original text and the target text, but also takes various roles in the translation activity — the original author, translator, reader and even patron — as the composition of social activities. It is these individuals who construct the network of relations in the translation field. From a sociological point of view, contemporary social translators obey the original work due to habitus but are also restricted by patrons and publishers. However, in the field of translation, translators are constantly trying to use new strategies to update such norms and habitus, allowing themselves to gradually move towards a position of creativity. As a result, translation will show a spiral upward trend; meanwhile research on translation will be conducted at a more in-depth level. Through the study of the field of translation, we found that from the perspective of the abstract field, various countries are also in the competition for power, in which language becomes one essential forms of such power. If the language of a country is in a relatively strong state (e.g., the English language), a greater proportion of works in this language will be translated into other languages to gain greater reading market in the target countries. Hence, the status of a language more or less determines the development of translation activities.

 3 Exercises

(1) Please summarize the three key concepts of Bourdieu's theories introduced in this chapter.

(2) What is your viewpoint on the connections between Bourdieu's theories and translation studies?

4 Reference and Further Reading

(1) BOURDIEU P. The Field of Cultural Production: Essays on Art and Literature [M]. New York: Columbia University Press, 1993.

(2) GRENFELL M J. Pierre Bourdieu: Key Concepts [M]. London: Routledge, 2014.

(3) JENKINS R. Pierre Bourdieu: Key Sociologists [M]. London: Routledge, 1992.

Chapter Seventeen

Mona Baker and *Corpus Linguistics and Translation Studies: Implications and Applications*

① An Introduction to Mona Baker

Mona Baker (1953–) is an emeritus professor of translation studies at the University of Manchester and Vice President of the International Association of Translation and Intercultural Studies (2004–2015). She received her DSc (Higher Doctorate) from the University of Manchester Institute of Science and Technology and MA of applied linguistics from the University of Birmingham. She founded St. Jerome Publishing, where she was editorial director until 2014 when the company was bought by Routledge. She also founded the international journal *The Translator.*

With such seminal publications as *In Other Words: A Coursebook on Translation* (1992), *Corpus Linguistics and Translation Studies: Implications and Applications* (1993) and *Towards a Methodology for Investigating the Style of a Literary Translator* (2000), she has initiated a wave of applying corpus linguistic methods to translation studies and become a pioneer in this research area. Her major theoretical contributions to translation studies include but not limited to the translation universal (TU) hypotheses, translational norms, translators' thumbprints, etc. These contributions have influenced the field enormously, showing how corpus linguistics could connect methodically to translation studies, thereby paving the way for what would soon become a thriving field – corpus-based translation studies.

② The Corpus Linguistic Approach to Translation Studies

I Moving Towards Corpus-based (Descriptive)Translation Research

For a long-time in history, the issue of equivalence has always been at the heart of translation studies, where the primary aim of all research was "never to establish what translation itself is, as a

phenomenon, but rather to determine what an ideal translation" (Baker 1993: 3). As a consequence, for translation activities that involve "products," "participants," "processes" and "contexts," a source text (ST) is endowed with an almost unrivaled position. In translation practices, much effort had been spared to minimizing any possible formal and / or semantic deviations from the source texts, in order to produce an "ideal" translation that sticks tight to the spirit, message and elegance of the original. Admittedly, what long has underpinned translation studies and guided translation practices was prescriptive in nature, in which scholars were more interested in designating what translation *should be*, rather than describing what translation *is*.

In the 1970s, however, this academic landscape began to change when the concept of "equivalence" is gradually losing its appeal and grip in translation studies. Researchers at that time like Holmes and Toury were increasingly critical about this traditional prescriptive and impressionist paradigm that saw translation as a rule-guided linguistic practice rather than an observable human activity. Against this backdrop, Holmes introduced in his important paper *The Name and Nature of Translation Studies* the concept of Descriptive Translation Studies (DTS) to his map of translation studies. This new approach to translation studies at that time is keen on "what translation is/was" instead of "what translation should be". As a result, DTS differentiates itself from the traditional prescriptive theories by shifting its focus from source language/culture to target language/culture with a special emphasis on the function of a target text (TT).

At the same time, Corpus Linguistics, with its emphasis on empirical methodologies and contextualizable results, was gaining increasing popularity in linguistic research in the 1990s. Such corpus linguistic approach to language research shares a lot of common grounds with the descriptive approach to translation studies. These similarities are generalized by Kenny in her book *Lexis and Creativity in Translation* that both are keen on using authentic language data, namely, language samples from real-world communication and literary publication, making best use of technological progress to identify recurring patterns of language(s) and placing research findings within the wider social, cultural and ideological contexts. Like the corpus linguistic approach to language research, the descriptive approach to translation studies, while providing theoretical foundations for translation studies, also offers methodological guides to analyze and interpret data. Therefore, it is a foreseeable trend for the two approaches to interact with each other to breed a fresh empirical branch – corpus-based (descriptive) translation studies.

In her paper *Corpus Linguistics and Translation Studies: Implications and Applications* (1993), Baker discussed the great potential of corpus-based translation studies to study features of translated language and seek evidence for Toury's "translation norms". Soon after, many scholars followed, making corpus an alternative tool to conduct DTS from the perspectives of translation products, participants or contexts. Generally, areas of research in corpus-based translation studies include but not limited to universal features of translation, translation norms and translators' styles. The former two areas are aptly discussed in Baker's paper, while the latter one is a burgeoning field and discussed in Baker's anther seminal paper *Towards a Methodology for Investigating the Style of a Literary Translator*.

II Universal Features of Translation

Translation universal (TU) describes a set of hypothesized linguistic features existed in translated texts of a language. In *Translation Universals: Do They Exist*? (2004), Chesterman divides TU into two categories: S-universals and T-universals. The former is based on the interlingual contrast between a source text and its translation, focusing primarily on the translator; the latter is about an intralingual comparison between a translated text and an original (non-translated) text in the target language. Baker's universal features of translation belong to the latter category, where she defines them as typical language features that appear in a translated text rather than an original (non-translated) text, and are independent of possible interference from linguistic systems of both source and target languages. To be more specific, a translated language shares certain universal features that distinguish itself from its non-translated counterpart. These features are believed to derive chiefly from translation processes, independent of source/ target language interferences.

According to Baker, some of major universal features may include such tendencies in target texts as explicitation, simplification, normalization/conventionality. Explicitation is the tendency to elucidate implied meaning in a source text for better cohesion in its target text, whereas simplification refers to the tendency to simplify language expressions of a target text. Normalization or conventionality, on the other hand, refers to the tendency of a translational language to follow the target language norms. In the paper, Baker summarized the studies by Blum-Kulka, Vanderauwera, Shlesinger and Toury, arguing that: (1) in a translated text, there's sometimes an obvious increase in the degrees of explicitness when compared with its source text; (2) a tendency of simplification and disambiguation is detected in a translated target text; (3) a target text may bear a "strong preference for conventional grammaticality," a tendency which is quite evident in interpreting activities; (4) a translated or interpreted target text tends to omit or reword certain repetitions occurring in its source text; (5) a target text will exaggerate certain linguistic features, when compared with its source text.

Since the publication of Baker's influential paper, great progress has been made in different studies of these universal features, where more complex features such as "sanitization", "imitation", "under representation", etc. have been analyzed in studies of translational languages. Yet, there are still some problems and issues worth further reflection in our quest of these universal features. For instance, the term "universal" has always been controversial, as some these "universal" features are quite "unique" and context-dependent. In his influential book *Descriptive Translation Studies and Beyond*, Toury pointed out that translation is a highly norm-governed human activity, it is believed that the hypothesized TU may bear certain contextual and receptive considerations from translators. At the same time, identifications of universal features of a translated language are more about understanding various constraints, pressures and motivations that may affect translators' decision-makings in translation, rather than simply demonstrating the existence of the "third code". Furthermore, the study of translation universal is not a simply a question of its existence, but a question of explanatory power, that is how to use various conceptual tools to better explain different phenomena in translation. It is therefore followed that one of the ultimate goals of TU research could be explorations of general rules that govern various translation activities. In addition, as most previous studies have only investigated those genetically close language pairs, their findings may be not easily applicable to Chinese and English, two languages that are linguistically and culturally distant. Therefore, TU features could only be confirmed "universal" when enough studies have been conducted between some genetically distance language pairs like Chinese and English, German and Japanese, Arabic and French, etc.

III Translation Norms

Translation norms could be hidden rules and mechanisms that shape the regularities of translational behaviors and products. It is a set of principles and conventions that take shape in certain social, cultural, political and historical environments throughout socialization. Different scholars have different ways of categorizing translation norms. For instance, Toury categorized translation norms into preliminary norm, initial norm and operation norm, while Chesterman divided them into "expectancy" norm and "professional" norm in his book.

Corpus-based research on translation norms often combines product- and function-oriented descriptive translation research, where scholars' interests have so far centered on the discovery and generalization of translation norms. In Baker's paper, she instantiated several studies by Toury, Vanderauwera and herself. These studies found that: (1) in Hebrew translations of prose fiction, there's "a high level of dependence on a repertory of fixed collocations derived from canonized religious texts"; (2) when translators translation some mystery books into Hebrew, the book titles are always very simple, without many complex or sophisticated renditions; (3) in the English translations of Dutch novels, foreign words/dialogues from the source language are often replaced or glossed in the target language; (4) compared with Arabic and French, the Japanese language is more tolerant of loan words in translation.

Although much has been achieved in the corpus-assisted studies of translation norms, there is still lacuna in terms of research scopes. To be specific, most previous studies were about seeking and confirming Toury's operation norms within different language pairs, while relatively few were keen on generalizing the preliminary or initial norms. According to Toury (1995), norms are often viewed as sociocultural phenomena, where explorations of translation norms are more about sociocultural contexts than translation products. However, this gap may stem partly from the limitations of present corpus tools in their effective capture of anything beyond linguistic forms. For instance, it would be rather difficult, if not impossible, to get extra-linguistic features of some translation norms with the current corpus tools.

Limited diachronic study is another issue. While most corpus-based studies of translation norms are synchronic in nature, only a few studies attempt to trace norm shifts in the inter-translation of different language pairs across time, and are thus diachronic. Of those diachronic studies (e.g. Yun Xia's *Normalization in Translation: Corpus-Based Diachronic Research into Twentieth-Century English-Chinese Fictional Translation* in 2014), the time spans between different translations are also relatively short, due perhaps to difficulties in obtaining the aged manuscripts; consequently, changes of translation norms are not fully presented. In addition, a translator's personal stances and experiences are sometimes excluded from corpus design. This is far from being reasonable, as translators, being the participants of translating activities, can also play a part in the shaping of translation norms. Hence, it would be necessary to include some details about the translators in the future corpus design intended for the studies of translation norms.

IV Translators' Styles

In translation studies, answers to such questions as "what is a translator's style? How is it represented? Why is it that represented?" could be significant, because they may help raise translators' visibility and reveal their subjectivity. Traditional studies of translators' styles tend to use impressionistic and prescriptive methods, with researchers' subjective intuitions and judgements at the heart of research designs. In those studies, the primary aim is to explore the degree to which a translator reproduces the original style of source texts, where a faithful reproduction of the ST style is often regarded as the "perfect" style. With the rise of descriptive translation studies, however, the focus of research has shifted from source texts and their authors to target texts and their translators.

Translation is then regarded as a sociocultural/sociopolitical activity, in which a translator is likely to leave his/her "thumbprints" in translation. Hence, some researchers attempted to answer these questions by seeking such "thumbprints" with corpus evidence. Of these researchers, Baker is the one who had made important contributions to this field.

Seven years after the publication of *Corpus Linguistics and Translation Studies: Implications and Applications*, Baker published another seminal paper *Towards a Methodology for Investigating the Style of a Literary Translator*. In this paper, Baker applied the corpus-based methods to examine translators' "thumbprints" by comparing three formal features (standardized type-token ratio, average sentence length and frequencies of report verbs) in several translations by Peter Clark and Peter Bush, respectively. The purpose of her study is to find out whether the two translators leave "thumbprints" independent of source text in their target texts. The results supported her hypothesis about translators' "thumbprints", which she also claimed as translator' styles. Essentially, Baker's study has two contributions: (1) it introduces the corpus linguistic paradigm to the study of translators' styles; (2) it views a translator's style as his/her "thumbprints" — the consistent linguistic choices a translator made in target texts, which are independent of source texts.

Researchers followed Baker by using corpora to describe a translator's style, but differed in their orientations and methodologies. Some scholars sought evidence of translators' "thumbprints" based solely on target texts: they are more interested in exploring forensic (formal) features of target texts at both lexical and syntactic levels with the aid of comparable corpora. For instance, in *Introducing Corpora in Translation Studies*, Olohan investigates the styles of Peter Bush and Dorothy S. Blair by examining their diverse frequencies of contractions use in translations. In *Translator Style: Methodological Considerations*, Saldanha studies the styles of Peter Bush and Margaret Jull Costa by focusing on their different uses of emphatic italics, foreign words and connectives after the reporting verbs SAY and TELL. With Baker's methodology, she also proposes two types of translators' styles: S-Type (source text-oriented style) and T-Type (target text-oriented style). Other scholar sought such evidence based on both source and target texts: they are often keen on identifying translation shifts in target texts with the help of parallel corpora. They felt that source text influence shouldn't be altogether excluded when describing a translator's style. For example, in *German Translations of F. Scott Fitzgerald's The Beautiful and Damned: A Corpus-Based Study of Modal Particles as Features of Translators' Style*, Winters investigates how two translators dealt with lexical items like reporting verbs, foreign words and particles of the source text in their German translations. Similarly, in *Stylistic Approaches to Translation*, Boase-Beier employs the cognitive poetics framework in her investigation of translators' stylistic differences in the Holocaust Poetry translating context from German into English. She checks the degrees to which the translators stick to the source text in their translations of these emotional pieces, evaluating the emotional effects of their TTs on the target readers.

As many corpus-based studies of translators' styles had confined their scopes to pure forensic (formal) features of a language, they may somehow ignore the stylistic picture beyond linguistic description. Hence, some scholars have turned to the functional or cognitive perspectives in their quest for a translator's style in more recent years. For example, in *Style in Translation: A Corpus-Based Perspective*, Libo Huang (黄立波) proposes a multiple-complex framework, which examines a translator's style by connecting their "thumbprints" and "responses" with discourse functions (e.g. speech/thought/writing presentations). In *A Corpus-Based Probe into Translational Language Features of Literary Self-translation*, Changbao Li (黎昌抱) and Jing Li (李菁) seek translators' stylistic features from both TT forensic features (STTR, lexical density, average sentence length, etc.) and their idiosyncratic renditions of ST wording in literary self-translation. These studies had made meaningful attempts to illustrate translators' styles with new perspectives, even though more systematic selection criteria for stylistic indices could be proposed and a tighter connection between linguistic description and literary appreciation could be established through possible corpus triangulation and corpus stylistic methods.

3 Exercises

(1) According to this chapter, what are the main areas of research in corpus-based translation studies?

(2) Please summarize and comment on the possible research gaps regarding corpus-based translation studies introduced in this chapter.

(3) Please comment briefly on the contributions Mona Baker has made to corpus-based translation studies.

4 References and Further Readings

(1) BAKER M. Corpus Linguistics and Translation Studies: Implications and Applications [M] // Text and Technology. Amsterdam: John Benjamins, 1993.

(2) BAKER M. Towards a Methodology for Investigating the Style of a Literary Translator [J]. International Journal of Translation Studies, 2000, 12(2): 241-266.

(3) CHESTERMAN A. Memes of Translation: The Spread of Ideas in Translation Theory [M]. Amsterdam: J. Benjamins, 1997.

(4) TOURY G. Descriptive Translation Studies and Beyond [M]. Amsterdam: J. Benjamins, 1995.